FENG SHUI

for

the

BODY

FENG SHUI

for
the
BODY

Balancing Body and Mind for a Healthier Life

DANIEL SANTOS

DOCTOR OF ORIENTAL MEDICINE

A publication supported by
THE KERN FOUNDATION

Quest Books
Theosophical Publishing House

Wheaton, Illinois ◆ Chennai (Madras), India

The Theosophical Publishing House
P.O. Box 270
Wheaton, IL 60189-0270

A publication of the Theosophical Publishing House,
a department of the Theosophical Society in America

The techniques and suggestions in this book are not intended to substitute for medical
advice. Please consult your health care professional before beginning any new exercise
program. Pregnant women are especially cautioned to consult a physician before practicing the exercises in this book. While every precaution has been taken in the prepara-
tion of this book, the author and publisher disclaim any liability or loss resulting from
the procedures and information in this book.

The author gratefully acknowledges permission to reprint "Flower of the Moon, Flower
of the Sun" by Miguel Torres.

Library of Congress Cataloging-in-Publication Data

Santos, Daniel, D. O. M.
    Feng shui for the body: balancing body and mind for a healthier life /
    Daniel Santos. — 1st Quest ed.
            p.   cm.
    "A publication supported by the Kern Foundation."
    ISBN 0-8356-0762-3
    1. Feng shui—Health aspects.   2. Alternative medicine.   3. Self-
    care, Health.   4. Mind and body.   I. Kern Foundation.   II. Title.
    RZ999.S33   1998
    613—dc21

                                                            98-5832
                                                            CIP

5   4   3   2   1   *   98   99   00   01   02   03   04

Printed in the United States of America

CONTENTS

INTRODUCTION

Feng Shui for the Body is about embodying a new awareness of our physical being so that we can live healthier and richer lives. Adopting a new fluid idea of our body opens an exciting panorama of spontaneous self-understanding, a panorama that meets our needs for adventure and spiritual fulfillment.

As an acupuncturist, healer, and doctor of oriental medicine for over twenty-five years, I have studied the causes of disease within the framework of traditional Chinese medicine and the healing modalities of indigenous cultures around the world. In a search for personal completion and a deeper understanding of healing, I have examined cultural ideas of the body and how these concepts not only restrict us, but predispose us to certain diseases.

As a healer, I naturally have a great interest in the body and the metaphor of disease. What I have found is that our bodies need spirit to build health around and a spiritual core from which to draw cohesiveness. We must understand that the body is a vehicle for achieving something greater, something that I describe as our connection to the Bigger Dream.

What I write about in this book is based on a wide variety of personal experiences. I hold acupuncture licenses in California and New Mexico. I am also a licensed acupuncture tutor in New Mexico, where I have taught private students for many years. I am the former chairman of the New Mexico State Acupuncture Board and have been a professor in acupuncture schools for many years, as well as a guest lecturer in hospitals and universities. I have traveled and studied in China, India, Mexico, and South America.

In looking deeply into the nature of disease, I have asked myself these questions: How can we take the knowledge of who we know ourselves to be and heal ourselves through that perception? How do the ancient Chinese models of flow and health, such as feng shui, allow us to see our health patterns more clearly? How can we use the Earth's power of gravity to help us heal and unite us with who we are? What is healing, and what is the role of the healer?

In seeking answers to these questions, I looked closely at our prevailing cultural views. I saw that hidden within them are forces that engender behavior patterns that impact our health—both individually and collectively. In turn, these patterns are reflected in our language and body movements, affecting both the quality and length of our lives. Because I studied the body models of many cultures, I saw that our cultural beliefs and perceptual conditioning give us a limited idea of the body; however, there is something beyond this constricted view. This led me to develop a more fluid idea of the body that I call "the feng shui of the body."

Feng shui means "wind and water" or "the flow of things." Westerners are starting to become familiar with this ancient oriental practice. The most common use of feng shui is to decide where to place buildings—both homes and places of business—and/or objects within buildings in order to capture a balanced flow of energy that enhances the lives and activities of those who live or work there. In this book, I extend the principles of feng shui to the body. I feel comfortable making this equation because of the nature of Chinese philosophy, in which concepts are fluid and used as metaphors for many different circumstances.

The body is the real house that we inhabit. We carry it around with us all the time. If we want to make deep changes in our lives—even before we rearrange the furniture—we have to change the way that energy flows through the body.

Through the practice of the feng shui of the body, we can change our fortunes out in the world; we can transform our relationships to those around us and enhance both our physical health and our spiritual growth. Acupuncture, herbs, meditation, and body movement all affect the body's feng shui.

The first step in creating positive feng shui for the body is to discover your Center. Finding your Center allows you to begin the journey of working with your personal feng shui by making your body's energy independent of your perceptual conditioning and your cultural beliefs.

Second, you have to remember that feng shui is a pattern in motion. Feng shui is not a static noun, not an object, but a sense of harmonious flow. Your Center also has flow. As you gather more and more energy away from your perceptual conditioning, or socially trained patterns of perceiving, you begin to move through layers of awareness, going deeper and deeper into the core of yourself, learning more clearly what this Center is and who you truly are.

Let me give you an example. A patient whom I'll call Don came to me with a variety of symptoms—asthma, allergies, back problems, dizziness. He also reported that he had been depressed for some time. His spirit—or *shen*, as the Chinese call it—was low. I concluded that his body no longer had a core to build around, and thus his energies were very dispersed.

In talking with Don, I realized that he lacked direction and that he wasn't nourishing his spirit—the Center of his being. During that first visit, as I treated his symptoms, I asked Don if he had a rich dream life. I was looking for some way that he connected with his spirit or Center. Don said that in his past he had had a rich dream life, but that lately he didn't recall many dreams.

I told him that what is important in curing disease and fixing the feng shui of the body is to give the body a core, an inspiration around which to create healing. I suggested that, in his dreams, he ask for a way to reconnect with his spirit and see all of his life from this vantage point. Second, I asked Don to recall times when he had felt complete and excited about life and had a sense of his spirit flowing through him. I encouraged him to focus vividly on these past experiences before going to sleep at night. It wasn't so much the activities he needed to recall, I explained, but rather the feeling of being connected to his spirit. It was that feeling that he needed now as a foundation on which to rebuild his health.

As Don continued to see me at my clinic, I watched him develop a core around which to heal. I told him that there was a big conversation occurring between the idea of who he thought he was and the world out there, and that he was in the process of learning a new language. The way to learn to speak this language was to direct his new feeling of completeness throughout the different aspects of his life. By using his personal feng shui pattern as the key, he could learn to focus on this interaction more clearly.

More specifically, I told him that he should take five or ten minutes, both before sleep and upon waking, to visualize his sense of completeness operating when he was at work, where he was having difficulty. I also suggested that he could apply the same process in his relationships with women and with his family.

As Don began to put these suggestions into action, his symptoms cleared up and his life changed. On the next visit he reported that his life was in some way different. He did not notice his back hurting very much, and he wasn't aware of any problems with his breathing. New things started to come to him—job interviews, different ways to deal with people, new activities and friends. Don had begun to feel more complete, and there was more flow in his life. At our next meeting, he told me that he was going out on a date and that he was playing music again. When I asked him about his dreams, he said that at first he had dreamed quite a lot, but that he hadn't dreamed much lately. I told him not to worry, because when we work with the feng shui of the body, we open up many avenues of flow. I reminded Don to keep following the feeling of flow and fullness and to radiate this feeling throughout his activities.

After another visit Don's physical symptoms had become unimportant and, for the most part, had disappeared. He no longer had time to be depressed. He had begun to reconnect to that urge within that sought completion, and he was in the process of incorporating this wholeness into his life.

In order to achieve such wholeness, we need a way to proceed. This book will show you how to take a hard look at how your learned behavior has limited you, and it describes a process for breaking out of your trained modes of behaving. This means getting back to your true nature while still maintaining a way of being that functions in the world.

As you learn about the feng shui of your body, you will begin to radiate this natural awareness out into your life. You will find yourself more in balance as you begin to perceive and work with your life from the inside out.

In my previous book, *Luminous Essence: New Light on the Healing Body, An Alternative Healer's Story,* I described our urge for completion as a pressure that our Luminous Essence creates within us. This pressure pushes us toward evolution. *Luminous Essence* followed my own path of healing and learning. In that book, I described my interactions with three teachers: Huang, my martial arts instructor who taught me to relate to the Earth's gravity; Esmeralda, who showed me how to be myself in the arena of human interactions and told me about the "male-female agreement"; and Eulogio, a healer, who educated me in the way that health and healing are affected by the longing for wholeness.

This book, *Feng Shui for the Body,* continues the format of interacting with these three teachers—Huang, Esmeralda, and Eulogio—in a storylike form. This narrative approach allows me to present a multidimensional look at our learned behavior, our cultural view of the body, and how we can change them.

Although my personal evolution has gone beyond what I learned directly from my teachers, I continue to write through their characters, weaving the knowledge that they imparted to me into the fabric of my more recent life experiences. Therefore, what these teachers convey in *Feng Shui for the Body* reflects how their knowledge has grown within me. In addition, the characterizations of the teachers have been embellished both for literary reasons and in order to further ensure their anonymity.

I have found that when we communicate with the world around us in a deep way, we access a great deal of energy and feel complete. If we have problems with health or energy flow, it's because we're not communicating or connecting effectively with the world. During sweat-lodge purification ceremonies, many Native Americans offer themselves by saying, "To all of my relations." They are referring to people, animals, spirits—all the ways in which we connect with the web of life.

The flow of this web of life is what I call the Bigger Dream. I use the term *Bigger Dream* because life in its larger sense is something greater than what we have been taught to perceive. It is greater than both what we discern in our waking lives and the projections of waking life that we experience in dreams. The Bigger Dream encompasses but is bigger than both our daydreams and our nightdreams. It is truly all our relations—the fluid womb that sustains us and from which all dreams flow, the river of life in which our being exists.

The Bigger Dream is something that cannot be described directly, because it is beyond language. In some ways, it is similar to what people call God. I don't use the word *God* because *God* has a multitude of social associations, and in our language it is a noun, a static concept. In anthropology, it is well known that language *is* culture. It may well be how our culture tries to harness the universal flow into a tangible structure. Thus, for me the word *God* relates to a limited view of life.

The Bigger Dream—or the web of life, the fluid womb, the flow of the sea of awareness—is something of which we are conscious when we feel complete. When we are disconnected from it, we become brittle, thus prone to sickness and disease.

I also use the terms *Center, the Watcher* or *the Observer, the Third Point, Luminous Essence,* and *the In-Between.* These are all names for something quite similar, yet each has a slightly different texture to begin to give us a feeling for the part of us that is our connection or doorway to the Bigger Dream.

Feng Shui for the Body also examines the role of the healer or doctor. We see that a healer, being the conduit of the Bigger Dream, can offer his or her patients a new way of being in the world. A healer realizes that the body is trying to heal itself. He or she is aware of the body's innate wisdom and knows that the spirit is working through the body, trying to reconnect it to the Bigger Dream

A healer can show his patient that sickness is an opportunity to discover his true self and to redirect his energies in more complete ways. The healer is there to assist in this process, to act as a coach. He tries to give the patient other ways of making contact with the world so that the patient can begin to understand the personal process of connecting to the Bigger Dream. In addition to being healed of a current malady, the patient may well experience greater energy, less future susceptibility to disease, and an increased life span.

Usually, the first step in learning to use our personal feng shui is connecting with our Center, as in the case of Don. However, sometimes a patient is very much in touch with their Center but has not learned a way to embody that awareness or put his personal feng shui pattern in order.

For example, a woman whom I'll call Olga came to see me at my clinic. Referred by another practitioner who had given up on her, Olga had chronic pain in her right arm. She had been to many doctors. When talking with her, I had difficulty following what she was saying. She described excitedly many different visions, hopping from one to another, seeking to find some meaning in them. It was as if she were trying to use our conversation to make sense out of them.

I realized that Olga had a very rich inner life. This indicated to me that she was fairly well connected with her Center, yet she had no way of expressing it. Her inability to get her energy out into the world was thwarting her ability to heal, particularly her arm. Although I treated the arm, the most important thing I did was to tell her that she needed a way of expressing her inner life experiences out through her body and back into the world. I quoted a saying from the Huichol Indians: "If God teaches you something, you need to go out and share it. If you don't, you get sick."

Olga was very involved with Native American teachings, so I also told her she needed to go share what she knew "with all her relations." She listened to what I said. She began sharing her visions with her friends, sometimes even translating them into dance. Her way of speaking became more focused and, as she learned to express her deep feelings through her art work, she began to relax and interact much more fluidly in the world. The condition of her arm quickly improved, as did her overall clarity.

In *Feng Shui for the Body*, we learn how to examine our learned behavior or perceptual conditioning and relax through it. From there, we can take the knowledge of who we know ourselves to truly be and heal ourselves.

To help you to put this goal of personal healing into practice, I have included instructions for exercises and activities. Some of these "Applications" involve body postures or movements. Others are what you might think of as meditations. Each Application can help you discover a new awareness of your body and balance its energies.

To further facilitate your understanding and growth, I have also provided the framework from which you can create an Awareness Journal to record your progress. It is divided into three sections: "Tracking My Awareness," "Mapping My Perceptual Conditioning," and "Embodying My Awareness."

Since you'll be looking at yourself from the inside out, you first need to track your journey into awareness. This is the first process to record ("Tracking My Awareness"). However, you will also want to examine the limitations and restrictions imposed on you by perceptual conditioning or learned behavior. This is the purpose of the second section ("Mapping My Perceptual Conditioning"). Finally, once you identify your learned behavior and begin working with it, you will embody your awareness and want to record your new perceptions ("Embodying My Awareness"). In this way, you will foster the spontaneous flow of your true nature through your being.

My intent is to describe to the reader the principles of embodying awareness. This opens a door that you can then walk through if you so desire. Because of my many years of experience as both a healer and a teacher, I am acutely aware that words, no matter how artful, can convey only part of the learning that goes on between our bodies and the world around us. Words can inspire you, show you a vision; they can point you toward an opening through which you can find the contacts in your life that will make this teaching a reality. The important thing is to begin cultivating your own life so that you bring your essence out through your body and into the world.

The Applications and the Awareness Journal, as well as the story of my own journey into awareness through my interactions with my three teachers, can help you use the principles of feng shui to find your Center, embody a new awareness, and devise a personal strategy for living a richer, more satisfying, and healthier life.

Dream well,

DANIEL SANTOS

PART I

BECOMING AWARE OF YOUR CENTER

Chapter 1

DREAMING THE BODY

*True dreaming is remembering who you really are. You will
learn to look at yourself in new ways that go far beyond the
way that you see yourself in your daydream and in your
nightdream.*

—Esmeralda

I awoke that morning in Esmeralda's house feeling no different than
when I'd arrived several days before: disoriented, directionless, full of
nagging frustration and doubt. I groaned out loud, curled up, and pulled
the pillow over my head. After a few nights of trying to follow her directions
about finding a new place to dream from, I had come up with exactly nothing. The few dream fragments I could recall seemed like gibberish, and they
had nothing to do with the issues I was confronting.

I thought back to the first time I met Esmeralda a few years earlier
when she had come into my clinic for treatment of a minor ailment. Esmeralda
was a petite woman of Mexican descent, full of laughter and grace and amazing vitality. Her rich, dark complexion contrasted strikingly with her most
beautiful feature: long, thick, silver-gray hair, which seemed to shine with a
light all its own. I couldn't guess her age—with a girl's springy gait and those
serene eyes that had seen everything and flinched at nothing, she could have
been thirty-five or fifty-five. Esmeralda set me immediately at ease, as though
she were an aunt or older sister I'd known all my life.

One day during her second or third appointment, I suddenly and
inexplicably started telling her about my personal life, specifically, my problems relating to women. She gave me a curious look and began to chuckle.
"A couple of nights ago," she said, "I had a dream about you." She went on
to explain that she regarded this dream as an omen. My broaching the subject of my personal pain was a completion of that omen, and it indicated

11

that she should offer to teach me.

Since that day, I had been to see Esmeralda many times. Under her mentorship, my inner landscape began to change dramatically, and soon I also drew two other teachers into my life: Huang, a martial arts instructor and master of what he called body mechanics; and Eulogio, a healer. What I had learned from these three had affected me in subtle yet profound ways.

The cornerstone of their teachings was the integration of body and spirit. I began to understand, as I applied this to my healing work, that sickness is a doorway to that integration. I saw how disease or feeling ill at ease with ourselves can be an opportunity to rearrange our idea of the body and to change the way we relate to the world.

Esmeralda, Huang, and Eulogio touched me with their vision of my inherent potential and how I could realize that potential in my daily life. They showed me a fresh worldview that allowed me to see beyond my cultural conditioning—what they called my learned behavior. They emphasized in each aspect of my training that if I changed my perception of my body and began to perceive through my whole body, I could then have more contact with the world and begin to feel energy flow through my whole being in a fuller, more unimpeded way.

Slowly, under the guidance of my teachers, I started to integrate and use the information they gave me. I began to gather more energy, feel more vital, and to increase my ability to contact the world in ways that were greater than my socialized, learned behavior and perceptual conditioning had previously permitted. As a result, my sense of self greatly expanded.

Then, seemingly out of nowhere, the changes I was experiencing snowballed inside me to create a very big personal crisis. My old boundaries began slowly and inexorably to disintegrate. Suddenly I was naked and very vulnerable. I experienced this inwardly as a disorientation from my usual sense of self. The outward experience was even more unsettling. In my work at my clinic, I began to acutely perceive the conditions of my patients, even to the point where I found myself taking on their pain. I could poignantly remember someone telling me that he had a cold and then instantly getting a sore throat; one night I limped home with the blazing sciatic pain for which I had treated one of my patients. This began to happen more and more until finally, at the end of every work day, I was exhausted in ways that I had never experienced. I seemingly had no way to protect myself from the onslaughts of the stimuli around me. In short, I was miserable, and I began to seriously doubt the value of what I had learned from my teachers.

Who had I become? What was I doing? Was the greater sense of self I had achieved worth all this confusion and suffering? Was I really better off than I had been before beginning my work with my three teachers? I arranged to take a few days off, and I went to see Esmeralda.

"Why do this work, anyway?" I asked Esmeralda. I had arrived in the early morning and she had made us a delicious breakfast of fresh tortillas, avocados, and *pico de gallo.* We sat now over cups of tangy hibiscus tea. "The more I open up, the more pain I feel, and the more I see other people's pain. I'm surrounded by a world of people in pain! What is so bad about the way I grew up, anyway?" My hands clenched the cup so tightly I thought it might shatter, and my face was stiff with tension.

Esmeralda began to laugh as if my misery were the greatest entertainment in the world. This reminded me of how she had chuckled when I first started telling her about my personal problems. "This is wonderful!" she declared. "At last you are starting to break through the shell of your perceptual conditioning." She lifted her cup and took a sip of the fragrant tea. "Seriously," she continued, patting my arm gently, "your present difficulties show that you have achieved a certain level of energy, and I'm delighted to see that happen." She gazed out the window for a few moments where a beautiful golden morning began to fill with birdsong and the cheerful murmur of the little creek that flowed beyond the patio. When she turned her eyes back to mine, they were somber with compassion. "Your question is a very important one," she began thoughtfully, "but it does not have an answer that can be put into words."

I moaned and dropped my forehead to the table.

"Listen to me, amigo," she said sternly.

I raised my eyes to hers.

"The real answer is bigger than any words I can think of—or that you can hear. The answer must come from your whole being-body. I can make allusions to it, but the only way for you to get your answer is to arrive at it yourself." Esmeralda went on to explain that I had not yet created a strong Center around which to orient the new energies that were being released. My teachers had described these energy flows as my own personal feng shui. *Feng* (pronounced "fung") is Chinese for wind, and *shui* ("shway") means water. Thus, feng shui is the flow of things; the flowing elements of the natural world.

"How do I do this?" I asked. "Are you referring to my personal feng shui that you, Huang, and Eulogio are trying to teach me about?"

Esmeralda smiled. "Yes," she replied. Then she suggested that I look for the Center of my personal feng shui through dreaming.

In the first days of my current visit to Esmeralda, she had taught me what she called exercises for the daytime. "One way to gather energy in the daytime to help search for the Center of your personal feng shui is through practices of the four elements: earth, air, fire and water," she said. "You've got to perceptually disengage from your normal interactions with the world."

Esmeralda ordered me to sit by the creek, to gaze into it and listen to its song, to immerse myself in the water occasionally so that I could detach from my normal thought patterns. "The important thing to keep in mind, Daniel," she told me over and over, "is that when you do any of these practices, you must have the right intent."

"What do you mean?" I demanded. "What is the right intent?"

"To know that you are doing them to move away from your learned behavior so that you can gather energy to find and then stabilize a sense of your true Center. It is your true Center, the basis of your personal feng shui." She had grinned at me and rapped me lightly on the head with her knuckles. "Remember it, *muchacho*!"

And so I had tried dreaming—I really had. But here I was, three days into my visit, and my dreams were leading me nowhere. I wanted to stay under the pillow and not get out of bed until my world had righted itself, but I knew that it wouldn't do so without my effort. I peeked out at a morning brilliant with sunshine and the fresh, clean smells of the desert. Crows argued raucously from the cottonwoods along the banks of the stream.

I flung back the blankets and got up to face another day.

Once again I sat with Esmeralda with a cup of tea in my hands, *galletas,* the little sugar crackers that she loved, and the rinds of cantaloupe and limes the only evidence of the breakfast we had just consumed. Even in my state of turmoil, I was able to appreciate the beauty surrounding Esmeralda's house. Beyond the lattice-roofed patio where we sat lay the vast southwestern skies and the looming mesas that changed continuously with the path of the sun. In the early morning light they were shaded mauve, violet, ochre, and pearly gray above banks of silver-green sagebrush. But the best part, for me, was the sparkling creek and its grove of lush cottonwoods. From the practice of water that I had been doing, I realized that there's nothing like the feeling of clear, flowing water in the midst of the desert.

I took another of sip of tea and regarded Esmeralda. She was dressed this morning in a full, colorful long skirt topped by a man's white shirt knotted at her slim waste. Her luminous hair was tied on the nape of her neck with a fuchsia scarf, and she wore simple sandals, her feet with their slender ankles propped on the extra chair. Here was living proof that women can be beautiful at any age, I thought, and something inside of me appreciated what she was trying to teach me. I began to remember why I was there.

"Well, you're not the best dreamer I've ever known, Daniel, but still, I think we can make it work," Esmeralda said. She grinned her mischievous grin. "But since you are so frustrated, let's change how we go about this a little." We got up and walked to the edge of the patio. She motioned with her chin towards the cottonwood trees next to the creek below. "I want you to spend most of the day in that hammock, suspended among the trees," Esmeralda said, "letting your mind disconnect and float. This is a practice of air. As much as you can, try not to focus on any one thing. Just observe. Feel the air flow around you and watch it move the trees. Drift. Then tonight, as you're going to sleep, keep the questions that you're asking in your mind's eye. I will help you by giving you a boost of my energy."

I spent the afternoon as Esmeralda suggested, suspended in the hammock, sensing the movements of the air. I listened to the sound it made in the cottonwoods, felt its currents ebb and flow around me, watched tree branches undulate and sway in the pressure of the breeze. It was as though my hammock were a boat rocking gently in a sea of air. Gradually I felt myself disengage subtly from the way I normally perceived myself. Somehow I reinforced and focused my intention to find my Center.

That night, as I was drowsing off, I thought about how working with my teachers had given me a greater overview of myself and the people around me. But this required me to experience a great deal of personal pain as well as an increased awareness of the pain of my loved ones and my clients. I saw that my increased awareness had allowed me to perceive my body as a luminous cell of light, and that when I was with another person, that person's luminous cell merged with mine. This created a larger cell within which I could intensely experience their being. If they were in pain, I felt that pain as my own. And even more disconcerting, I now saw that all people are in pain. I did not know how to live with this.

I often remembered what Esmeralda had told me about pain. "Pain is really only more energy than we are used to dealing with. You must learn to see the world not in terms of pain but of energy flow."

Oh, wonderful, I thought. *I'm not in agony—I'm just feeling increased energy flow. No problem!* But no matter how much I tried to change my perception, what I still felt was pain. I needed to search for the Center of my personal feng shui.

As I drifted into sleep, I held the question in my mind: Why do this work if all I'm going to experience is more pain?

I stand before an immense oak tree whose branches reach out to me. It radiates a sense of well-being. There is a glow around it. It is a wonder to behold, and I enjoy being in its presence. I am filled with a sense of exuberant life. I see the ebb and flow of energy moving up and down through the tree; it pulsates with wholeness. My enjoyment of the tree is interrupted when the question "Why?" reverberates through me. Is it Esmeralda's voice?

Suddenly a shadow, a sheet of cloudy, thick plasticlike substance, falls across my vision. I can still see the tree as an opaque presence, but now only one branch and a few leaves seem alive. The rest of the tree is gray, shadowy. The sense of well-being is gone. Instead I feel an immense longing and tiredness that I relate to in a very deep and profound way. From the state of the tree, I sense what is missing within myself. The tree and I both long for wholeness. We are sadly aware of the loss of our life energy. I move toward the one branch that still seems to be alive. I glide along it like a snake, sensing its contours, moving out into its leaves.

Suddenly I am among a group of people of all ages. They are building houses, raising families, working at different activities. I watch, fascinated. They are busy, but they lack exuberance; their movements and expressions are heavy, tired. I perceive a sense of incompleteness, a sadness similar to that which I had felt with the tree. But these people seem to have no way out of this situation, no way to fulfill their longing.

I watch them build a house for a new family. There is a baby, full of energy as the tree first was. Time speeds up; the baby grows older. As I watch it mature, the same plasticlike substance begins to opaque its image until it is engulfed in the same sense of longing. The word "Why?" reverberates through me again.

Now the tree superimposes itself on the scene with the people. I shift and look at the tree with the plasticlike substance in front of it. Only one branch is alive. My vision shifts again. I see the people and feel their longing. Suddenly I become both the tree and the people. I am suffocating, stifled. I don't know what to do. The feelings of the tree and the body I inhabit are indistinguishable. I am frustrated and incomplete, wrapped in thick, claustrophobic plastic. I desperately want to break out but I can't—I am bound on all sides! The only outlet I have for self-expression is limited as if, like the tree, only one branch of myself is alive and able to contact the world. I want wholeness. I want to be everything I feel! Again, "Why?" reverberates through me.

I go back and forth, from tree to people to body, until I can't tell where one ends and the other begins. Suddenly a fire ignites in my abdomen, sending its sap out through the branches of my body/tree. My body fills out and is whole, exuberant, iridescent. Eulogio the healer appears. He shows me pictures of energy flowing in the body. I have seen these once before in his presence, but now they have a strange kind of brilliance, more life. I understand. Rainbow colors burst forth from me and light the scene. Waves of energy surge through me and I bathe in them joyously. I am complete, whole.

I awoke feeling ecstatic. It was the middle of the night, and a three-quarter moon, fat as a ripe peach, had risen over the shadowed mesas. I could still feel the fire, the explosion of life within my being, the exhilarating sense of wholeness, as I had switched back and forth between my body, the young child, and the tree. Cradled in this exquisite feeling, I slept again.

In the morning, Esmeralda sat across the table peering at me as I finished telling her about my dream. She picked up her teacup and leaned back in her chair, looking pleased. "Well, now. This is the beginning of the answer to your question," she said. "You want to know what I think?"

"Do I have a choice?" I laughed.

"Not really," she said with a smile. She knew full well that I couldn't wait to hear her interpretation. She paused briefly, then began. "We want to experience everything that we are," she said. "We want to feel total, full, have maximal contact with the world. The keen longing cannot be explained. It is such a massive force, beyond reason and the linear thinking processes, beyond language, even. That is why I said you must experience it for yourself. It is the mystery of our Luminous Essence. And it is the most natural thing for people to desire this ecstatic completeness." She paused and we both sipped at our tea, today something with cinnamon and oranges.

"There is an old Sufi saying," Esmeralda continued. "'The fruit is not the result of the tree; the tree is the result of the fruit.'" She laughed at what must have been a look of confusion on my face. "We are being pulled towards the ripening of who we are, just like the peach on the tree!" I thought suddenly of the moon I'd seen during the night when I had awakened from my delicious dream. "It is for this that we are created. This yearning inside is what keeps us struggling to fulfill our potential. It is beyond the realm of reason. It is in another world, the world of our greater selves, the world of our connection to the Bigger Dream."

I remembered the sheet of cloudy, thick plasticlike substance that enveloped my dream tree, then the baby, and finally me. I shuddered involuntarily. "What was that awful plastic stuff that made me feel so suffocated and stifled?"

Esmeralda arched her eyebrows, her eyes flashing with challenge. "You know that answer, Daniel. Stop avoiding it! You tell me."

I nodded sheepishly. "My perceptual conditioning."

"Bingo!" said Esmeralda. "Our learned behavior is basically our acculturation—a fancy word for ways of acting that are passed down through generations. Because it is unconscious, it runs us like a tyrant and keeps us from experiencing our completeness and our affection for the world."

"And because it's focused on reason," I continued, "it blocks out all the juices, the colors!" I couldn't contain my excitement as the puzzle pieces of my dream began to tumble together into a clear picture. "It's the suffocating sheet of plastic coming between us and experience."

Esmeralda smacked her palm against the table top and tea danced over the edges of our cups. "Do you see how, in your dream, that happened with the tree and the baby?"

"The baby?" I repeated. In my mind's eye, I saw the plasticlike substance grow around the baby, sucking its energy and cutting it off from directly experiencing the world around it. I shivered. "The baby," I began thoughtfully, "as grew older, showed me how learned behavior kidnaps our life energy for its own ends."

Esmeralda leaned toward me. "Get it through your head, boy," she said, tapping me on the head with her teaspoon, "society does not care for us as individuals or as complete beings. Society wants our energy for its own uses." She waved the teaspoon in my face. "Our job is to get our energy back. And for you, right here and now, your task is to create a Center for working with your own personal feng shui."

I put my hands up, pretending to fend off the lethal teaspoon. We both laughed.

"Your challenge is to get your energy back. You need a lot of energy to be able to redirect your perceptions beyond your learned behavior."

"Okay," I replied, buying time. I was trying to draw together the threads of this revelation and how it related to my reason for coming to see

Esmeralda in the first place. I broke up pieces of an unfinished tortilla and tossed them toward the edge of the patio where half a dozen little gray chickadees waited patiently for a snack. We watched them as they happily plucked at the fragments, their black eyes darting with spirit and intelligence.

"But what does all I've been going through—feeling vulnerable, experiencing the pain of others, feeling my own pain, all this confusion—have to do with learned behavior?" I asked, thinking of the pains I'd felt after a day with clients in my clinic. "I just want to know how to get rid of this pain!"

"Hold on, amigo, and listen closely," Esmeralda said, raising the teaspoon with a smile. "You don't know what pain is until you feel the sting of this old spoon."

In spite of myself, I laughed. I was continually amazed at how unaffected Esmeralda was by my moods. She never seemed to have time to indulge me and I was sincerely grateful.

"What you call pain is the result of gathering more energy, which gives you more perspective," she said. "The pain and confusion come from the fact that you now have more energy than you're used to dealing with. Your learned behavior—those old habits—gave you a false sense of self. You're moving beyond that now, but you haven't yet established a strong Center around which the new energies can flow." Esmeralda smiled. She did not raise the spoon, but I could feel her thinking about it. "I've told you before and I'm telling you again, you need to look at the world in terms of energy flow—and your own personal feng shui—not in terms of your pain and confusion." Esmeralda arched her back and stretched out her arms.

"And—" I started to ask.

"—how do you do this?" she said with a grin, taking the words out of my mouth. "You know, I should let you talk sometimes, but it's just so much fun to say everything myself!" Esmeralda could be such a ham, and she loved to laugh, even though at times it was at my expense. "You're already doing it," she went on, standing up from the table. "As I said before, it takes a lot of energy to experience who you are beyond your learned behavior."

She stood behind my chair and placed her hands on either side of my head. "Now, turn your head!" she ordered. I tried but Esmeralda's hands held me fast. "It takes a lot of energy to turn your head around to establish another perceptual Center, to fight against the current that is plastering you, or I should say 'plastic-ing' you into your worldview. Keep trying!" She continued to hold my head until at last, slowly, I turned it to the right. Esmeralda's hands relaxed and she rubbed my shoulders vigorously. "You begin to see now!" she said, and we both laughed.

Chapter 2

THE IN-BETWEEN

The In-Between is what links us to the Bigger Dream.
—Esmeralda

A fter dinner that night, Esmeralda asked me if I had felt her presence in my dream.

"I'm not sure," I said. "I may have heard your voice, but I don't remember more than that."

"Just wondering," she said with one of those enigmatic smiles. "Whether you feel me or not, I'll dream with you again tonight. Try and gather what you've learned, and ask for more."

As I lay in bed before going to sleep, I carefully went over my dream and my talk with Esmeralda. I realized that there was a greater force moving through my dreams and through Esmeralda's explanations. My awareness of this force would come and go sporadically, but something in me always knew when it was there. How could I connect with it and stay connected? Was this the Center that I was looking for?

What I felt was like a thread in a magical tapestry moving in and out of various situations, people, dreams, my waking life—even in my deepest sleep. Was this what lay beyond my daydreams and my nightdreams? Was this what Esmeralda called the Watcher or the Observer?

She had told me that once I found the Center of my personal feng shui, I would notice, as I gathered back energy from my perceptual conditioning, that my Center contained layers upon layers. There are, she had said, many levels of who we really are and of our interaction with the Bigger Dream. Esmeralda had broken down learned behavior into what she called the four perceptual motions: the ways we use sight, sound, body movement, and breath. It is through these mechanisms that we learn to stabilize our reality according to the cultural standard. It is also by breaking down our learned behavior into these building blocks that we can learn to undo the bindings of our cultural matrix.

At that time, Esmeralda had given me the task of seeing what would happen when I stopped the four perceptual motions. These four motions are conditioned very early in life, and they determine our perceptions of the world as we grow. I had attempted to stop the movement of my eyes, my inner dialogue, my physical motions, and alter my breathing as best I could. When I described the experience to Esmeralda, she brought me to the realization that there was something greater within me that was observing the four motions. She called it the Watcher. She said that the Watcher is always there, linking everything together, but is often clouded by learned behavior. She suggested that the Watcher is a neutral space and that within the Watcher are layers of awareness.

APPLICATION: AWARENESS OF THE WATCHER

Sit still. Open and relax your joints. Don't move your eyes (eyes can be either open or closed). Quiet the thoughts and watch your breathing. Become aware of what is watching. When your attention wanders, gently refocus. Do this for ten minutes. Notice who is watching.

As I lay in bed doing this exercise, a memory surfaced. A friend held a string of amber beads in front of his eyes, telling me that each bead was a separate experience or emotion linked together by the thread. As I drifted off to sleep, I grabbed on to the sense of the Watcher, the Center of my feng shui, that which connects the events in our lives, the thread and its flow.

Gossamer wings tilt. Iridescent ribbons of light shimmer along them. Filling with light, the creature moves. I follow on wings of my own. Soon I notice that if I tilt in a certain way, I am in motion and my wings disappear. If I tilt differently, they reappear and I am stationary. I play back and forth, zooming through currents of light. When I wonder about the wings, they appear.

I am steering a sailboat. There is no water—or is there water all around? A current moves the boat. I am the boat, the current, the water, the wind. I become and embody them all. I am the thread.

I am in a room with a black-and-white checkerboard marble floor that stretches as far as I can see. I swoop down to look at the tiles. They separate and I see that rivers of energy move between them. I am absorbed in this flow. I tilt my wings and they disappear. I am In-Between. The tiles move farther and farther apart, up and down; now they are geometric cubes moving in currents of energy: apart, then together, then apart again as I float between them. I am the eye—the center—of the storm, but I'm not afraid. Gigantic waves crash around me, a tile bobs past. I land on it and feel it solid beneath my feet. Then— whoosh! I am back in the current, a dolphin moving in and out of the water. Life ripples through my form. A new sensual language explodes outward from my body.

I see a long strand of dazzling jewels. I move up and down the strand, through one colored jewel after another. I stop inside one that shimmers blue. I am suffused with brilliant light; I tingle as though I'm filled with tiny bubbles, like icy sparkling water. I feel exhilarated in this world of light and color. I see a lake glinting in the sun, surrounded by dense trees, bushes, and ferns. I enter the trees just as a brilliant red bird swoops down before me. I put out my hand and realize that I have a body. I am the thread, and strung on me are brilliant jewels. I go inside a jewel and am instantly filled with warmth and fragrance. Flowers grow against a sunny garden wall; their delicate petals fall around me in a perfumed shower.

Like a fish, I flick my tail. As the thread in the necklace, I penetrate another jewel. I stare down into a plant. Now I find myself perched on a leaf. I feel a shell around me, and many legs coming out of my body. I see the world through kaleidoscope eyes.

Next, I am the ocean breaking on the beach, pulling back and breaking again and again. I am a line of pressure amid the ebb and flow of opalescent waves. I am alive, buzzing with energy, pulsating, an electric thread. I am In-Between. There is Esmeralda! She waves.

I awoke breathless, waves of energy coursing through my body, crescendo after crescendo. I found myself staring out the window and through the trees at stars scattered against the velvet-black sky like the brilliant jewels of my dreams. After a while I smiled, punched up my pillow, and sank back into sleep.

I opened my eyes to the sound of someone tapping on the window. I turned my head to the bright sunlight and saw Esmeralda's face smooshed against the glass. She laughed and waved before turning toward the garden. She carried a hoe over her shoulder.

Later, I sat at the kitchen table, eating sweet ripe tomatoes from Esmeralda's garden. On a plate were half a dozen delicious fresh tortillas wrapped in a blue-checked cotton towel, and there were beans and salsa as well. As I munched contentedly, I admired bunches of green herbs, garlic, and bright red chilies that hung among the pots and pans. The walls of the white room were smooth, hand-troweled adobe. I realized for the first time how living in a house made from the earth provided me with a serene sense of security and well-being. The thickness of the adobe, its massive quality, had a very solid feeling to it. At the same time, it permitted the inner stillness of the house to flow easily, blending with the vast desert beyond.

Esmeralda came in, carrying a huge bunch of creamy white radishes. She left them in the sink and washed the dirt off her hands. "Oh, what a lovely day," she exclaimed, drying her hands. She wore her work clothes: much-faded jeans and an even more faded purple T-shirt. She had twisted her hair into a thick coil on the nape of her neck and tied a bright green scarf over it to protect it from the sun. She took a glass from the counter, filled it with water, and joined me at the table. "Did you dream well last night, Daniel?" she asked with a grin. She pulled the scarf from her hair and wiped her gleaming face with it.

I grinned right back at her. "Yeah! And you were there—I saw you!" I said. "How do you do that, anyway?"

She dismissed my question with a wave of her small brown hand. "That's not important," she said airily. "What is important is the feeling of your dream. Want to tell me about it?"

26

"So much went on, there was so much change and motion. Most of all, I was aware of something greater than myself, and I flowed within that energy."

"Sounds exhausting," Esmeralda said slyly.

"Not at all! It was exhilarating—energizing, actually."

"This is true perception!" she exclaimed. "The Bigger Dream is alive, and it has breadth and depth. It moves and yet is still. It invigorates but does not tire. It goes on forever. And I think you're beginning to find your Center. Now you need to build on it just like a spider spins her web."

"Maybe I'm making too much of it," I told her uneasily. "Maybe it was just an ordinary dream after all."

"Maybe so, but I want to hear all about it. Let's have some tea and talk."

We took our mugs out to the patio, and as Esmeralda fed the chicka-dees, I told her what I had experienced. "But I can't really put the feeling into words," I concluded.

"What is happening is that you are expanding," she said, glancing at me. "The compartmentalized parts of yourself—which were made, shaped, and glued together by your early environment—are now flowing with each other more freely. The space between them is widening. You are beginning to realize that you are not really these parts, but that which they are made of and that connects them together. The In-Between. And you are becoming aware of a new integrity."

"And maybe I'm just going bonkers!" I countered. "How do I know who I am anymore, where I'm acting from, how I'm functioning in life?"

"What do you mean by functioning in life?" she asked, chuckling. One of the little gray chickadees hopped close to Esmeralda's feet as she scattered bits of *galletas,* the little cookies she liked. She crooned softly to the bird, and it tilted its head to look up at her.

"Don't we have to make decisions?" I asked. "How do I even com-municate with other people? Is this the learned behavior that I have to leave behind?"

"In a way it is, and in a way it isn't," Esmeralda said.

"Well, that clears everything right up! Thanks, Esmeralda." I threw up my hands, startling the chickadee. It flew into a nearby shrub and cheeped at me.

Her grin widened; clearly she was enjoying my confusion. "Really, we don't lose our ability to function, we just take away the emotional charges that keep us attached to it." Esmeralda went on to explain that through our socialized, learned behavior we become enmeshed in a kind of electromagnetic circuitry with each other, in patterns of action and reaction. We are taught to communicate with other people with a charged expectation. When we send out a signal, we expect a certain reaction. If we don't get that reaction, we feel threatened.

"Another place where we can observe this charged circuitry in action is when we have a decision or choice to make." She reached over, grabbed the salt and pepper shakers, and placed them in front me on the patio table. "Salt or pepper?" she asked. "You often think you have to make a decision between one thing or another because these two options have a charge between them that doesn't allow you to see anything else. So if you are considering one option—say the salt—all you can see is its opposite—pepper!"

She pushed the salt and pepper shakers together, then pulled them apart. Her eyes lit up as she looked at me and said, "You see? Salt. Pepper. All the same thing." She laughed again. "Whenever you make a decision within the continuum that you have been taught, you are in this situation. Doing one action calls for its opposite reaction: pepper, salt." She touched each in turn for emphasis. "*No* brings up the idea of *yes*; *arriving* makes you think of *leaving*," she continued. "This is how we are fooled into continually giving power to our learned behavior. We actually think that we have a choice. But we don't realize that, either way we choose, we're still looking at the world through the same limited perceptual lens." She leaned back and smiled at me, as if she had just revealed to me the greatest secret in the world. Perhaps she had, I reflected wryly.

"Take, for example, a woman who, by reason of her upbringing, is highly sexually charged." She raised her eyebrows and looked at me, then laughed at the expression on my face. "She could say 'yes' and become a go-go dancer and live out her sexual fantasies," Esmeralda continued, "or she could say 'no' and become a nun. Either way she hasn't really converted her sexual energy. She hasn't changed the continuum offered by her learned be-havior, nor the diseases she will be susceptible to. What she needs to do is decharge the polarity and use this energy to move In-Between and begin to find her true Center."

Esmeralda paused for a moment and studied me. I nodded that I understood.

"The way to decharge these polarities or to create more options," she went on, "is to sink into a greater place that is beyond, yet includes, your learned behavior. It is a place where you are not thinking in terms of deci-sions, but in terms of flow—your feng shui. Know what I mean, *calcetín*?"

I laughed at her Tex-Mex rhyme. *"Calcetín"* means sock in Spanish.

"Then other ways appear," she said, moving the sugar bowl in be-tween the salt and pepper shakers. "Let's call this sugar bowl the Third Point." She stuck her finger into the sugar and licked it, smacking her lips. "And these new ways sure do taste good!"

"They'll also rot your teeth," I countered.

Esmeralda laughed. She had the whitest, most perfect teeth I'd ever seen, and they were all hers. "Seriously, this is a difficult point to explain, because explanations are in the realm of linear reasoning, and linear reason-ing is in the realm of learned behavior. We are much, much more than that. So let's add some multisensual pictures."

Suddenly visions of female breasts popped into my mind, and I began to chuckle. When I told Esmeralda, she waved her finger at me with a mock-severe expression. "No, no, no!" she said—and then complimented me on my ability to become multisensual.

After we had stopped laughing, Esmeralda continued more seriously. "If you create a fixed idea of your body, then the field of undulating life that you exist in will twist and shape its opposite." She paused for what seemed a long time. Finally, in a soft, hypnotic voice, she said, "Relax. Try and sink into that greater place that is beyond. Bring in pictures with feelings. I'll get you started, but as I talk, allow your being to show you more, to become spontaneous.

"See the branches of a tree in winter, casting shadows against an adobe wall. Let the pictures keep coming." I closed my eyes. "As you shape an idea of your body, a charge is created between you and the shadow that forms to mirror you."

As I listened to Esmeralda, my image of the stark branches and their shadows changed. *I am running in the desert in the late afternoon, trying to catch my shadow. . . .*

When I became aware of Esmeralda's voice again, she was saying, "In order to feel complete, you are compelled to seek the other half of your creation. But because your learned behavior is static, your idea of your body is static. You are separated from your Center of flow. So, erroneously, you seek another object for completion. It is the seeking, the action, that is the crack In-Between. You endlessly pursue your shadow self, but what you are actually looking for is the flow that is creating it."

I knew, even with my eyes closed, that she had poured sugar between the salt and pepper shakers. She said, "The answer is In-Between."

I opened my eyes just in time to see her put her finger in the sugar, place it in her mouth, and smack her lips. "And no peeking!" she chided. She couldn't even maintain a straight face as a hypnotist, I thought, laughing silently.

She went back to her hypnotic voice. "The light hitting your static idea of your body forms a shadow. You chase it to find completion, but you're looking in the wrong place. What you are really seeking is the totality of your being. To find that, you need to look toward the light."

As I run through the desert after my shadow, I begin to get very tired, so tired that I stop. At last I turn around and look directly at the sun. As I watch, the sun changes from yellow to white. Looking at it makes me feel full and complete. I look down again—I have no shadow.

"Think of braiding hair," Esmeralda said. "Look at it, feel it, touch it, watch." I opened my eyes. Esmeralda pulled the pins from her hair and let it cascade in a silvery stream over her left shoulder. As she spoke, she divided it into three sections. "One part goes over the other, over and over," she explained, braiding slowly. "It ends up looking like just two strands, one over the other. But there are really three. The third one gives motion to the other two and allows them to flow. Without the third section, there would be only opposites, disunited, without function. In Chinese philosophy, it is the space inside the pot that can be filled, the hole in the hub that makes the wheel useful. And I say that it is the space In-Between that allows you to move through duality.

"When you get caught in a situation of either/or, watch out! You're missing the Third Point." Esmeralda put her finger in the sugar again. "The way out is to expand into the space In-Between and decharge the duality. Then the flow can continue. Three gives motion. If you are locked in deciding between salt and pepper," she said as she picked up one and then the other with a comically puzzled look on her face, "you need to bring in the Third Point to break the deadlock."

Huang, my martial arts teacher, taught the same principle that Esmeralda was describing. Huang's method for teaching me how to reach the In-Between was movement. He showed me that thought patterns activate only a small percentage of the possible pathways in the body and that are so-called normal movements. Normal movements lock us into the duality of learned behavior. He then demonstrated new ways to move that spread energy throughout the body. In this way, I could expand past my learned behavior. As a result of Huang's exercises, I could see how moving in this bigger way, which was similar to focusing on a more inclusive Third Point, had created space for new actions and spontaneity in my life.

My attention returned to Esmeralda as she put her finger in the sugar again and licked her lips with a grin. "I know you want some!" she said, giggling. She loved to tease me about both my dislike for white sugar and my behavior toward women. "It's the Watcher, it's the Observer, the Center—and it sure does taste good!"

We both laughed, and she continued. "So one's work is to flow with the process that brings in the Third Point. And the Third Point is sugar—flow, the In-Between. So, to become the Third Point means to identify with the process of focusing rather than that which is being focused upon. The difficult part is to be aware of this in the midst of a world that has taught you to focus in very prescribed ways. This world of learned behavior is a world of subjects and objects, but the spirit likes to flow."

Esmeralda asked me to stand up. "You'll become a stale tortilla if you sit there much longer. And even if you put salt and pepper on a stale tortilla, it still tastes like a stale tortilla." She laughed and suggested that I do in a very slow and deliberate way one of the warm-up exercises that Huang had taught me.

"There is always something In-Between," she said as I began moving, "another point of focus." She walked around me, hands clasped behind her back, like a drill sergeant. "This becomes very clear when we look at our idea of the body. We are taught a very static idea of the body—it is either a subject or an object. Don't forget now, the spirit likes to flow, and from the spirit's point of view, the static idea of the body that we learned to inhabit is calling for the Third Point—other points of contact—to release it from the bonds of duality." Without warning, Esmeralda nudged me off balance, laughing at the situation she had created. She motioned for me sit down. "The spirit, or our true being, wants to be released from the bonds of duality because it seeks maximal contact with the world outside," she said, sitting down across the table from me. "We are that which focuses. We are the Watcher, we are the In-Between. The In-Between is everywhere."

She looked at me intently. "The spirit loves to flow and not be pinned down. From the perspective of our learned behavior, it may appear that we are active or inactive. But from the inside, with the eye of the spirit, we are always in motion—In-Between. We need to see ourselves and the world through the eyes of the spirit."

I heard Esmeralda's words and remembered my dream. "Look," I told her, "I think I understand what you're talking about, but I don't see the practicality of it. I still feel so frustrated! Am I a hopeless case?"

"When you realize that you are trying to change without any hope of changing at all, that's when you change. When you accept yourself, you can move beyond yourself. If you are not busy with positive/negative reactions to your idea of yourself, your idea of yourself dissolves and you can move beyond it. It's in this area beyond that you'll find the Center for your own personal feng shui." With her marvelous eyes twinkling, Esmeralda put her finger in the sugar and licked it one last time.

Chapter 3

JAGGED BODIES:
THE NIGHT DREAM

We as a society create a collective limited dream, within which we share the same framework of separation. So we collectively create an agreement or a consensual dream of how to separate ourselves from our true nature.

—Esmeralda

Following dinner that evening, Esmeralda and I went outside into the courtyard. The last of the sunset colors were fading into darkness and stars had begun to peep out shyly. The air grew chilly as it always does in the desert at night, and Esmeralda asked me to make a fire. As I arranged kindling and logs, Esmeralda told me that she wanted me to work with the element of fire.

"The practice of gazing at fire is like gazing at water. You look into it and listen to it and allow your perception be taken in. After you have fixed the fire as your object of meditation, every time you have a thought, I want you to throw a little stick into the fire and watch it burn."

She had me do this for a couple of hours.

After my fire meditation was finished, Esmeralda came out with thick mugs of steaming chamomile tea. As the fire sank into embers, we drank companionably and talked about how splendid the night sky was, unmasked from the light and air pollution of the city. Finally my eyelids got heavy and I told Esmeralda I was going to turn in. As I walked toward my room, I heard her call my name softly. I turned back toward the courtyard.

"Just one more thing," she said, lifting her finger. The glow of the dying fire caught her eyes and for a millisecond I saw the familiar teasing twinkle. "I hope you dream well."

Before I dropped off to sleep, I focused once again on formulating my question. Esmeralda had said that through dreams—whether daydreams or nightdreams—a greater conversation occurs. Between wakefulness and sleep is the In-Between, our connection to the Bigger Dream. As I lay there, I thought about this ephemeral place that I could not define with the intellect, but for which I had begun to develop a feeling, a sense, an awareness.

I knew that the more clearly I posed my question, the clearer my answer would be. But I also knew that I had to begin asking questions that could no longer be stated in words. These questions needed to find expression in feelings and impulses. So I sought to create a fluid metaphor that would take me to the Center of my being and allow me to understand the perceptual condition that kept me from being there. My question took the form of an image of myself about to open a door. I felt anxious and uncertain. I didn't know what I would find on the other side.

I am in a foreign place. Sounds, visions, rippling and floating sensations come at me from all sides. I try to look around, but my eyes don't work in the usual way. Unfamiliar pictures flash in the middle of my head. I can feel my body undulating.

I am a dolphin! I am surrounded by other dolphins as we swim joyously through the warm, clear waters of a tropical sea.

Below, above, on all sides, communication pours into me. I flip my tail and feel a ripple through my body. I am aware that my companions feel my motion as a ripple through their bodies. We move together in perfect synchrony, rolling and playing. Sound, sight, movement, immeasurable amounts of information flow through and between us. I am exhilarated and full. Again I send a ripple of energy up my body, and my companions respond with ripples of their own that circle back to me, back to them, and then back to me once more as if we were capable of being both individuals and a single harmonious organism.

Suddenly I am in a human body with a group of people around me, talking, looking, moving. I send a ripple through my body from my foot to the top of my head and out through my arms, but there is no response. It is as if these people live in another world. I undulate my body from my pelvis up to my shoulders. A couple of people give me curious looks before resuming their conversations—no response. I feel suffocated and frustrated. They are my own kind, but they will not talk to me!

I am by a lake, near some trees. I feel soothed, round, and full. I am a geometric shape, a bubble. Warm affection fills my bubble. Suddenly jagged shapes start coming at me. The people surround me again, talking, looking, moving. Their jagged shapes fit into one another's, as though they were puzzle pieces. They are pressuring me to join their conversation. I feel their jagged edges tearing at my round bubble, trying to force me into shapes that will match their own. I pull away.

I awoke in a cold sweat, panting. My heart raced as I sat up among the twisted sheets. I looked around in the darkness for a moment and then I remembered to relax. As I rearranged the bedding and allowed my body to grow heavy, I recalled that my teacher Eulogio had once told me that relaxing is the only way to effectively move through things; it is always the first step toward increased awareness. Soon my breathing slowed to normal and I slid easily back into sleep.

I am on a mesa. I look down and see the face of an Indian. I am a baby being held up to the sky. The Indian points to the sky and turns me to face it. He says, "This is your father." He points to the earth. "This is your mother." He smiles and gives me to the woman at his side.

Once again I find myself in a crowd, feeling other peoples' hooks grabbing at my skin, trying to pull me into shapes that fit theirs, trying to fix me in one spot, to calcify me into a single posture. I can't breathe. I feel suffocated, burdened, tired, gray, and dull. There is no end. A sense of resignation radiates from everyone around me. I shoot up over the crowd and look down. I see how these people are suffocating. They are actually getting sick and dying from being locked together by their jagged hooks. They are strangling from the death grips they have on each other. I see that I have to fight against being hooked into it myself, but the more I struggle, the deeper the hooks sink in. I feel as though I'm being sucked into quicksand as I rapidly approach exhaustion.

I simply stop, relax; I no longer care whether they get me or not. I look up and see the white sun. Suddenly I am a reed in a pond, hollow, in between heaven and earth. I am full, complete, relaxed. In the next instant, I am standing on the ground. The jagged-body people are here too, but I feel relaxed now; not engaged. I simply observe and watch without being tangled in their hooks. I bend and dance; I play lightly with their jagged shapes. Their hooks cannot penetrate me. As I walk away, some of the people throw their hooks at me, but they bounce off harmlessly.

I am standing in a vast cultivated field with a hoe in my hands, working my row. I look across the field. There are others hoeing their rows. There is someone near me. I catch her eye. I wave and Esmeralda waves back.

I woke up feeling solid. I was smiling, my whole body aglow. I looked out the window at the stars in the sky. I could feel my world stretching far beyond the house to the land around. I floated in the web of light created by the song of the crickets and sank back into sleep.

The sun on my face nudged me slowly into wakefulness. I yawned, stretched, and got up to prepare for breakfast. I was ravenously hungry. As I entered the kitchen, I heard a voice from outside calling, "Hey, Daniel! Out here!" I looked out the door, and sitting at a table under one of the towering cottonwoods was Esmeralda, waving me over. I could feel the undulations of her body as she waved at me. I waved back. It felt as if we waved back and forth together.

"Do you need anything?" I called.

"Pick a flower on your way down. I have the vase here already," she replied.

I stopped at a clump of irises. Because of their beauty, scent, and incredible toughness, they were one of my favorite flowers. I enjoyed allowing my eyes to wander deep inside their luscious folds. I looked at them all and was drawn to one. It was iridescent violet with a white heart ruffled out in yellow.

As I knelt down before it, I began to sing to the iris as I had learned to sing to plants when I was in the Peruvian Amazon. I reached out beyond myself and suddenly I became an iris, just as in my dream I had become a dolphin. Becoming the iris, we were the same, and cutting it was like cutting myself. The iris understood. I reached beyond and between myself, and my knife severed the stalk. Tingles ran through my body, a sensation of gratitude for the wisdom the dolphins had given me. Then I felt the wonder of moist earth under my knee. I stood and walked towards Esmeralda.

Esmeralda always amazed me. It seemed as if she did whatever she wanted, yet there was a direction and exuberance in her actions. I never knew what to expect. Today, on a picnic table under the trees, it was pancakes topped with fresh strawberries and whipped cream, along with pan-fried trout. We ate to the soft flutter of the breeze through the cottonwood leaves and the ubiquitous chatter of birds, who sounded as though they were planning their day in minute detail.

After we finished eating, we sat back with cups of mint tea. Esmeralda looked at me with a twinkle in her eye, and said, "Spill the *frijoles*. What happened to you last night?"

As I told her my dream, she listened carefully without interruption. When I finished, she said, "Well, it looks like you got your answer."

"What answer?" I asked, bemused.

"You've dreamed three nights running now, and your question has been resolved," she replied.

"But I'm not sure I know any more now than I did before," I protested.

She laughed in the same way as when I had first arrived at her house and began cataloging my frustrations. "Your answers have come in a language that you are only beginning to understand," she said. "The you that you think you are doesn't understand. But you're beginning to connect to a bigger you that does, and you are beginning to find a sense of your Center in the midst of it. From there, you can create your own personal feng shui. Believe me, the answer is in there. Even though the immensity of it cannot be understood by your little mind." She tapped her head with her index finger and smiled. "You will grow into it. The answer will begin to pour out of you. Your Luminous Essence has found new ways through your idea of your physical body and through your relating body—the way you move in the world with others—to make contact with the Bigger Dream out there," she said, opening her palms toward the sky.

"Well, maybe you can help explain some of these things that you think I already know," I said. One of the things that endeared me to Esmeralda was that she did not react to my sarcasm, but rather seemed to enjoy it.

"Ask," she said, amused.

"Who were those jagged people in my dream? And why were they attacking me? What were they after?"

"They showed you the real world," she said. "They were everyday people. Your parents, your friends, even your children—if you had any. They were trying to fix your motion, to make you into an object to which they could react so they could fit you into their view of reality."

The puzzlement must have shown on my face, for she continued. "To find our Center, we need to discover what's in the way, and that's what you've done," she said with a wink. "We live in both a horizontal and a vertical world. The vertical world is how we line ourselves up between heaven and earth. In other words, how we connect or line up with our Center. From there, the right perspective is created. So you see how important it is to find the true Center of your being around which your personal feng shui can be formed.

"Our feng shui is how our energy flows out into the world from our Center. So, once we're lined up vertically with the right perspective, we spread the energy from our Center out through our physical body and our relating body and into the world. I see it as a cross." Esmeralda made the sign of the cross on her body with her right hand, then winked at me again.

Her description of the horizontal and vertical lines making a cross reminded me of Native American cosmology. The vertical is what connects us to heaven and earth. The horizontal is how we flow with the four directions. There is one road—the black road—that has to do with the rising and setting of the sun, the coming and going of things, the way we interact with the world. Then there's the red road of the spirit. It intersects the black road and creates the "cross of who we are."

I thought of how in my dream I had seen the face of the Indian and how he had pointed to the sky and said, "This is your father." Then he made me look down at the earth and said, "This is your mother." Looking up, then down—this I could see was vertical. I told Esmeralda my realization and asked her if this applied to what she was talking about.

She nodded with a smile. "But, more simply put, the horizontal world is the way we relate with people, and the vertical world is our relationship to our Luminous Essence and to our spirit. At this juncture in our history, the spirit is under siege. That's what your dream was showing you.

"Our horizontal world," she continued, "has become very jagged. This jagged world, which you saw in your dream, begins to effect us as soon as we leave the womb."

I nodded. I was beginning to see how jagged my relating in the world had been and still was.

"When we are babies, we have no defenses," she went on, brushing silver hair out of her eyes. "We need the help of adults to interact with our surroundings. In order to relate to them, we learn very quickly to adopt modes of behavior that interlock with their needs and expectations." Esmeralda paused and interlocked the fingers of both hands. She kept them locked as she continued. "These modes of behavior are critical when we're tiny and helpless—they're literally a matter of life and death. The problem is that we learn to identify these behavioral modes as our true selves—and we loose our connection with our Luminous Essence, therefore with the Bigger Dream. Ultimately we're almost cut off from our true Center."

Esmeralda allowed me to absorb this for a few moments. I recalled my own early childhood when the adults around me loomed like giants; they had seemed like gods.

"We should, in a perfect world," Esmeralda continued, "grow up learning to have interchangeable modes. In fact, so interchangeable that we identify ourselves as that which lies in between them." Esmeralda unlocked her fingers and began softly rubbing her hands, one over the other. "These behavior modes are made up of electromagnetic action and reaction patterns," she continued, "with all kinds of associated thoughts, emotions, and physical actions."

As she spoke, I was suddenly surrounded by memories of people I had healed in my clinic. After studying with my teachers, my awareness had become clearer, and I had begun to see people in terms of electromagnetic energy. I could now see that these people had jagged edges, and that my job as a healer was to not interact with them in the same jagged way that they were used to. Instead, part of my role was to relate to them in a different way so that their edges would round out—just as Esmeralda was doing with me. I saw how I had been doing this more and more all along without knowing it.

I thought of one patient in particular, a woman named Sharon. She had spoken to me at length about how bad she felt. She wanted to convince me of it because this was the jagged edge she had learned to use in relating to her family and her friends. It seemed to be the only way she could get their attention. I could see now that Sharon had been struggling to maintain her internal pattern of flow, or feng shui, from the wrong center—the one based in learned behavior, rather than the true Center of her being. The end result was a very jagged pattern of flow. She had tried to fit me into her jaggedness, like a puzzle piece.

After I had put acupuncture needles in her body, her energy flowed in a much rounder way, more from her true Center rather than from her learned behavior. Her perception of herself changed as well. I was then able to relate to her with more of myself. I spent fifteen or twenty minutes with her in this altered state, interacting in a new way, stabilizing this fragile, not yet familiar, energy.

I could see now, through Esmeralda's explanation, how the people I treated in my clinic and the people I saw in the street were all connected horizontally and how they depended on these horizontal connections for a lot of their energy. I also saw that they were unbalanced vertically, so much so that it was difficult for them to be self-sufficient. They did not have the power of the cross that Esmeralda had told me about. Inwardly I asked, *Why are they stuck to these limited horizontal electromagnetic patterns?*

Like thunder follows lightning, I was struck by a startling image: I saw a mass of horizontally relating energy feeding itself by sucking children up and spitting out diseased old people, a monster that gorged itself on babies and defecated the elderly into rest homes and hospital beds. A series of advertisements flashed before my eyes: pictures of men riding horses, smoking cigarettes, drinking beer, and other ads of women preening their legs and acting suicidal over dingy laundry.

I chuckled to myself and began to experience what it was like to laugh at the weird juxtapositions of my mind. It felt good. I was beginning to see why my teachers, Huang, Esmeralda, and Eulogio, were always telling me not to be offended by their laughter. They would always tell me that they were laughing not at me, but at themselves. At this moment, I could believe them. In fact, Esmeralda was laughing that very moment.

"What are you laughing at?" I asked.

"I'm laughing at you laughing," she said. "You remind me of how I laugh with myself, and that's funny. What was your joke?"

I told Esmeralda what I had seen. She beamed as I went through my images.

"It's like being in a mob with its feet off the ground," she said, interlocking her fingers once more and moving her hands back and forth. "All these people, locked together and moving a little bit back and forth, but never touching the ground. They need to keep indoctrinating new people, like juicy little babies, in order to sustain their jagged energy. They do this because they falsely believe that their sustenance is dependent on learned behavior, rather than on the spirit. They believe that they *are* their learned behavior." She paused a moment for dramatic effect. "These behavioral modes are really their ideas about their own and each other's bodies," she said as she pinched her left biceps. "I believe that there is a way to keep our vertical and horizontal worlds in balance so that the energy of heaven and earth can spread out." Esmeralda leaned forward and traced a cross on the tablecloth. Then, as if that weren't enough, she grabbed my knife and crossed it over hers.

"When you are strongly grounded between heaven and earth, you can touch the world of people lightly," she continued, reaching over and softly touching my hand. "You can become resilient. The horizontal world loses its charge, and you begin to find your Center and become the Watcher. Then, the field is cleared for the flow of pure affection."

I nodded, but still I was not clear as to how to accomplish what

41

Esmeralda was talking about. She stretched, reaching her arms out and rotating her wrists. "Your strength comes from relaxing into your natural alignment between heaven and earth," she said. "Then the poles of your electricity are hooked up vertically, and you can dance and play horizontally, no longer needing hooks and jagged agreements for security. And don't forget about those guys riding horses and smoking cigarettes. They are pretty cool." She laughed, as she put two fingers to her mouth. "And last but not least, those women going suicidal about their laundry!"

I laughed, too, knowing where she was headed.

"These hooks," she said, locking her index fingers together again, "this jaggedness, all this interlocking behavior, are at their core based on the male-female agreement. This interlocking behavior, this limited view of the body, predisposes those who partake in it to certain sicknesses, diseases, and eventual death, and this happens on a societal scale."

I remembered Esmeralda telling me about the male-female agreement—the culturally derived unconscious ways the sexes relate to one another that is the matrix of all other social mechanisms—as a way of categorizing and understanding our learned behavior. When we look at learned behavior through the male-female agreement, we can see how society's concern for its own preservation robs us of our natural perceptual birthright and thus the gateway to the Bigger Dream. Energies diverted by the male-female agreement are not available for us to align ourselves with the Center of our being—they are taken up by the jaggedness of horizontal relating.

Esmeralda had expanded on this concept by saying that through the male-female agreement, the ways that men and women relate to each other are established. In order to keep this relationship intact, men are trained in specific ways to relate to other men (the male-male agreement) and women to other women (the female-female agreement). Our social structures and social interactions are created and regulated by this collusion. It is where the jaggedness comes from. Therefore, Esmeralda asserted, we as a society and as individuals are predisposed to certain illnesses. Because our energy is diverted into limited views of both ourselves and the world, we do not have the energy to maintain our fluid connection with the Bigger Dream. We need to gather energy to break the stranglehold of learned behavior in order to take back our connection with the Bigger Dream. Esmeralda made it clear that if we could reestablish this link, we would live full, healthy lives with incredible vitality and amazing vibrancy.

These concepts had forced me to reexamine my ideas of disease and what constitutes a cure. I had begun to conclude that a change of perception was needed. What I saw as a healer was that disease is cured only when people have the energy and the direction to round off their jaggedness and make their lives more fluid.

"Why aren't we connected to the vitality around us?" I asked Esmeralda as I returned to the moment. "There must be a part of us that knows better."

"Of course we know better, but we have been hoodwinked," she said. "We have to take our energy back and redirect it. It takes a great deal of energy to lose your jaggedness, to round your body off," Esmeralda rubbed her belly with a circular motion, "to become smooth and fluid, to reconnect to the Bigger Dream. We don't have the energy to face ourselves, so we hide behind laziness."

"How so?" I asked.

"Laziness is a facade that masks our fear of facing our loneliness. We're afraid of loneliness because loneliness means standing outside the consensus of perceptual conditioning. Without that consensus we think we're nothing. Loneliness is the door to your vertical integrity."

"The reason that you are becoming aware of your own pain and that of others is because you are facing your loneliness. You have gathered enough energy so that you now have a perspective on your learned behavior," she said smiling. "You can feel the pain created by the restrictions of your learned behavior, and you are acutely aware of that pain in those around you. You are very lucky to have your work as a healer to see this so clearly." She chuckled. "You are now identifying with the part of your patients that is in pain and seeks release. What you need to do now is identify with the process of letting go of this pain."

I suddenly realized that I had been doing this all along but that I hadn't been aware of it. I remembered a patient that I had seen recently. Merlin had come to me in a great deal of pain because he had just separated from his wife of seven years. At first I had empathized. Then I realized that Merlin had stumbled into a great opportunity. I explained that he now had the time, space, and the energy supplied by the pain he was feeling to over-haul his life. I added that these opportunities did not come along that often and that now was the time to act.

I then used this perspective to treat him. I employed acupuncture to balance the flow of energy throughout his body. In that way, his jagged-ness—or attachment to perceptual conditioning—was lessened, and he was able to begin discovering what was behind the pain. Not only did this help Merlin to discover new perspectives and options in his life, but it gave us a new premise through which to relate to each other.

I related this story to Esmeralda and added, "But he wasn't totally cured, was he?" A little doubt had crept into my mind.

She laughed. "It's a process that goes on day by day, hour by hour, minute by minute. Look at yourself. Are you cured? You now see that your life seemed dead and meaningless because of the doldrums created by repeti-tions of your learned behavior. You've allowed more energy into your life. You feel more connected to the flow of life around you. You may even begin to see that breaking out of your learned behavior is what was causing the disorientation and frustration you were experiencing when you arrived here," she said with a smile. "And you now have time for bigger thoughts.

"But you have only started. You have gathered enough energy to begin to shatter your learned behavior and to get a sense that there is some-thing beyond. You are clearing away the debris from your true potential so that you can begin to consciously dip in and out of the womb of creation."

I was contorting my face, trying to understand what she was saying. Esmeralda contorted her face back and started to laugh.

"Don't laugh at me! I barely have a grip on this," I snapped.

"Yeah," she said, laughing some more, "this grip thing is a famous excuse! It's just the kind of grip you are looking for that's the problem."

I was exasperated and thoroughly confused. "So how am I supposed to understand unless I *try* to understand?" I demanded.

"Often," Esmeralda continued, "if you keep going when you think you barely have a grip, you find out that you had a grip all along. The key is not to stop and intellectualize the process. You must keep flowing. Now, I want you to get up and move, get your energy mobilized."

She told me to begin walking around. We had been talking so intently that I had gradually closed out the beautiful morning around us. I stretched toward the sky, loosened my shoulders, and following Esmeralda's directions, I began to relax. I noticed right away that movement began to change my static thoughts as well.

As if reading my mind, or maybe my movements, Esmeralda continued, "The kind of grip you wanted was a grip that would stop the flow of things so that you could look at them as objects. But we're not talking about objects, we are talking about flow—finding a Center of flow."

I nodded and immediately began to hear the murmur of the water in the nearby stream. The sun was higher now, and the water danced and sparkled, coming to life.

"Remember the Sufi saying: If you want a new thought, put your body into a new posture." Esmeralda paused, then added, "Those old Sufis, they sure knew what they were talking about. We are much more than just the thoughts that we have when we're sitting still or lying on the couch. Do you see how your idea of your body and who you are changes as you move?" Esmeralda got up and walked beside me. "We forget about the body's relationship to gravity and the body-to-body language that is always going on," she continued, smiling. "You can ignore it, but it still affects you." In a fluid motion, she playfully nudged me, saying, "We're just like dolphins, though we live in a different kind of water."

Chapter 4

THE BIGGER DREAM

We all sense that there is something out there—what is it? The Bigger Dream is an immense black womb full of liquid light. That is to say, black, warm, and nourishing, yet full of swirling energy that contains dream worlds without measure.

—Esmeralda

That night, Esmeralda and I sat in her living room by the light of a single candle. We had finished dinner and were enjoying the silence, feeling the soft glow of the candle and the flicker of shadow on the walls around us. We were practicing yet another act of perceptual reorganization, using the element of fire. In this case, it involved keeping one's attention on the flame while interacting peripherally with another person.

After a time, Esmeralda began speaking. "Your dreaming was very productive. Now you understand better your feelings of frustration. They were caused by gathering more energy without knowing how to apply it. It's important to give that newfound energy a focus. You have to become a particle in the midst of the flow of things. You need to find the true Center of your being and create a new self-identity from that place. It is imperative that you do this. Once you've broken out of your perceptual conditioning, your old sense of self no longer works. You need to organize yourself by remembering who you really are. And that is just the beginning of the adventure."

Esmeralda suggested that I relax into my chair, a heavy, old-fashioned overstuffed piece that she had picked up at a flea market for a couple of dollars and lovingly refinished and recovered in a coarse, heavy cotton the color of sage. Over its back was folded a brightly striped *serape* to protect against the inevitable evening chill.

"Once you move out of your self-concept—the limited dream of

47

learned behavior—you start to make full connection with what we all sense is out there—something bigger than the daydream and the nightdream—what I call the Bigger Dream."

I slowly nodded. She had my rapt attention.

"The Bigger Dream," she began, "is an immense black womb full of liquid light. That is to say, black, warm, and nourishing, yet full of swirling energy that contains dream worlds without number, running through it like the golden strings of a harp. When we dream, we brush up against these strings." She paused for a moment. "When we are complete and full of flowing affection, we become little sparks of light moving in this immense blackness, this nurturing womb, like fireflies in the warm summer night."

She picked up a slim book and opened it to a poem, "Flower of Moon, Flower of Sun," based on Zapotec mythology. It was written by a good friend of hers, Miguel Torres. Esmeralda began to read:

I am a flower of a thousand colors
and one aroma,
that of the dreams,
the feminine.

The solar rays close my petals
and I sleep navigating in them
to the meadows of the stars,
to the sunsets in strange worlds.
I go to eternity,
my origin and my end.

The moon arrives to interrupt my dreams
and it opens my petals,
I dream awake.
We share the nights together
when all are asleep.
We move the sea
and the cycles of the Earth.

We run with the wind,
we sing with the water
and we bleed with the women.

But in the quiet nights
The moon and I
observe the dreams
of the dreamers
when they leave to fly.
We see them between the fog,
going to the cosmos,
going to themselves,
to die
before returning to the world.

I am the flower of one color
and a thousand aromas—
those of the world,
the masculine.

When the moon arrives
my petals close.
I stop the world
and go to dream
with a sigh
that I have wings
that unite me with the sky.

The sunlight dissolves my wings
and I return to the world,
to my roots,
which unite me to the earth.
I stalk daily events
with my aromas

and share with the sun
life and its colors,
the crystal waters,
the invisible winds.
We contemplate together the enigmas
of the clouds telling stories.

Today is the day of clarity, year zero:
It begins with confusing lights in the sky.
The flowers, we open and close
our petals in the confusion.
We swing between dream and vigil
in the middle of the eclipse of fertility
that unites us like one single flower.
Only today we fuse,
Flower of Moon and Flower of Sun.

This is how you were born,
nostalgic seed of wisdom.
You are a mystery.

When I dream, I feel your word
in all my being.
I don't know if I understand it.
I open my petals but can't see you.
All that is there is the sleeping flower of love.
And I feel a terrible nostalgia
that shakes me,
from my deepest
until my last petal.

Where is the fertile land
that makes you bloom?

Where is the silent water that will feed you
and the wind that will tear you apart
to make you born?
What is the fire
that will temper you?

I see you come
with the color of solitude
and the aroma of freedom.

APPLICATION: EXPLORING THE WATCHER

This exercise helps you find the place between your daydream and your nightdream, a place from which we resonate but for which we have no language.

Your learned behavior, through which you perceptually function during the day, is often reflected in the way you create and perceive your image in your nightdreams. The first step in learning to work with your personal feng shui is connecting with the self that is in between your daytime self-concept and your nightdream image.

In order to do this, you need to shift your perception and gather the energy necessary to transcend your ordinary self-concept. Here are some simple applications that I have found helpful.

DAYTIME

The following practices are structured around the four elements that make up the daytime world—fire, water, air, and earth. Spend some time each day (forty-five minutes would be ideal) over a period of days engaging in the activities described below. Remember as you practice that your intent is to move away from your perceptual conditioning so that you can gather enough energy to become aware of your true Center.

FIRE. Gaze into or listen to a campfire, a fireplace, or even a candle flame so that your perception gets taken in. If you catch yourself drifting away into thoughts or feelings, bring your concentration back to the fire.

You can practice this alone or with others. When others are present, try interacting with them while keeping your main focus on the fire. This will help you to maintain the position of the Watcher in the midst of other activity. As a variation on this practice, throw a stick into the fire every time you have a thought; then watch it burn.

WATER. The practice of water is similar to that of fire. Gaze at or listen to water. Moving water, such as a fountain or river, is ideal, but even a rainstorm can be useful. When you catch yourself drifting into thoughts or feelings, bring your concentration back to the water. As a variation on this practice, drop a flower petal or a leaf into the river every time you get a thought or feeling; then watch it float by.

You may also immerse yourself during this practice; sense the flow of water on the skin.

AIR. During air practices, you are suspended above the earth—in a climbing harness, lying in a hammock, or dangling your legs off the side of a suspension bridge or a tree limb. Concentrate on being suspended. The purpose here is to disengage from your normal way of touching gravity and thereby your normal way of touching the world.

Falling Practices of Air. Pick things up repeatedly and let them fall through the air. Use, for example, leaves, flower petals, or seeds. Grab a handful and raise your hand. As you let them fall through the air, gaze at and listen to them.

Rising Practices of Air. Gaze at steam, fog, or smoke (as from burning incense). If you catch yourself drifting into thoughts or feelings, bring your concentration back to the falling or rising medium.

EARTH. Bury part of your body in the earth (the beach is ideal for this practice). Concentrate on and sense the pressure of the earth around you. If you catch yourself drifting into thoughts or feelings, relax back into the pressure of the earth.

As a variation, sit or lie on the ground and feel gravity as a darkness wherever your body touches the earth; sink into it and let the feeling of gravity pull you down.

Remember that in doing any of these practices you must have the right intent: you want to move away from your learned behavior and perceptual conditioning to gather energy to establish your true Center.

If you can spend time doing a variety of these practices over a period of days, your awareness of the Watcher or your Center will increase, and you will have more energy to work with during your nightdreams.

NIGHTTIME

During sleep, if you become aware that you're dreaming, relax, wait, and observe. Be the Watcher in your dream; wait for something else to happen. Act within the awareness of the Watcher.

SIGNS OF PROGRESS:

◆ You notice that you're watching yourself in your nightdreams. In daydreams, you see that you're a little further from your normal way of perceiving yourself. You begin to feel freer and more energetic as you disengage from learned behavior.

◆ If you gather enough energy to stay away from perceptual conditioning, you can learn to act from there, settling into a new identity around which to create your own personal feng shui.

AWARENESS JOURNAL

This is where you can begin to create your Awareness Journal, in which you write down anything you notice about your experiences as you go through the Applications in this book. (To review a more detailed description of the Awareness Journal, see page 8 in the Introduction.) Specific suggestions for what kinds of observations to make in your journal are given below and in the Applications to follow.

In "Tracking My Awareness," write down anything you notice as a result of doing the preceding applications for daytime and applications for nighttime.

For instance, you might describe difficulties in keeping your at-

tention focused while gazing at fire or water. How long did you do the practice? Did your concentration improve over time? In what part of your body did you experience most strongly the fire or water? What were your body sensations while you were suspended or while your legs were buried in the sand? Did you feel as though another part of you gained energy because you weren't focused on your internal thinking process?

Record your nightdreams and to what extent you were successful in being the Watcher.

PART II

EMBODYING YOUR AWARENESS

Chapter 5

Huang

The idea is to create an internal way of doing things that you can integrate into your everyday life. You take your idea of the body with you no matter where you go. Your idea of the body is the centerpost of your perception of reality. It is through this idea that you define who you are and what you are not.

—Huang

It was Friday afternoon, and Huang and I were in my truck, headed for a resort in the mountains where he had set up a one-week workshop. I had been looking forward to this workshop since I had last seen Esmeralda. I thought that I was beginning to understand about my connection to my Center and to the Bigger Dream, how we are restricted by the male-female agreement, and how this affected my personal feng shui. But I was not really sure how it applied to the body. I was hoping that during this workshop with Huang I would find out.

Huang was the martial arts teacher with whom I'd been studying for years. Even sitting still in the passenger seat of my truck, Huang's compact body radiated calm energy and boyish exuberance. Like Esmeralda, his actual age was always an enigma. Huang continually conveyed a contagious feeling of well-being. It was as though he changed the quality of the air so that it was charged with clear brightness.

My initial meeting with Huang a few years ago coincided with a point in my internal search and my training as a healer when I knew that something was missing. I saw clearly that I could not progress any further unless I could ground the principles or truths of my new perception through my body. Esmeralda supported this decision and encouraged me to train with a martial artist and master of body mechanics.

Training with Huang enabled me to properly open up my body to become a container for the new energy and information I had gathered. He taught me that an interconnected body translates into interconnected information. What I learned from Huang also helped in my healing practice. I was able to take all the mental formulas and models I'd studied in Chinese medicine and actually feel them in my body. This had given me a greater understanding of this ancient art of healing and a strong sense of confidence in my work. At the same time, I observed that the trust level of my patients increased. I could be much more myself with them. I also learned the very physical aspects of how bodies talk to bodies and the principles of how to stay in contact with myself, even in very intimate situations.

I thought about this as we drove through the mountains. My mind was very clear. The air rushing in the window was cool on my face. It was a very tactile experience. Because of the work that I had done with my teachers, my natural sense of balance was being reestablished. This indicated to me that my personal feng shui was getting better.

As Huang admired the mountain scenery, we talked about what kind of fish to order in a Chinese restaurant. Whenever I went to a Chinese restaurant, ordering was always difficult. But Huang always knew the most delicious combinations of things without ever looking at a menu. As I glanced at him briefly, I saw him run his hand meditatively over his short-haired scalp. His body rippled with energy. Huang finished enthusiastically describing a few different ways that the Chinese prepared fish and the various sauces that could be used. Now that my mouth was watering, he decided to change the subject.

"Daniel, how you are enjoying the exercises I taught you? Have you seen any changes in your life?" He also wondered if I had found a way to use the inner principles in my everyday movements, such as walking.

Suddenly a piece of the puzzle fell into place. I thought about a ritual that Esmeralda had put me through early in my training. She had given me four dolls to carry on my back as we hiked miles to an old bull ring. There she had used the dolls as props so that I could tactilely experience the linchpin that held together our learned behavior—the male-female agreement. Esmeralda had gone on to say that society's urge to perpetuate itself is, of course, fine. The problem is that society, in its paranoia, has become tyrannical and rules out any other use of the dynamic energy centered in the lower part of our bodies. This is one of the things that damages our feng shui, our potential for flowing in the world.

After I had set the dolls up in the bullring, the two male dolls on one side and the two female dolls on the other, Esmeralda told me to walk between the male and female figures. As I strolled back and forth, she explained that the first important event following birth is the distinction between self and other. Then society imposes on us its idea of male and female. It is through this perceptual conditioning that our contact with the world becomes limited and, when our Luminous Essence cannot flow unimpeded, our feng shui suffers.

Later, Esmeralda broke down learned behavior into the male-female agreement, the male-male agreement, and the female-female agreement. Through these, the male-female agreement becomes the basis for all of our family structures and social interactions. She stressed that this is because society believes that for its own preservation it must control the sexual and procreative energies.

What triggered this entire memory was that the whole time I was moving back and forth between the male and female dolls in the bullring, Esmeralda kept reminding me to walk the way that Huang had taught me. I related the experience to him and asked, "Why was it important that I walk that way?"

Huang looked back at the road, thought for a long moment, then turned to me, rubbing his hands together enthusiastically. "Two answers: one is that Esmeralda wanted to establish a way of walking that was different from how you normally walk. In that way, you were put In-Between. You started to contact your Center. You had to move through the world in a new way. Second, walking with your whole body more efficiently connected to gravity is a superior way to walk, especially when you are actively in the midst of confronting learned behavior. Your learned behavior makes you walk and move in very fixed ways. To counter this you need a very natural way of positioning yourself with the flow of things," he said. "This is the way that a conscious warrior wages war, by maintaining his natural flow in the midst of all conditions."

What Huang said made sense. After the experience with Esmeralda at the bull ring and being with her recently at her house, I was slowly beginning to see how dealing with my learned behavior was a constant war. Maintaining continual awareness from the place of the Watcher was the only way to combat its unrelenting onslaughts.

"Esmeralda wanted you to involve your whole idea of the body and its relationship to gravity as a way of knitting together a multisensual exposure to your male-female agreement," Huang continued. "She also wanted to pound into you that, as a result of learned behavior, all repetitive movements are a ritual that creates the feng shui we live in. The way you are learning to move with me is an efficient way to get beyond those repetitive movements."

I nodded as Huang continued.

"The way I'm teaching you to move comes from within yourself. Using this internal focus when you walk, as Esmeralda had you do in the bullring, separates you from your normal way of moving. Then you can see that your usual movements in everyday life are repetitive—the ritual of learned behavior. For real change to happen, your fixed idea of your body and yourself has to change, and you need to relate to the world from a new Center."

I thought about this as we entered a long, dark tunnel and then emerged to an incredible Rocky Mountain vista. "What exactly do you mean by my fixed idea of my body? Isn't my body my body?" I asked, rubbing my chest.

Huang started laughing, rubbing his belly and patting his head at the same time. "If you are dealing with a whole idea of the body, you are dealing with a full deck," Huang continued, still chuckling. "When you are using just the mind or the idea of the body that you have acquired through learned behavior, it's like five-card draw. You get only five cards. You have very few variables at your disposal. You can stand pat, discard, or draw new cards. But you still have five cards, not fifty-two. When you're using your entire body, you have access to a full deck with all its variables."

"And what if your deck is all jokers?" I asked, only half in jest.

"The body in motion, lined up properly with gravity, gives us a full deck. What I teach is the study of lining oneself up most efficiently with gravity. It is through this recognition that we can move beyond to our greater essence and also allow that greater essence to flow through us into the world," Huang said. "All the information we need is in the body. That applies even to jokers like you."

After we stopped laughing, Huang continued. "I try to have you experience this in my classes. As you well know, when you make a proper movement against someone in the martial art that I am teaching you, it is as if you didn't do anything. Something greater takes over. You make contact with a larger aspect of yourself that is in touch with the Bigger Dream."

When he demonstrated his martial-art techniques, Huang always stressed that something greater than his idea of himself was at work. He always said that motive is supremely important. To take powerful new ways of moving and use them frivolously could easily cause harm to oneself as well as others. This had always rung true to me, but I felt that I had never fully understood all of the implications. I was hoping to learn more about this during the workshop.

Huang often told me that the way to get beyond our idea of the body is to be in the body in a much more complete way. He once gave an example from his earlier Buddhist training: One day a disciple asked the Buddha, "Lord Buddha, where do I look for enlightenment?" Lord Buddha pointed to the disciple and replied, "In your infinitely long body."

Late in the afternoon, we arrived at the resort. The mountains were beautiful this time of year. The snow had melted and left everything green in its wake. Wildflowers bloomed everywhere. Being around nature and sensing its flow was an inspiration.

The camp was set up on the side of a mountain overlooking a town in the small valley below. Even though the ski season had ended, the town still bustled with vacationers. It felt exhilarating to be away from my usual surroundings and in such a gorgeous natural setting. There were several small cabins scattered around a large meeting hall. I dropped Huang off at his cabin so he could get ready for that night's class and went off to find my own cabin.

It was just after sunset and the sky was still light when we gathered in the meeting hall. There were about ten of us and we stretched and did warm-up exercises as we waited for Huang. Huang arrived wearing yellow sunglasses with bright green stripes, a Mickey Mouse T-shirt, and plaid work-out pants. I tried unsuccessfully to stifle a laugh—my venerable teacher resembled a Chinese-Scots golfer. When he saw me grinning, Huang flashed an offended scowl. "I paid a lot of money for this outfit!" he declared. He endured some more good-natured jibes before calling us to order.

He had us form lines, assuring us that this was the hardest thing we would do all week. True to form, it took us several minutes to get lined up to his satisfaction. Because Huang knew so many martial arts forms, I was a little nervous about whether I would be the only one who didn't know the one Huang would select. But before I had a chance to become too self-conscious, he said, "Begin." And he started moving.

I automatically started doing the Tai Chi form he had taught me and was relieved to find that everyone else was too. I found quickly that moving with a group felt very different from doing it on my own or simply following Huang's personal instructions. I watched other people peripherally as they turned and twisted, and I tried to synchronize myself with them. There were ten of us, and we each occupied about five square feet of space with our movements. I enjoyed lifting my arms, twisting my torso, and pushing my feet into the shiny wood floor.

I began to focus on moving my entire body with my arms. When I was lined up properly and my joints were open, I could lift and move my feet by twisting and turning my arms. As I moved, I could feel the energies of the bodies around me, all concentrating on the same movements, all learning from each other. We even seemed to be breathing together. I flashed on a sudden memory of a school of brilliant yellow fish I had seen one time while diving in Mexico. They had moved as a single organism, changing direction with flawless synchrony as they glided elegantly through their sun-dappled sanctuary. Now, here in a mountain studio, the atmosphere felt like that same peaceful, underwater world. I slipped in and out of time as my thoughts turned off and on. I was learning to engage the world in a new way.

I could see and feel our individual luminous cells surrounding us, much like the placenta surrounds us in the womb. As I watched, our luminous cells merged into one big cell, and within it flowed concentrated energy. Was this what it was like for the yellow fish in that far-off Mexican reef? I could feel information flowing into my body from all sides, subtly altering the way I moved. I felt carried along, my focus augmented by the concentration of the group. It was exhilarating to have so much energy to work with. On the other hand, it was almost painful to have more energy than I was used to. But then the memory of what Esmeralda recently told me came to mind: Pain is simply more energy than we are used to, and we must sometimes experience pain in order to grow and gather more energy. In this situation, there seemed to be much more energy than my body could handle for long. But the thought that I was learning kept my focus intact.

When we were done, Huang congratulated us. He always seemed to know how much and how hard we had worked. One of the things that I most admired about him was his fairness. If you worked hard, he taught you. If you didn't work, he didn't have much to teach you. It was irrelevant whether you were his friend or someone he barely knew. What was fair was fair.

"You have all studied with me for at least two years," Huang began. "Our bodies have learned to talk with each other in a different way than we were originally taught by our parents and society. You have been learning a new language. This week, we are going to use this new language in a very practical way, one that extends far beyond what is normally thought of as martial arts. You will begin to find out what your particular learned behavior is and how it affects your personal feng shui. We will take our new way of moving, this new language of the body, and juxtapose it against our normal way of moving so that we can explore our potential."

A male student in his mid-thirties asked, "I've never heard you talk about a body language before."

Huang beamed enthusiastically and motioned for the student to come forward.

This student, Henry, was one of the few people in the room that I had met previously. He was tall and shy. What struck me about him was the difference between how he moved when we did exercises together as opposed to when we were just talking. During exercises Henry was relatively fluid. Otherwise he stood stiffly with his head thrust forward, seemingly disconnected from his body. Now he approached Huang in this awkward, stilted way.

Huang said, "The way you walked toward me was the way that you talked to me."

Henry flushed with confusion and embarrassment.

"Now, Henry," Huang continued, "begin doing the Tai Chi form that I taught you."

"Wh-where?" Henry looked around in confusion.

Huang chuckled. "Right here."

At first, Henry moved self-consciously. But soon, as he became absorbed in the Tai Chi form, his movements became graceful and fluid. After a few moments of watching, Huang spoke softly. "You're talking differently now, using a different language. There's more of you interacting with the world now, and I can feel it." Huang glanced at us with raised eyebrows. We all nodded back: we could feel it, too. Henry returned to his place, his face still flushed, but now experiencing himself in a new way.

"Now," Huang continued, "put that fluidity that you just experienced while doing the form into your motion as you walk toward me again."

I could tell this took Henry by surprise, but he recovered quickly. This time when he approached Huang, he walked differently. He wasn't stiff; his joints were more open. Although he wasn't quite as fluid as when doing the Tai Chi form, there was a visible improvement. Huang clapped his hands delightedly. "Good! Now you are learning a new language."

Beaming, Henry returned to his position in the group. I wondered what it would be like if Henry maintained this new language of fluidity beyond our group practice. I thought it might be fun to find out.

APPLICATION: CONTACTING YOUR ENERGY BODY

Stand with your arms at your sides. Begin slowly moving them as if they were strands of seaweed under water. Do this until you feel a tingly or fuzzy sensation in your hands. Try to feel that sensation throughout your body as you continue to move your hands. This is a way to begin contacting your energy body. After a while, you may be able to sense this tingly or fuzzy energy without moving your hands. Try to sense it while you're walking down the street or even at work. See if you can keep it as you relate to other people. Next, attempt to engage the tingly feeling before you go off to sleep. See if it makes any difference in your awareness at night.

AWARENESS JOURNAL

In "Tracking My Awareness," note how well you are able to maintain this tingly sensation while at work. Does it affect your awareness during sleep?

For example, in my own Awareness Journal, the first thing I noted while doing these applications was that I felt as if I were in two places at once. I was acting normally, yet there was another part of me that was a keen Observer. I also noted that my energy did not dissipate as quickly during the work day, and I had more ability to focus on the needs of others around me.

Continuing, Huang addressed the group. "We are accumulating a body of knowledge together, a new language of moving in the world. It's very different from the manner of relating we are accustomed to in our ordinary lives. We are going to take this new way of moving and extend it out into what we think of as ordinary life. We will pit it against our old way of being in the world.

"Although we may not be conscious of it, the form of our movement in everyday life is a multisensual ritual that confers upon us certain ways of being. When you practice this multisensual ritual in the right way, an unimaginable sense of flow will begin to develop in your life. This will be good feng shui."

Huang looked us over for a moment, then said, "Marlene and Joseph, I would like the two of you to walk over to the door and back."

As we watched Marlene and Joseph did as they were instructed.

"Looks normal doesn't it?" Huang asked, looking at us. "And feels normal too," he added, smiling at Marlene and Joseph. They nodded in agreement.

"And that," Huang continued, "is the problem. Those movements are so normal to us that we not only do them repetitiously, but unconsciously. Watch this." Huang snaked across the room, undulating with fluid grace, to the door and back. It was always a marvel to see Huang move.

"Looks weird, but it sure does feel good," he said when he returned to his place in front of us. We all laughed. "In order to properly juxtapose the massive amounts of input that our learned behavior has trained us to receive, we need a more efficient and inclusive system that fully engages all our senses," he continued. "We can't rely on changing our thought processes alone. We need a system that contains physical components, and one of those components is movement."

"What do you mean by 'physical components'?" Henry asked.

Huang motioned for Henry to stand, then walked up to him and said, "Watch me push you over." Huang scrunched up his face, made claws out of his hands, and huffed and puffed. Henry didn't move. Huang laughed and said, "Boy, this Henry is strong, I can't move him with my mind."

We all laughed.

Then Huang stuck out his arm and pushed Henry—who went flying across the room.

"Get it?" Huang smiled. He loved being an entertainer. He had pushed Henry in a carefully controlled way so as to give a jolt without injury. Henry now sat on the floor, grinning sheepishly.

The more energy Huang got moving through us, the more we wanted. "Learned behavior affects us physically. You can't just have some mental idea of how you want to be and pit that against your learned behavior. It doesn't have a chance." He pointed at Henry and we all smiled. "I know that some of you have been exposed to the ideas of the four motions and how they help us see the degree to which our learned behavior affects us."

Marlene spoke up. "I'm not familiar with them. What are the four motions?"

"I thought you'd never ask," Huang replied gleefully. "Listen closely, you will probably hear about them only about fifty times during these next few days." We laughed again.

"What we call the four motions," Huang explained, "are movement, breathing, the use of the eyes, and the use of sound. These are four ways of breaking down our physical indoctrination to a very limited system of being. However, we can also use them to free ourselves from this indoctrination. If we are going to pit another system against our learned behavior, it needs to have a strong physical component. That's why you need each other to do this. By learning to move in a new way around each other, something in you will say, 'It's all right to move this way.' You need each other to stabilize another way of being in the world."

Huang motioned a female student to the front of the class. She was a tall woman with short brown hair. I had not met her before, but found her quite attractive. Huang smiled at her. "I don't draw very well, so I need your help, Keisha," he said.

Huang picked up a piece of chalk. At the blackboard he drew a big ellipse with smaller ellipses for arms and legs, and a round head. He pointed to Keisha's body and said, "Physical body." He then made a thick line down the center, from the top of the head to the bottom of the torso. Huang turned to Keisha and pointed up and down the front of her body and said, "This is really inside of her. We'll call it her Luminous Essence." Next he drew a large egg shape around the figure on the blackboard and said, "Relating body." Huang turned to Keisha and touched her shoulder.

Huang pointed to the line in the middle of the blackboard figure. "So this is our Luminous Essence—the real Center of our being—who we really know ourselves to be at a very deep level. It is directed out through our idea of our physical body," he said, pointing to the blackboard and Keisha's body. "And then it moves through our relating body, the way we interact in the world," he said, motioning to the space between the ellipses and the outer circle. The manner in which these energies flow constitutes our personal feng shui."

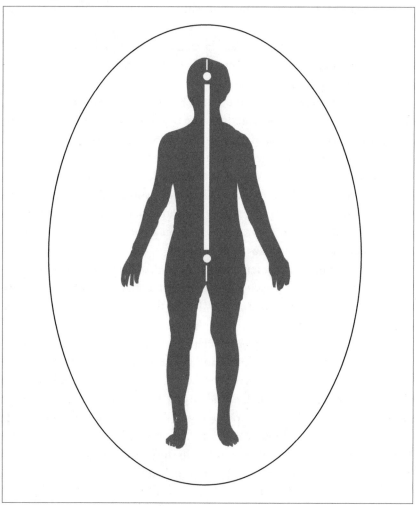

ILLUSTRATION 1: *Luminous Essence, Physical Body, Relating Body, Other World.*

APPLICATION: THE FEELING OF THE WATCHER IN-BETWEEN

You want to get a sense of the In-Between—that feeling between the daydream and the nightdream—our Center.

◆ Sit in a quiet place. Imagine this feeling as a column extending up and down the middle of the trunk of your body from the top of your head to the perineum.

◆ Let the sense of your true self flow out into your physical body.

◆ Return to the sense of the Watcher or Observer.

◆ Extend that feeling, again creating a central column, to what you perceive as your physical body, and then to your relating body: first, to all the ways that you relate to people; second, to all the ways you relate to other beings (including animals and plants); and third, to the earth itself.

AWARENESS JOURNAL

In "Embodying My Awareness," make an entry describing what you experienced from this application. One of the things that I experienced was the realization that I was a lot bigger than I thought I was. I realized that I wasn't just my physical body, but I was also the way that I connected and related to others.

Application Reminder: When doing any of the applications, remember the importance of intention. Look carefully into the reason you are doing the applications, and remember to continually explore this motive. You're trying to connect all of your parts together to make yourself whole. Remember to find and continually redefine your Center. Note this in your Awareness Journal under "Tracking My Awareness."

Redefining your Center is important because most of the applica-

> *tions will be about directing the energy from your Center into manifestation. Be sure to note the evolution of the feeling of being in your Center. Remember, it has a motion.*

Huang smiled at Keisha and asked her to remain where she was. "Now let's start talking about the body computer," he said, looking at me. "Daniel, are you a body computer?" Huang motioned me to the front. "Do you remember me telling you about this?" The question was directed to everyone in the class. "The trunk of the body is really the computer," he said, gently poking me in the ribs. "The head, " he reached over and mussed my hair, "is the computer screen. So far so good." Huang smiled.

"Now I'm going to pose a question to both of you." He looked at Keisha and me. "How do you interact or relate?"

Keisha and I stood there awkwardly, not knowing what to say or do. "Very good," he said. There was a ripple of laughter. "Well, reach out and touch someone." Huang chuckled.

Keisha and I tentatively touched each other's fingertips.

"Right," said Huang. "That's how we interact with the world around us—with our hands or feet. We walk with our legs and feet and reach out to the world with our arms and hands." With childlike artistic zeal, he began to draw an amusing picture on the board, a combination human being-computer, with electric plugs emerging from the limbs. "Our body is a computer; our head is the screen, and with the hands and feet, we plug into the world." He finished the drawing with a flourish.

APPLICATION: PLUGGING INTO THE WORLD

As you move around, at home or out in the world, notice how many objects you pick up in the course of an hour. During the same hour, notice how fast or slow your legs and feet move as you walk. Notice how your legs turn your body to change direction and how your feet respond to different surfaces or inclines.

During the above practices, notice how you interact with the world around you through your limbs; how your limbs are your plugs into the world. Notice what your hands and wrists do, what your elbows and shoulders do, what your ankles and feet do, and what your knees and hips do. Re-member yourself.

AWARENESS JOURNAL

Under "Embodying My Awareness," write down your observations and experiences of the ways your body connects you to the world.

"We've got to get the energy out into our extremities in order to relate to the world," Huang said. He lightly touched me, sending an electrical shock through my body that put me on the floor. As I picked myself up off the floor, everyone laughed but me. Then I laughed, too, dramatically dusting myself off.

"This is what can happen when we plug into the world," Huang said, chuckling. He motioned for me to stand again next to Keisha. He walked in front of us and pointed to our heads, moving his hands and making buzzing sounds to indicate energy moving between us. "If they're operating from the head," he said, pointing to my head, "we know what that's like." Everyone laughed.

"One of the things we're going to work on while we're here is how to create a sensory checklist so that you can see where you begin and end in the midst of relating. But we're not going to get into that just yet. That's another story." Huang grinned. "For now," he continued, as Keisha and I stood next to each other, "I want you to remember: Thinking . . . " Huang pointed back and forth between our heads. "Feeling," he said, gesturing between Keisha's chest and mine. He pointed back and forth between our abdomens. "Being." For emphasis, he wrote on the blackboard: "Thinking, Feeling, Being."

"And remember that just thinking separates you from the lower parts of your body. And when you feel, you also think, but you're not really in

71

contact with your whole being. But when you're in contact with your whole being," he said, rubbing his abdomen, "you can think, feel and be all at the same time."

Huang asked me to lift my shirt. He pointed at my belly. "This our navel," he said, then added, "No, not really, this is Daniel's navel."

Everybody chuckled.

"It may look like a common, ordinary, everyday navel to you, but it is actually the physical primordial connection," he continued. "This is where we hook into the great womb that we know as the world. This is our primordial scar. It is what we call the Celestial Pivot, where the energies of heaven and earth meet. When we align ourselves properly with gravity and allow thinking," he pointed to Keisha's head, "to fuse with feeling," he touched her upper back, "and that, in turn, to fuse with our sense of being," he said rubbing his belly, "we become united naturally through the laws of gravity."

Huang thanked Keisha and me and we resumed our places in the group.

"This uniting then allows us to become physically aware of our Luminous Essence," Huang went on, "and sets the stage for our volition or our Luminous Essence to properly flow in and through the physical body, through the relating body, to make total contact with the world at large."

Chapter 6

THE BODY EYE

I awoke early the next morning, just as the sky began to lighten. I dressed in the dark and left my cabin for a walk. Stars were still out and the ground was wet with dew; the scents of the vegetation were sharp and clean. I breathed deeply and the cold, sweet air swept the last vestiges of grogginess out of my head. Below me, the valley was swaddled in darkness with only a few lights to show where the town lay. I watched as the sky above the crests of the mountains faded from deep blue to purple, then violet, rose and finally gold as a perfect new day was born. Standing shin-deep in wildflowers, I saw a doe leading twin fawns across the meadow below me. Briefly, the fawns broke out of formation, bounding in circles with the natural exuberance of the young of every species. The doe monitored her babies' play for a few moments; then coughed and stamped an authoritative hoof to call them back into line. As I watched them disappear into the mist I took a deep breath. I felt a thrill of reverent awe at the scene that had unfolded in front of me. Silently, I thanked the deer for showing me the beauty of the flow of energy around me.

It was in this frame of mind that I went to our first session of the day. Huang taught us a very light touching technique as we practiced martial arts movements in pairs. This exercise taught us to be very sensitive. We would work for ten minutes or so with one partner, then change to a new partner. It created a tingly awareness in my body that allowed me to perceive the intentions of my partner. Later on, this light touching was done in combination with other practices to create strength inside the body. The ideal result was to feel very strong on the inside and very sensitive on the outside, or what could be described by the Chinese idiomatic expressions "steel wrapped with cotton" or "iron wrapped in silk."

During these movements, I was able to begin integrating what Huang had told us in class the previous day. His discussion about thinking, feeling, and being became something that I could sense in myself and in my partner. I began to physically incorporate a way of observing these feelings in myself and then maintaining this state of being while interacting with my partner. I watched emotions and thoughts pass through me without getting hooked by them. Next I realized that I could also perceive my partner's energy and, seemingly, to some extent control it. I started exploring the combination of my energy with someone else's that occurred when our luminous cells merged. What allowed us to stay merged, I realized, was contact—in this case, physical.

APPLICATION: CONTACT WITH ANOTHER THROUGH CONTACT WITH YOURSELF

Sense your thoughts in your head; let that energy sink into your chest where your feelings reside. Then, let it sink down into your abdomen. Get a sense of how these three areas relate to each other when you're alone. Begin to see the state of being that comes from having your attention in the abdomen and how it encompasses the other two states of feeling and thinking. Practice alone for five or ten minutes at a time. When you become familiar with this sense of beingness, begin practicing around others. This will help to establish your sense of Center in the world of relating.

AWARENESS JOURNAL

In "Embodying My Awareness," describe what you experienced from this application.

When I did the above application alone, I watched the identification with my thinking process dissolve into an identification with something greater—the Watcher. When I did it around others, I noted that it was harder to stay aware of the Watcher. It seemed that the stimulus of being around others made me want to identify more with my thinking and my feelings.

We started working with an exercise that Huang called "activating the body eye." This movement was an extension of the previous light touching exercise, except that here we learned to make light contact with another not just with hands and forearms, but with our whole bodies whether close in or far away from our partners. We would continue light contact even as we spun around, shoulder to shoulder and back to back. Even our legs would sometimes be points of contact through which we could see-feel each other's intentions.

Here I found that I could sense what my partner was doing and what his or her intention was. I could do this, not only with my hands, but with all different parts of my body, even my back, as long as I maintained contact with my partner using this very sensitive light touch.

Not only could I perceive where their next movement would be, I could tell when they were even thinking about doing something. But I realized that I could do this only if my entire body was connected to my sense of being. This meant that I had to let go of my learned behavior and my usual sense of self.

Later in the morning, I was very aware of my movements as I walked to the hall where the workshop classes were held. Huang was already there, chatting enthusiastically with several students. After everyone had arrived, Huang called us together and began. He rubbed his lower abdomen and said, "The source of the energy of the body is here. This energy is the motor that powers the machine. However, our society chooses to interpret it primarily as sexual. The learned behavior we have acquired through the male-female agreement and social contracts fixes and limits it. The key to expanding beyond learned behavior is to relax this area.

"We want to try and loosen our energy and move it through our being in other ways than those that are prescribed by our learned behavior. To loosen the grip of learned behavior, we have to establish another way of being to juxtapose against it. That way must be based not on learned behavior, but on a new and more complete way of seeing the world that includes a new idea of your body," he said. "This is what we are doing, beginning to create a new idea of being in our bodies."

"Sometimes you talk about the body and other times you talk about the idea of the body," a gray-haired man named Alfred said. "You seem to jump from one picture to another, and I get very confused. So what's the difference between the physical body and our idea of it?"

Huang's eyes lit up. "Excellent question," he said, beaming. "Sometimes I wait years for such a good question!" He laughed. "You're not as confused as you think you are. This question gets down to the essence of our inquiry."

I was again amazed at Huang's resilience and brightness, particularly when he responded to one of us. "What I am trying to describe to you," he went on, "is an idea in motion. It's not a static idea that can be described in a single way, and it is not just a visual experience. It is a force, a multifaceted, moving experience. So in trying to explain it to you, since our mental faculties can cover only a small area, I have to hop around from one way of viewing things to another and another." To accentuate what he was saying, Huang shifted from foot to foot while pointing his finger at imaginary objects in front of him. "What I'm doing is describing this idea in motion to you in different ways," he said, "then you have to put it together.

"To make it even clearer," Huang continued, "it's like the old East Indian parable of the blind men touching the elephant." Huang closed his eyes and mimed. "Each blind man touched a different part." Tugging here and pulling there on the imaginary elephant, he said, "One the tail, another a leg, another the trunk, another the ear, and the last one who sat on the elephant's back. Each had a different idea of what the elephant was, and each in his way was right! But together they could have arrived at a total concept. Likewise, our idea of the physical body is only one limited way of looking at it, just like the blind man pulling the elephant's tail." He chuckled, pretending to pull a big tail. "By touching our living experiences—our physical bodies and the patterns that we use to relate to the world—in enough different ways, we can eventually get to the concept of the animals we really are.

"Now, to get back to your question," Huang said looking back at Alfred. "The physical body is the storehouse of our relating patterns. The *idea* of the body, however, is bigger than that. As I said last night, the relating body is how we relate to the world. Together with the physical body, this forms the idea of the body. Normally, the physical body takes its shape through a repetition of perceptual patterns, repetitive ways of viewing oneself. It is a point of being in relation to other beings and to the Earth itself. It creates a location for you in space. From it, you can then relate. It is the platform upon which your idea of the body rests. When a change is made and integrated into the platform, everything resting upon it is affected, and the way you perceive your body and yourself changes.

"I repeat, the physical body is the very concentrated storehouse of our perceptual patterns. Another, but related way, to look at this is that our idea of the body has to do with where we think the body ends and the rest of the world begins."

Alfred spoke up again. "What if someone changes his physical body by something like weight lifting? Or running? Doesn't that change the idea of the body?"

Huang smiled. "No, it probably won't. Ask Joseph sitting next to you. He tried to look like a bodybuilder, but look at him now."

Joseph struck an exaggerated bodybuilder's pose, and we all giggled.

"Both of the things that you mentioned, weight lifting and running, if used with the right intention, could change one's idea of the body," Huang went on. "But they are rarely undertaken with that intention. They are usually done to concretize an idea of the body that has been given to us by our learned behavior. Even the martial arts are rarely used in the proper way. Without the proper intent, the martial arts are no better than weight lifting or running." For emphasis, Huang performed a karate chop through the air. "It is possible, and very common, for a person to change the way he looks by simply repeating the same pattern. In the weight-lifting example," Huang continued as he began to pump imaginary iron, "a person will look different if he practices this discipline diligently. However, if you examine carefully what he is doing, you will see that he is simply repeating his same patterns, only on a grander scale. This makes him feel better and look better in terms of his idea of the body. But he hasn't really changed his basic idea— his internal perception of who he is."

Now I was beginning to understand how our idea of the body reflects our connection to the Bigger Dream and how this related to the physical body. I also realized that, if I changed my limited idea of myself, it would be reflected in my idea of my body. For this lesson alone, I thought, coming to this workshop had been worth it.

"These weight lifters, for example," Huang continued, "are still limited to the same ways of making contact with the world. They continue to use their muscles, their breathing, and so on, in the same way to substantiate their view of the world, only in a more exaggerated fashion. Perceptually they are no freer than they were before. In fact, they may become further entrenched in their worldview because their intent and practice are based on supporting and enhancing their learned behavior rather than moving beyond it. But really they're perceptually the same as they were before." Huang bent over and hefted imaginary barbells. He jerked them over his head a couple of times and laughed. "Although the physical body may look as if it has changed, the preexisting patterns have only been accentuated. Look at Joseph here, our beach boy." Huang grinned, enjoying himself immensely. "Did you know that Joseph used to be a beach boy?"

Of course we all riveted our eyes on Joseph. He grinned back at Huang and then the rest of us.

"When he got stronger by lifting weights," Huang continued, "he could then go back and kick sand in the face of the guys who used to kick sand at him. But that didn't change him inside. The fact that he moved higher in the beach-boy pecking order meant only that he epitomized those action-reaction patterns even more. The higher he moved, the more power he perceived himself to have. That made it harder for him to move beyond his learned behavior and expand his idea of the body. That was because, after lifting weights for years, he had even more invested, and was even more entrenched in that way of being. That made him an even harder nut to crack. Until, of course, he met me." Huang chuckled.

Chapter 7

KEISHA

I went to the resort town in the valley for lunch, filled with a burgeoning sense of excitement. The material Huang had gone over was starting to fall together, and I was making connections between what Esmeralda had said and what Huang said about the relationships between learned behavior, the male-female agreement, and sexual energy. I could now see how our idea of the body could affect our personal feng shui, thus creating illness, and how repetitive patterns stopped us from making a fluid connection to the Bigger Dream. Slowly, a clearer picture of how the patterns of learned behavior affect health and the way we relate to the world began to emerge.

I walked along the main street until I found a cafe. A big blond kid of sixteen or seventeen with a lot of hardware in his earlobes was washing the front window, and it sparkled in the bright sunshine. He flashed me a dazzling grin as I paused to examine the menu posted behind the glass. Bright yellow gingham curtains adorned the lower half of the window below a veil of lush-looking ivy, philodendron, and asparagus fern in white hanging planters. Just as I concluded that the plants were real and that the buckwheat cakes with my choice of wild honey or real Vermont maple syrup were just what I needed, I heard a soft tap on the glass. I stepped back, startled, and then saw Keisha, seated alone on the other side of the posted menu. I'd been just inches away from her the whole time. I blushed with embarrassment, then laughed, as she waved me inside to her table. As I settled into a chair across from her, I felt the same attraction that I'd felt in class.

As we ordered, I noticed the silky quality of Keisha's short brown hair, the shine in her eyes, and how she seemed very secure within herself. I was impressed by the calmness and clarity that I felt in her presence. She told me that she had been Huang's student for about six years and that the experience had transformed her life. Huang had put together a special series of

79

exercises designed specifically to enhance her feng shui so that she could live a healthy, flowing life. Without the slightest hesitation, she offered to show them to me later.

Keisha explained how, by doing these exercises, she had watched her old ways of being peel away like the layers of an onion. As a result life had become, on one hand, very exciting and, on the other, very dreamlike. Even the way she saw the world had changed. She became aware of the many tendrils that extended from her and hooked into the world. Eventually she was able to feel these tendrils gradually unhooking as she disentangled herself from the social patterns she had been taught. She became more the Observer and began to experience increased energy in her life. As she spoke, I admired her ability to articulate her experience. She reminded me a little of Esmeralda.

We started to talk about how people could change themselves. Keisha described her brother and sister and the burdens that weighed them down and made their lives heavy and dull. Her own life had been transformed when she learned to work with her personal feng shui, and she wished she could teach her siblings. "But," she concluded a little sadly, "they're so afraid to try anything new. It's as though they'd rather be miserable than to have to change their view of life."

We had long finished eating. Suddenly, I looked at my watch. I realized the afternoon class had already begun.

Keisha laughed. "It's okay, I've been to these workshops before. I know what Huang's going to teach next. I'll fill you in." She suggested a place up in the mountains where we could go for a long walk. As we rode in my truck, Keisha said, "I used to live in a lot of fear. I first went to Huang to learn martial arts so I could protect myself."

"I originally went to see Huang because I felt sick and very stuck in my life." I confided. "I can see now—with the luxury of hindsight, of course—that I was also in a lot of fear too, especially of myself."

Keisha smiled. "After Huang began working with me and I felt a little stronger," she said, "he mentioned that after you change the energy flow in your body, you can change your relating body, and that in turn changes how you interact with the world. And boy, did that ever happen to me! He also said that when you begin to arrange your own personal feng shui in a more harmonious pattern, the way the world hits you changes too. Once you get more flow in your life, you experience everything differently."

I smiled. "Yes, I've gone through some of that, too. Like you, doing exercises, changing my experience of my body, have really affected how I relate to the world around me. But only now, talking to you, do I realize the extent that it has changed me. What I remember Huang telling me," I said, "is the wonderful effect of consciously aligning ourselves with gravity for many hours a day."

Keisha looked at me curiously, as if she didn't quite understand.

"My problem," I continued, "was that at the time I met Huang I would move as little as possible and lie down every chance I got. I didn't know what else to do with myself. One of the first things Huang told me was not to let myself lie down all day. He said I needed to let the earth's gravity move through me as I stood and walked. He showed me some exercises and explained the underlying principles in these movements. I've got to tell you, my life was real exciting back then." I laughed, amazed at the difference between then and now.

APPLICATION: MOVEMENT AND FLOW

More movement and flow in your life supplies more doorways through which the spirit can speak to you. To the extent that you are a sedentary person, think of putting more flow into your life by letting the earth's gravity flow through you in different ways. If you find yourself lying down or sitting a lot, get up and move more. You may find that standing consciously takes less energy than standing unconsciously. Be conscious of moving until you become one with the movement. When you are sitting, create a movement through noticing; make conscious contact with the environment around you.

For about one week, make a point of moving more and focusing on moving in your life. Note the results of this under "Embodying My Awareness." Make an entry once a week to keep track of yourself.

"Remember how differently Henry walked yesterday after Huang showed him how to incorporate more fluidity into his movements?" Keisha reminded me.

"Yeah," I said, "that was dramatic. You could tell just by the look on his face that all of a sudden he *got it.* The energy shift was visible to everybody in that room. I doubt Henry will ever again move in that old way."

She was smiling at me as I stole a brief glance at her, then looked back at the road. We were approaching a wooded area. "Since I've incorporated Huang's teachings into my everyday life," I said, "I feel as though I get more sparks of energy off the earth's surface. Huang said that aligning myself with gravity would take the jaggedness out of my luminous cell so that nothing could hook on anymore."

"Well," Keisha continued, "That's the new language that Huang was talking about last night. It's a very vibrant language of tactile resonance."

"Tactile resonance?" I echoed.

"That's a term I coined myself," she said proudly. "Do you like it?"

"Yeah," I said, "but what exactly does it mean?"

"For me, it describes how bodies vibrate and interact with each other," she responded. "It's the language that our multiplied senses have with ourselves and each other. And—Oh, turn right here, Daniel!"

With the style of a Grande Prix driver, I executed a turn after a split-second check of my mirrors.

"Wow!" Keisha exclaimed. "How'd you learn to drive like that?"

"Trial and error," I deadpanned, opening the door of the pickup and stepping down into the parking lot. "This was actually only the second time I've done it without turning the truck over."

I came around to Keisha's side as she jumped out. Her eyes were solemn as she asked, "You're not serious, are you?"

I couldn't keep a straight face. "No, I'm not," I confessed. I burst into laughter.

Keisha began making fake martial-arts jabs at me. "Don't mess with my head!" she laughed as I threw my hands in up mock self-defense. Suddenly she stopped cold and looked at me. "Why are we acting this way with each other? Did you feel how our energy just shifted?"

I looked back at her pensively. "I think it's what one of my other teachers calls the male-female agreement," I said.

Keisha raised her eyebrows in a silent question.

"The ingrained behavior between men and women."

"Yes," Keisha responded after a moment, "I see what you mean. We laugh and have a good time as if it were the most natural thing in the world, but somehow it feels like we're going through predetermined motions."

"Yeah, you're right," I said. "But at least we are now able to see it, and I think that's one step beyond being totally immersed in it."

Keisha nodded somberly. "Let's walk," she suggested, heading toward the path leading up the mountain.

I enjoyed watching the spring in Keisha's step. I noticed how agile she was, and how much contact she had with the ground. After a long climb, we reached a beautiful meadow laced with lupine. Overhead the sky was cloudless, brilliant as a sapphire. There was still snow on the highest peaks surrounding us, but the breeze was sun-warmed and mellow. We flung ourselves supine on the ground and watched birds—eagles, maybe; they were too far away to tell—riding down the sky in lazy spirals, carried by invisible thermal currents. I drew a slow, deep breath and let it out easily. I felt incredibly relaxed, as though my energies were perfectly integrated and flowing smoothly. I described the feeling to Keisha. "This must be what it feels like when our feng shui is really working," I concluded. I turned my head and looked toward Keisha. Her eyes were closed, and her cheeks were bunched delightedly in a smile.

Suddenly she was on her feet. "C'mon, Daniel," she said, extending her hand and pulling me up. "Let me show you some of the movements Huang taught me."

She began with simple movements of the arms—or they *looked* simple, anyway. "Is that it?" I asked her.

"There are really only four major ways to move the arms," she said. "They all have to do with different ways of pumping the energy from the torso out to the palms and fingers. All other wrist and arm movements are simply infinite variations on the basic four." Keisha demonstrated them again, this time more slowly so that I could follow along. "These movements are the building blocks of all the forms Huang teaches," she told me.

"This seems too simple," I said, perplexed.

She laughed. "Appearances can be deceiving, can't they? The trick is to practice simple basic movements over and over, so that they become so imprinted that you can do them without having to think about it. Then you can get down into the little details—the real nitty-gritty."

"Nitty-gritty," I repeated. "There's a venerable Chinese term for you. It probably originated thousands of years—"

"Daniel, you're incorrigible," Keisha giggled, executing a flawless movement that looked so graceful and effortless that I was sure I could do it just as she had. I couldn't. She stopped and led me through it again, gently correcting me and guiding my movements with her hands.

After I repeated the movement several times, she clapped her hands. "Excellent!" she exclaimed. I felt like a first-grader who has just gotten a gold star. "You know," she continued, "in many ways, a simple exercise is better than a complicated one. With a more advanced exercise or form, we have a tendency to get into a loose general pattern in which all refinement and nuance are lost. We like the idea of learning something big and flashy!" Keisha made a flamboyant leap above the wildflowers. "But it takes more concentration to stay focused and learn a simple movement. When you approach your practice by slowly and patiently mastering the simple components, then eventually you can build them into more complicated forms—and you'll find that your focus is so precise that it becomes effortless, like breathing."

As Keisha talked, I had continued practicing the simple movements. It was fascinating to see how subtle they could be, how I could experience a difference in my energy flow when I paid attention to the details. Keisha nodded approvingly. "Sometimes," she said, "we don't even have to go beyond the simple ones."

"I hear you," I said.

We continued to practice, and Keisha kept up her supportive critique with very precise instructions. Then we took a break and lay down in the grass again. While we were resting, we decided to develop those basic arm movements into some two-person exercises. Moving synchronistically, we practiced testing out each other's senses using our body eyes. The purpose was to learn to be flexible and strong at the same time; as Huang would say, steel wrapped with cotton.

As we began our walk down the mountain toward the parking lot, I recalled doing movements with various people and how it reminded me of the way ants communicate. I'd once spent the better part of a morning watching ants in a long line transporting tiny bread crumbs to their nest. Two ants would meet and touch each other with their feet and antennae. Each person I had practiced movements with was a totally different world, and this is how it felt with Keisha. Her fluidity and presence had flowed through me in a way that enhanced my sense of well-being.

I understood more completely her term "tactile resonance." It was a way to describe all those sensations and simultaneous combinations of senses for which our language has no vocabulary. In this situation, "tactile resonance" described how I could comprehend Keisha in a complete way.

We stopped to rest and sat on rocks by a pond. We took off our shoes and walked in the mud, squishing it between our toes and laughing like kids. Thinking about the movements we had done, I complimented Keisha on her fluidity and acknowledged how much I'd learned from her, even in this short period of time.

"That's part of the payoff," she said. "I'm glad to not have to deal with so much of my old behavior—not that it was easy to let those parts go. And I love to pass on what I've learned to people who truly value it."

Her words piqued my interest. I asked her to describe the letting go.

She scooped up a handful of pebbles and threw them, one at a time, into the pond as she spoke. "At first it was pretty nerve-racking," Keisha said.

"Huang warned me that when I began using the exercises, all that old learned behavior would intensify before it lessened. And, boy, was he right. I magnetized circumstances and people that presented me with patterns that matched my fears. The more I persisted in doing the exercises, the more energy I gained, the more intense the situations became."

"Wow," I breathed, interested.

"It was scary," Keisha nodded. "I had to learn to relax and stay neutral in the midst of them. I had to take the ideas and feelings from meditation and martial arts and bring them into all my life activities in order to break down my learned behavior. I had to learn to stay in deep contact with myself, even in the midst of these trying conditions."

We enjoyed a few moments of companionable silence, and then Keisha suddenly laughed. "Oh, I just remembered when it really broke open. As I gained more energy, I attracted a lot more men."

I began to get even more interested. I gave Keisha my full attention.

"I was in a bar," Keisha said, "and there was this man who'd had too much. He was loud and he began to get hostile, as though he was waiting for just the right cue to become violent. He reminded me of my father. When I was a kid, my father, when he drank, would hit me. I tried to be as good as I knew how, but no matter what I did, he still hit me. Now, with this guy in the bar," she continued, "I needed all of my concentration to relax and stay in my body so as not to be frightened that he was going to hit me. I remembered how to relax, as Huang had taught me. The more I relaxed, the stronger my fears got and the more the tension built around me. This drunk, he began looking my way. The relaxing made me acutely aware of the situation. My body was experiencing so much energy that I began to tremble. But I just kept relaxing. As I sat there, centered and feeling very present, a sense of spontaneity burst forth and I began to laugh. And do you know what that guy did?"

I shook my head. "Don't keep me in suspense!"

"He gave me the oddest look, as though he simply couldn't see me anymore, and he turned away. I knew then that his hooks could no longer grab onto me."

"That's wonderful," I said.

"And, in the following months," Keisha went on, "as I continued doing Huang's exercises and learning to relax, my energy continued to build, and I pretty soon I didn't even run into those kinds of men anymore. Weird, isn't it?"

I smiled. I liked hearing Keisha's story, and it did something to me. It allowed me to understand that when I connected with someone on a very deep level, I could transform my sexual energy into a way of relating that was beyond the male-female agreement. I was able to tap into a part of myself that was beyond learned behavior—it no longer affected me as it had before. I became more of an Observer. I had a new direction to my life that I wanted to explore.

"Another funny thing," Keisha added, "was that at first it was so hard to push myself into doing the exercises. Then the more I did them, the less effort it took."

"Yeah," I said. "It reminds me of when Huang instructed me to keep moving rather than lie down all the time. It was hard at first, but after I got used to it I enjoyed it more and it became easier to do." I thought about how fortunate I was to have my three teachers and to meet new people like Keisha who were willing to provide examples of what clear relating could be. I also realized that I had caught a glimpse of what I was capable of and that this reflected a growing energy within me.

"C'mon, there's a beautiful lake a little further on," Keisha said, tapping me on the shoulder as she got up. We walked in silence until we reached a crystal-clear lake that reflected the sky, now filling with billowy, marching white clouds. We sat on a fallen tree and watched as fish broke the surface of the calm water. I began to tell Keisha about the times in my life—and they were not frequent—when an unusual energy would take me over. "The last time it happened was about three or four weeks ago," I said. "I was walking along with a friend of mine and all these big dogs—about four or five of them—began fighting. I recognized one of the dogs as my neighbor's Australian shepherd. Without the slightest hesitation, I jumped into the middle of the melee, kicking and pulling them apart. The dogs were stunned—they actually backed away from me. I was stunned, too! When I thought about it later, it seemed like an incredibly dangerous, stupid thing to do!"

Keisha grinned at me. "I know what you mean," she said. "Sometimes I find myself acting in inexplicable ways, doing things that are way out of character, feeling as though something has taken me over and is acting through me. What Huang says is that the exercises we're doing allow us to tap into our higher selves or a greater way of being. When we do this, a flood of energy comes from the highly centralized core of our being. This may start happening to you more often."

"Are we talking about connecting to the Bigger Dream?" I asked.

Keisha gave me a blank look. I told her what Esmeralda had said about what can happen when we tap into higher levels of the Observer, where we make direct contact with the power of the Bigger Dream.

Keisha pondered my words for a moment. "It's so hard to talk about concepts that are beyond the words we've been taught." Keisha paused. "But I think there's something else here," she said. "The added twist is that if we can move this greater knowledge through our bodies, we can create and stabilize permanent changes based on a connection to that flow of greater energy—what you call the Bigger Dream." Keisha sighed, swinging her legs from the high end of the tree trunk. "Sometimes I get into a state of heightened, almost magical sensitivity," she continued. "I mean *incredible*. I can hear someone's heartbeat from a thousand yards away and I can feel them thinking. It's even more intense than when you feel someone staring at you."

"Another way people experience that altered state," I said, "is just before an accident. You know how everything slows down and your perceptions become incredibly keen but you can't really move? I think what Huang is after is teaching us to move our bodies within that place of awareness."

APPLICATION: REMEMBERING ENERGY

Sit back and rekindle the memory of instances of heightened awareness when time and energy were compressed around you. Your awareness focuses down to a point. Sensations become acute. You may even find yourself floating above the scene. You have disengaged from the way you normally experience consciousness in your body; you move into another dimension of awareness. Now bring that awareness into the present. Try moving it through your physical body and your relating body.

For example, when I do this I feel a sense of expansion in my physical body—my body actually feels bigger. I begin to experience my essential connection to the outside world through my relating body, and my judgments of the outside world begin to fall away.

AWARENESS JOURNAL

In "Tracking My Awareness," jot down those moments. When you remember more instances of expanded consciousness, add them to your list. For example, not only can I remember being in an automobile accident, I also recall spinning around in a truck before it stopped in the middle of an icy road. I have also had such experiences when running, which is also a repetitive series of physical movements. After a while it would seem as though time had stopped: I was in a state of heightened awareness.

"In working with Huang," I went on, "I've learned to focus more, be more in the present, trust who I am, and it's given me much more courage to be myself in close, personal relating." The sun had just dropped below the western edge of the mountains, and the clouds were beginning to take on a decidedly golden radiance. "In fact," I continued, "the most important thing I've learned is to stay in contact with my Center. When I can do that, I'm able to read another person's energy, and I feel safe because a greater part of me knows what it's doing."

"Yes!" Keisha responded excitedly. "Integrating this energy can change everything—your health, your job, your relationships, your appreciation of the world. Everything."

When we arrived back at my truck, Keisha told me that she felt different, somehow nourished by our interaction. Then a realization hit her.

"You know," she said, "studying with Huang and moving along this path, I've learned that for my real being, knowledge is food. Thank you," she smiled at me appreciatively.

I smiled back. "Looking at how knowledge is food for my being," she continued, "and touching and moving with you has been great, I feel full. Sharing with you in this way and learning about the Bigger Dream has filled me with energy."

On the drive down the mountain, Keisha told me about when she had been a secretary. "After I began studying with Huang and changing my personal feng shui, my life opened up. I started taking time off work. I didn't know why. But now I can see that I was giving myself a new container within which spontaneity could arise—just like the spontaneity that came through me with that guy in the bar—but on a bigger scale. I'd taken time off before when I was exhausted or sick, but this was different. And my energy kept building. I began remembering things that had excited me in the past. I took up art again, but this time I had the enthusiasm and persistence to keep going with it. And, of course, the chronic pain in my right hip and shoulders went away."

I remembered how I used to have lower back pain and how studying with Huang and opening myself to the world in new ways through movement had taken those pains away. I also saw that it was really more than that. I have watched people in my clinic change in similar ways when they remember their spirit and follow its call.

APPLICATION: FINDING DIRECTION

If you're lost and you lack a sense of direction in your life, go back and remember specific times when your life was full. These experiences can happen at any age, from childhood to where you are now. For example, perhaps there was a time when you were totally absorbed in a project—everything fell into place. Remember the specifics: the feelings you experienced, books you read, movies you saw, music you listened to, people you spent time with—everything that was connected to this feeling of fullness. Look for a thread of connection that is similar in all of them. Bring that thread into the present, then project it into the future and feel as though you are that thread. This is another way to reconnect with your Center, the source of flow that is your personal feng shui.

AWARENESS JOURNAL

In "Tracking My Awareness," write out as much as you can remember of the peak experiences of your life. Include details like colors, odors, tastes, sounds. This will enable you to reconnect with that feeling and bring it into your life now.

Chapter 8

PACKING THE BONES

That evening, following the afternoon with Keisha, I took a walk in the moonlight. I felt superbly alive in the crisp mountain air under the canopy of stars. I recalled that the ancient Egyptians called the night sky *Nut,* and thought it a goddess who arched her spangled body over the earth. I smiled, remembering those people far away in time and place. I came across a series of ponds and knelt down at one to admire the reflection of the sky. The water was as still as polished obsidian, and it mirrored the heavens so flawlessly that I had a brief, acute sensation of standing on my head.

At that moment I was startled by a movement in the short grass nearby. A pair of frogs was mating. I wondered how long they had been joined, and I began to think about what Huang said about sexual energy. I also remembered Esmeralda's opinion that moving beyond the male-female agreement—or our societal training for the use of sexual energy—was the key to correcting our personal feng shui.

A question came to mind: How can you use sexual energy to make the body stronger? I had always thought that there must be deeper layers of potential in sexual energy than those commonly acknowledged in Western culture. I was looking forward to the following day because Huang had mentioned that he would be addressing this very question.

These were the thoughts I carried back to my cabin where I undressed without turning on a light and slid as easily as a newborn into a dark, nourishing sleep.

In the morning all I could remember of my dreams were sketchy images of dancing skeletons, hardly a clear answer to my question of the night before about sexual energy. I tried unsuccessfully to make sense of their meaning, but then I remembered what Esmeralda had once told me: "Sometimes your answers will come if you look not in your nightdream, but in your daydream." I stored the residual feelings from these dreams and began the day.

Huang's first topic of the morning was circulation. As we stood around him in front of the chalkboard, he explained, "Maintaining right circulation in our bodies is how we maintain health. Right circulation is created by aligning our bodies properly with the force of gravity so that it not only pulls energy down, but pumps it up as well. The resulting circulation then spreads energy all the way out to the skin." He paused to give us his famous grin, the one that always accompanied his rendering of abstruse philosophical or spiritual concepts into language that even those of us born into the culture of reason and materialism could understand. He was good at it, too.

"Circulation is synonymous with concentration. When our concentration flows outward to support a fixed way of being in the world, we lose energy. If, however, we disengage our energy from those habitual patterns, we can store it inside until we gather enough to start constellating new avenues of perception and new ways of making contact with the world. This requires gathering concentration."

"Is that the same thing as circulation?" Henry asked.

Huang nodded. "Didn't I tell you that this guy is smart?" We got another flash of white teeth and an explosion of smile lines over his otherwise smooth-skinned face. "Let's concentrate." He lined us up and told us to merely stand and notice how much circulation we felt in our legs. "Now relax your bellies." He strolled slowly up the line. "What do you feel, Marlene?"

"I definitely feel more circulation in my legs and feet."

"Good!" Huang enthused. "That's what we're looking for. Now, bend your knees," he continued. "We want to saturate our bodies with more stimuli than we're used to. We can do this by becoming more interconnected, feeling the relationships between all our body parts. I know you're not used to doing this, so let me reemphasize: the more interconnected we feel, the more energy circulates through the body, and vice-versa. As your body becomes more and more saturated with stimuli, you will begin to open up to more variables, and thus your consciousness will expand." Huang reached the end of the line and turned back.

"Now, to create even more circulation, relax your shoulders and elbows. . . . Do you see how circulation is enhanced by relaxing? Energy flows outward and upward as well as downward, did you know that? It's just like lightning." Huang paused at the chalkboard and drew a jagged vertical line. We couldn't entirely stifle our chuckles.

Huang turned to us in bewilderment. "What? Don't you like my lightning?"

There were a few deadpan disavowals from his captive audience. "Well, this is what it looks like in China," he said, not trying very hard to hide his smile. He turned back to the chalkboard, where his attempts to improve his drawing resulted in something that we all agreed looked like an explosion of overcooked spaghetti. Huang threw up his hands at last, erased the lightning and replaced it with a smiley face. We groaned. "Guess you'll have to take what you can get," he beamed.

"Anyway, to get down to business: lightning is the result of energy that comes from both the earth and the sky simultaneously. It actually flows up and down at the same time. Are you with me?"

A few of us nodded.

"Good, because this is a good model to follow. When you can get the energy flowing back and forth, up and down, in and out—you get the idea—what you end up with is an interconnected body."

APPLICATION: FEELING THE PRINCIPLE OF CIRCULATION

◆ Assume the Horse stance (as if you're riding a horse). The feet should be shoulder-distance apart, pointed straight ahead, knees slightly flexed.

◆ Feel how much circulation your feet are putting on the ground.

◆ Open the pelvis by relaxing your belly.

◆ You should feel even more circulation. Your normal body awareness is becoming saturated. You could be experiencing a minor shift in
consciousness.

◆ Relax your shoulders. Let them drop into your torso.

◆ As if you are grasping a tree in front of you, stretch out your
arms and embrace it. Open your shoulder, elbow, and wrist joints. At
this point your arms are horizontal, making as big a circle as possible
with your finger tips almost touching. This gives your body even more
stimulus, more than you normally experience.

◆ To finish the posture, lift the top of your head, as though a
string suspends you from the crown. Feel the increase in your circulation. At this point, you should have all your joints open and feel circulation throughout your body.

◆ Focus on the perceptual changes in your body. Use this posture
as a launchpad to explore your physical presence.

Huang had us stand and concentrate on this feeling of perceptual
saturation as he walked around us, pausing occasionally to correct someone's
posture or offer encouragement. "Saturation is an excellent way to bypass
the four motions of learned behavior," he said. "Who remembers what they
are?"

"Movement, breathing, the use of the eyes, and the use of sound,"
Joseph responded.

"Let's start with breathing," Huang continued. "Good circulation
bypasses our normal breathing patterns. Normally we breathe in a wave that
moves up and down our bodies. This breathing pattern is one of the most
basic ways we define ourselves. As some of you have heard me say before, a
traditional yogic practice for understanding and calming the mind is to observe the breath. The way we breathe reflects what's going on in the mind."
Huang growled. "When we get angry, our breath gets really rough and choppy.
When we are peaceful and calm, we are like that," he pointed, with a big
grin, at the smiley face on the chalkboard. We all shook our heads.

"Nevertheless," he continued, "as you stand there and saturate your body with stimulus, notice what happens. Your breathing begins to change. Instead of a wave up and down the body, it moves into the middle of your body. We call this core breathing.

"Core breathing comes from the middle of the body and spreads out uniformly and naturally, unforced, into all the body parts. By freeing the breath from this learned wave pattern, you free your energy as well. You move your energy back to the core, where it concentrates so that it can stream back through your connective tissues in an integrated way."

Huang had once described interconnectedness using the embryo as a metaphor: life begins as a single cell that divides into two, four, eight, sixteen cells, and on and on; yet these cells remain interconnected. Even when organs, bones, and tendons develop, the body still resonates with the original tissue from which it was made. This was, he had asserted, somewhat analogous to the Western concept of connective tissue, or fascia, and it is through the limitations imposed on us by our learned behavior that we begin to disconnect from our innate structural integrity.

I returned my attention to Huang as he continued. "The energy that you gain in breaking down your patterns can be retained if you create the right body receptacle to integrate it into your life. You begin to unite yourself with your body of knowledge. You are not negating the fact that you breathe. What you are doing is moving to a third point, a point of observation, where you are not even thinking about breathing. You make good circulation in your body and breathe naturally. Focusing on saturating your body in this way will naturally begin to unwind you from the inside out. Not only can you do this here, you can learn to do it in your everyday life. You can learn to face your learned behavior by saturating your body with more stimulus than it's used to.

APPLICATION: FIRST MOTION—BREATHING

Put yourself in the Embracing-the-Tree posture. If you need to, go back and reread the previous application, which describes how to create circulation in your whole body. Relax your belly and saturate your body with stimulus. Let gravity pull you down. Notice how this changes the way you breathe and quiets your mind. You can use this to calm yourself down whenever your mind is in turmoil. It also makes a good daily five-minute standing meditation.

AWARENESS JOURNAL

Under "Embodying My Awareness," describe how this application affected your breathing and its resulting influence on your thought process. For example, when I did this application, I noticed that I would experience pauses in my thinking or that I wasn't identifying too strongly with my thinking, but rather was watching my thinking.

Huang called Joseph to stand in the front of the group. "Joseph, punch me in the stomach as hard as you can."

Joseph hesitated. "You sure?" he asked.

"Go ahead," Huang insisted.

Joseph shrugged and drove a fist into Huang's lower abdomen. Nothing happened.

"No, no, no, you weren't doing it very hard," Huang laughed. "Do it with everything you have." Again Joseph hesitated, then pulled his arm back and let loose at Huang's abdomen with all his might. I winced involuntarily as I heard the impact of his fist in Huang's flesh. Huang remained as immobile as the wall of a cliff, but Joseph jumped back, shaking his hand. "Whew, man!" he exclaimed, dancing a little.

"That," Huang said with a broad smile, "is what creating strong circulation can do." He thanked Joseph and motioned him back to his place. "Now, with your circulation intact, the next thing you must learn is to concentrate it." Huang gestured us to our feet and asked us to assume correct standing posture. When he was satisfied that we were properly aligned, he began directing us.

"Interconnect your body properly, as you did before. Now, concentrate the energy from your skin down through your flesh, then your tendons and ligaments, and finally into your bones. Concentrate your circulation there. This will give you great strength, and will replenish the storehouse of energy in your bones. Life energy flows from the bones out to the rest of the body."

On the chalkboard, Huang drew a picture of a bone with arrows of energy pointing toward it.

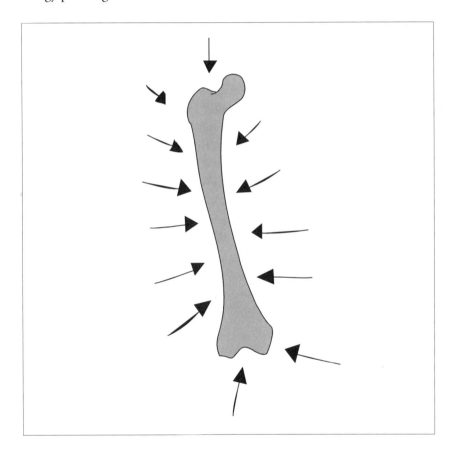

ILLUSTRATION 2: *Bones*

I suddenly understood the gravitational mechanism that creates osteoporosis, a disease that affects post-menopausal women and sometimes men. The bones get stripped of their calcium; they turn brittle and begin to degenerate. I could see that when the body becomes weak from lack of circulation and needs energy, the blood pulls energy from the bones where it has previously been pressurized and stored. I also began to see that with correct posture and circulation exercises, women should be able to slow down and perhaps even prevent bone degeneration. I was very excited about sharing this information with my patients once I got back to my clinic.

Huang directed us to do a simple repeated exercise with our arms, keeping the lower parts of our bodies still, in order to pack our bones with energy while in motion. To an observer it would have looked as if our arms were two windmills. As we kept moving, Huang continued explaining that we could use any simple exercise to pack energy into our bones so long as we kept the circulation moving in our bodies and concentrating on the bones.

He also said that it was important to take a perception, move it through our bodies, and integrate it into the four postures—standing, moving, sitting, and lying. "It is important to stabilize a perception in all four postures," he said. "Otherwise, you may learn to do something in one posture, but you can't translate it to another."

He described friends of his who were quite accomplished at sitting meditation. They could reach very exalted states in that posture. Yet when they had to get up and move, the exaltation dissipated rapidly, and they were as locked into learned patterns of motion and behavior as anyone else. "What you are doing," he told us, "is preserving your fluidity and allowing your own volition to flow through your body unimpededly—no matter what posture you are in."

We continued the exercise, focusing on the movements of our bones and the spaces between them. Huang drifted around the group, speaking softly to each person, correcting the turning of a wrist here, the position of a head there.

After Huang had corrected my movement, I closed my eyes to concentrate better. Suddenly I could see all the bones in my body moving together. I couldn't believe it. I continued packing energy into my bones. Then

I found I could expand my field of inner vision to include my whole body, so that I was actually a moving, feeling skeleton. I could see and feel every little bone and joint. It was one of the wildest sensations I had ever experienced, but it was only the beginning of my astonishment. When at last I slowly opened my eyes, I was stunned to see the bones in all of the people around me. I was surrounded by living skeletons, moving together in a dance of bones! The image of my nightdream suddenly made sense.

Gradually, as the half hour wound down, I began coming back to a more normal sense of perception. The first thing I noticed was that the floor was dotted with little pools of sweat. Huang told us to take a ten-minute break. We milled around, drinking water, talking exuberantly.

Later, Huang gathered us into a semicircle on the floor. "We have just explored one way to strengthen the body by concentrating energy in the bones," he said. "The physical body is a platform from which we can take an infinite variety of flights. It is important to keep the platform strong by using the strength of gravity."

He stood up laughing, tapping his chest. "All you guys do is sit around all day and you never think with your bodies. Sometimes you have good ideas, but unless you put them into your bodies they don't stick, they don't work. Stand up, everybody!"

When we were all on our feet, Huang continued. "When people start to gather energy, the first thing that happens is that their sexual energy goes off the chart."

"You call that a problem?" said a small voice behind me. It was Octavia, a trim, leathery seventy-year-old with amazing blue eyes who was full of life. She once told me she had spent her late teens and early twenties capturing and breaking wild horses in Arizona before settling down on a vast ranch near Socorro, New Mexico.

Huang laughed. Even he was amused by Octavia when she decided to open her mouth. I made a mental note to seek out Octavia later and ask her about her own experience with bone thinning, if indeed she had any.

"No, Octavia," Huang answered, "not in the proper context. What I mean is that this," Huang placed his palms over his lower abdomen, "is the place where our energy flow is most constricted due to the patterns we have learned to restrict sexual behavior. What you have to recognize is that this energy is not merely reproductive, but has many other potentials as well. Now, please find a partner of the opposite of sex—I don't mean to marry—just for the exercise."

"Good," Octavia intoned to no one in particular. "Because I don't intend to get married again—unless he's young and has plenty of money."

Huang threw up his hands and rolled his eyes as we all laughed. Luckily there were equal numbers of men and women, so we arranged ourselves in male-female pairs. Octavia had three offers and finally chose Henry.

As I stood next to Keisha, Huang told us to stand back-to-back, relax, and see how it felt. Huang told us to begin turning slowly, maintaining light contact, until we were facing each other. Huang directed us to notice how we felt as we went through this process. As I turned slowly against Keisha, I was decidedly uncomfortable. I felt a great deal of energy that I didn't know what to do with, and it left me feeling felt naked, without protection.

"Do you feel a lot of energy now?" Huang chuckled.

We laughed, releasing some of the tension. Huang told us to separate and relax.

"Before we were building our energy by concentrating on our bones," he recapped. "What I was showing you here are the patterns that you'll have to face when you begin accumulating a lot of energy. It will probably happen in more subtle ways, but I wanted you to really get the point. What do you think this energy is that you're experiencing?"

"Sexual energy!" Henry called out.

"Not so fast, my friend," Huang said, raising his hand with a smile. "It's just *energy*. But so often when people get more energy than they know what to do with, they express it sexually. We're trained to do that. And what is the result if the energy is always expressed sexually?"

"You'll have a great time," Octavia said, "but you won't learn much that's new."

Huang beamed at her. "Precisely! If it is always expressed sexually, you cannot discover different ways of making contact, and the old patterns are just strengthened. It's similar to the beach-boy weight lifter who attains more energy, but who doesn't really change his idea of himself." Huang then told everyone to turn around and face him and give him all their "body attention."

"When gathering energy, it is important to have a strategy." He placed his hands on his lower abdomen again. "It's this energy down here. If you let your energy out only in the ways of your learned behavior, the pattern doesn't change. If you negate the pattern and don't even let the energy drop down into this area, the old pattern remains intact, too. Daniel there, if he could stop thinking about Keisha for a moment, will tell you that maintaining these old energy patterns can cause a web of disease throughout your body."

I felt my face glow red as everyone laughed.

"When we make a strategy," Huang continued, "the first thing we need to do is break out of normal patterns so that we can allow the awareness in our core to build. When you take a break from learned behavior, you become the Observer. This liberates energy! I want you to understand this—that becoming the Watcher, becoming neutral, moving back a step, builds energy. The closer you are to the true core of your being, the more energy you have available.

"This relaxing creates awareness that will seek release through other channels. What you will eventually learn is that it isn't sexual energy that you have an abundance of; it is just energy, seeking to flow."

It was wonderful to watch someone with so much exuberance when he communicated. Energy radiated from Huang's body, and it was contagious. I could see that Huang used his body to express his ideas, enabling me to understand what he was saying at a very deep level. What I realized was that Huang was not just talking about relaxing—he was integrating relaxation into a bodily sensation, a dynamic process of gathering energy.

"Your connective tissue gets plastered together by your learned behavior, especially below your navel," Huang said as he clapped his hand on his lower abdomen. "In order to release it from the inside, you need to build circulation in that area. This is done by deep, concentrated relaxation. In order to properly expand the connective tissue here, it has to be done from the core of your being, from your Luminous Essence, from the inside out. You need to continually establish a core around which to create your personal feng shui. I can't overemphasize this. It will add stability, constancy, and progress to your growth. Manipulations from the outside will never release the patterning in a way that is long-lasting. The body has to be integrated from the inside out. After you have gathered some energy, it will seek to express itself in new ways."

This made me reflect upon what Esmeralda had once told me. She had said that when I relaxed through my learned behavior, I would find myself in a new world.

"You will be up against those barriers of fear that plastered your connective tissue together in the first place—the emotional charges behind your learned behavior," Huang continued. "What you can expect then is that all the fear, guilt, shame, and taboos that you've learned will start to come up in your daily life. As you get more energy in your connective tissue, the tendency is for it to flow in the old patterns; in other words, the old way of relating will come after you."

"So what do you do when you are faced with this?" Joseph asked.

"That's the old Chinese story that I'm just about to get to, Beach Boy," Huang grinned. "The first thing is to take a break and become the Observer. The presence of the Observer creates strong relaxation and circulation. You've studied how to make good circulation in your body and how it can disrupt your old breathing-wave pattern. Therefore, in the midst of anxiety-producing situations, where you are going up against your old patterns, you can create an internal circulation in your body by relaxing, and this will help neutralize the outside pressure to conform to your old ways. The important thing is to understand that you have to allow more and more energy to flow through your body, and to be committed to it. You will then begin to expand in a very natural way."

Huang paused, then added enigmatically, "This movement—this process of expansion is who you really are."

AWARENESS JOURNAL:
RELAXING IN THE MIDST OF CONDITIONS

Write in "Tracking My Awareness" about how relaxing in the midst of conditions—or becoming the Observer—has changed your life. How has it affected your perceptual patterns? This will give you a sense of continuity and constancy in your journey of awareness.

For example, there was a time when I went through a confrontation on the phone with my father. I was able to relax in the midst of those conditions with the technique of relaxing into my abdomen. Although there was no tangible result in that instance, the next time I spoke with my father, there was a new spontaneity between us that allowed us to experience our connection in many new ways.

Chapter 9

RELEASING THE JOINTS

At the start of the next day's class, we stood in a semicircle around Huang before the chalkboard. The subject under discussion was loosening our joints. "Patterns of motion are ingrained at an early age," he said. "They form a companion to the breathing patterns that imprint us with our learned behavior. We become restricted and repetitive in the ways we move, and the result is that our spectrum of possibilities is limited to a small range.

"In order to free ourselves from these limited patterns and make the body a fluid platform from which to operate, we need to gather energy and expand our range of motion." Huang began undulating his upper body in a snakelike fashion as he continued speaking. "It's a way to gather more energy so that we begin to embody the idea that we are more than we have been taught to be." He paused for a moment with a knowing smile and grasped his left elbow with his right hand. "One method of expanding range of motion is to release the joints. This increases energy flow to the connective tissue that holds the joints in place. When you really think about joints, what are they?"

"Hinges," Keisha volunteered.

"Good," Huang nodded. "What else?"

I thought of my dancing dream skeletons and the vision I had enjoyed during our session of the day before. "The spaces between the bones," I offered.

"Precisely!" Huang affirmed, continuing to move his body. He made me think of seaweed floating in a gentle underwater current. "These spaces must be opened to allow energy to gather and flow. If they are closed tight by repeated patterns, our range of motion is compromised. The flexibility and health of any area of the body is dependent on the openness of the nearby joints.

"Now, I want you to line up!" As usual it took a while before Huang was satisfied with our alignment. Then he led us through a progression of movements to open the joints, beginning with wrists and ankles, then elbows and knees, and finally shoulders and hips. He ended by showing us how to maintain circulation in the spaces between the joints, even between the vertebrae in the spine.

APPLICATION: SECOND MOTION—OPENING THE JOINTS

Adopt the Embracing-the-Tree posture. Relax your abdomen. Let your pelvis open up like a flower. Let this relaxing open your hip joints, knees, ankles, and lower back. Let the imaginary string pull up on the top of your head, loosening the joints in your upper spine and neck. This will finish opening up the spine. Now relax your jaw and open the jaw joint. Open your shoulder, elbow, and wrist joints as if you're embracing a tree. Concentrate on keeping your joints open. This helps you to develop the "muscle" of saturating your body with stimulus beyond your normal awareness. Stand this way for five minutes.

Once you feel that all your joints are open, begin to slowly move your body, maintaining this feeling. Move your arms and twist your torso as if you were seaweed moving in water. This practice will imprint the feeling of having the joints open into your body's memory.

AWARENESS JOURNAL

In "Embodying My Awareness," describe how doing the application affected your joints and how the necessary mental concentration influenced your thinking.

Application Reminder: Combining applications

Remember that even a simple posture and movement done correctly and with awareness provide the platform for more complicated and integrated concepts.

Basically, you can combine movements in any of the previous applications, such as building circulation, opening the joints, and so on, as *well as in the ones in the chapters that follow. To start with, do each practice for twenty minutes. Eventually, they will all come together so that you can do them simultaneously.*

"Now let's put this concept into a fluid motion," Huang said. "We'll do our Tai Chi form very slowly, concentrating on these principles. Focus on keeping the joints open in order to embed the concept in body memory."

We began to move slowly as Huang circulated, fine-tuning our posture and movement as though, I mused, we were musical instruments. "One of the things that can be done with a well-tuned set of movements," he said as if reading my mind, "is that we can play many different ideas, concentrating first on one, then on another. Each idea is part of an interlocking pattern." Huang chuckled at the image he was seeing in his mind. "We are like a sheep dog working a herd of sheep. A sheep dog is constantly vigilant, even when he's asleep. He's just one small dog responsible for maybe dozens of sheep, and he knows he can't take them all on at once. So he concentrates on the ones that stray out of line. He works them patiently, heads them off and back into the herd. We can use the same technique, working one principle at a time, then moving on to the next 'stray.' Just like that sheepdog, our minds cannot concentrate on the massive input coming from the body all at once; we have to concentrate on one sheep at a time. Eventually, through patience and focus, we can herd the entire body into the desired form."

He motioned for us to resume movement, then added, "Physically, we are loosening ourselves up from the outside in, moving from seemingly difficult principles to simpler principles that encompass them. This herding gets easier the more you do it, because the finer techniques upon which this system is built encompass all the previous cruder ones. We are building a system that actually gets easier as we go."

It took us an hour to slowly go through our sequence of movements. The room was electric with our concentration.

During the break, I stood chatting with Joseph. Because we had just concentrated and moved together in a way that was different from our learned behavior, I discovered that I felt more open and affectionate around him. At dinner and later on that evening in the cabin, I was much more at ease with my fellow students.

Because of the movements and amount of concentration I had experienced in class, I was very energized that night. I couldn't sleep. I tossed and turned in my bunk. In the middle of the night, I had to go out for a walk. The moon was out as I made my way down to the pond, which had become an inspiring place for me. I sat for a while, then got up and began doing some of the exercises we had learned in class. Then, as if in a dream, I remembered an interchange I once had with Huang.

In the dim light of Huang's studio, I stood on the brick floor playing with my shadow. Huang laughed and said, "When foreigners first came to China, they saw people practicing Tai Chi and called it shadowboxing. Let's do some real shadowboxing."

Huang instructed me to keep moving. "Your real shadow is the opposite of your idea of the body, seen through the eyes of the spirit. It is the shadow of your idea of the body, cast onto the world by your insistence on your own identity. We run around forever, seemingly trying to catch it. So let's catch it!

"Imagine your shadow in front of you, and when you do this exercise, see yourself becoming one with it. As you move one way, it moves the other. As you move back, it moves forward. As you strike, it blocks. As you kick, it parries. It is your perfect reflection. Concentrate on it, see it."

I thought about this as I moved through the exercises by the side of the pond. Gradually my surroundings receded. All I was aware of was the shadow I was pushing against. I could feel the pressure in it building as it pushed back. Huang's words continued in my head.

"Grasp the energy between you and your shadow. The process of reaching out is what connects you with your shadow. Become the energy that is In-Between."

With the memory of Huang's words, I felt a shift and actually started to become that energy. I could feel my body dissolving, and the shadow along with it. And then, suddenly, a wave of fear rose up like a tidal wave and I backed off, sweating, shocked. I was by the pond again, hearing frogs and crickets, and the damp, cool breeze against my face was comforting.

APPLICATION: CONVERSING WITH YOUR SHADOW AND FINDING THE IN-BETWEEN

This should be done in a darkened room using only a candle for light. You stand so that the candle is behind you and you see your shadow on the wall in front of you. Assume the Horse stance and, as we have done before, move your body and arms like seaweed under water. Be aware of the tingling or fuzzy feeling of energy moving through your body. As you move, watch your shadow and regard it as something outside yourself mimicking your movement. Now close your eyes and keep moving. Create a "shadow" that is your exact opposite: as you feel your arm move forward, see in your mind's eye your shadow's arm moving back. As your other arm moves back, you see your shadow's arm move toward you. Keep doing this until you find the fine line between you and your shadow. That is your point of focus. Stay with it and keep moving. Do this for ten minutes and you will tactilely get in touch with the In-Between.

AWARENESS JOURNAL

Under "Embodying My Awareness," record your experiences from the application above.

The next day we did a series of two-person exercises. They involved moving very closely with another person in a predetermined set of movements. After practicing for a long while, I was feeling both tired and exhilarated from the strenuous effort. Finally, Huang told us to stop and gather around him.

"What I want you to do now," he said, "is the same exercise, but now you should incorporate into it the ideas of keeping your joints open. This takes a little more concentration. Working in close with a partner will bring up all different kinds of learned responses that will threaten that concentration. Keep in mind that this new way of flowing is a direct attack on your conditioned way of moving. That's what this old Chinese torture that you're having to endure now brings out in you. Just be aware that you've got to keep up the pressure on those old conditioned ways of moving." Huang flashed us a grin, and at that moment it was easy for me to imagine him as an old Chinese torturer.

"The first stage of incorporating a new way of moving is to learn to do it alone," Huang said, holding up one finger. "This allows you to stay in your concentration while doing it, with less distraction. Then learn to do it with a person standing next to you." Huang held up two fingers. "Next, incorporate this new way of moving while facing another in a staged way, as we are doing here in class." Holding up three fingers and smiling, he said, "And, for the grand finale, learn to do it in the movements of your everyday life."

"Yeah, like when I'm taking out the garbage," Octavia muttered, off to my left.

"When I'm doing my dingy laundry," Marlene quipped.

"Cutting my toenails!" Joseph volunteered.

"Yeah, yeah, yeah!" Huang grinned. "But what we really need right now is some of that secret Chinese practice known as hard work. Go back to your original partners and do the movements while facing each other."

Keisha was my partner once again. As I faced her and began moving, I found that it was indeed very difficult. It took a great deal of concentration to maintain sensitive contact with her body and keep my own joints open at the same time.

"Now try it with your eyes closed," Huang said a few moments later.

It was much easier for me to concentrate on keeping my joints open with my eyes closed, but not being able to see my partner made me feel very disoriented. I realized that Huang was right. Each part of the process took a bit more concentration.

During our break Huang disappeared. When he reappeared, he carried a stack of full-face masks of clear, lightweight plastic. They were molded into faces of men and women. Huang told each of us to pick one of the opposite sex. When we put them on, we found that the plastic allowed the colors of our faces to come through but blurred the lines of expression. Through the cut-outs, eyes shone with vivid intensity.

"Now resume your two-person exercise," Huang said.

At first, not being able to see the expression on Keisha's face made me uncomfortable. I also became aware of how exaggerated my normal facial expressions were. Gradually, I felt my face relax, and I realized it was because Keisha couldn't see my face.

It was a new and pleasant sensation, to be able to relax my face while facing another person. Normally it was very difficult for me to look somebody in the eyes without feeling self-conscious or threatened. With the mask, it was much easier. I wasn't quite sure if it was because I didn't have Keisha's facial expressions to respond to, or because she couldn't see mine.

The thought flashed in my mind that it's easy to look at babies because their faces are so relaxed and undemanding. It's easy to let my own face relax when I look at them. I began to chuckle to myself as I wondered if there was a law against people wearing masks into banks. I had an image of us walking into a bank while wearing our masks. Without facial expressions to guide them, how could anyone measure our intent?

Huang asked us if we had begun to notice our faces relaxing. He pointed out how learned behavior is stored in our patterns of facial expression, just as in the rest of the body. Our faces relaxed when we put on the masks because we didn't have to worry about our revealing ourselves.

"When your face relaxes," Huang said, "all of the energy you are holding there starts to fall down through your body into your abdomen. It's just like turning off a car engine and letting the oil run out of the engine down to the crankcase."

After a while longer, Huang collected the masks and turned to us.

"Now, can you keep your faces relaxed without the masks?" he asked with a laugh. "Our faces are full of motion. In the same way that we can stop the energy from flowing out of our bodies in habitual patterns, we can take the outflow of facial motion and send it back inward. We can use our faces to help us reconnect our bodies. We can actually learn to keep the oil down in the crankcase while we express ourselves," he said. "Move your faces into a smile," he ordered. As we followed his instructions, he stopped us, laughing.

"No, no, no, not like that! We don't want that plastered-on Miss America smile. Smile from your *navel*." He rubbed his abdomen gleefully. "Feel how your mouth is connected to your navel region. See how dropping the old patterns down into your abdomen then allows you to function or smile from down there." He rubbed his abdomen again, chuckling. "Now, keep the mouth and the navel connected. Try to move your navel and see if your mouth goes into a smile." He watched us approvingly.

I was astounded to discover that I could actually feel the areas on either side of my navel move upwards simultaneously when the corners of my mouth lifted. My whole body was smiling.

Huang examined us critically, a bit more satisfied. "This is just for you to experience how your bodies get cut off by your automatic responses to the world," he said, rubbing his hands over his face. "By using the relaxation of your face to reconnect your face to your abdomen, you move your energy back to the core, just like the oil running down into the crankcase." Huang chuckled, seeming to revel in this metaphor. "From there the circulation concentrates and streams back through your connective tissue. This lets you be in the world in a unified way, maintaining contact with your integrity."

APPLICATION: THIRD MOTION—USE OF THE EYES

This application can be done either with a friend or looking in a mirror. Find two masks where only the eyes are visible. Put the masks on and look at your partner or yourself in the mirror. Does your face feel more relaxed? Does the patterned conditioning in your facial muscles disappear as you realize that, since you can't see your own expressions and you're not reading another person's expressions, you can be more relaxed? As your face relaxes, does your abdomen also relax? This application will show you, in a very tactile way, how deeply your socialization is ingrained. Do you notice that it is very easy to maintain eye contact with this other person or yourself in the mirror when you've relaxed your face? For fun, try wearing a mask while you do the applications in the Embracing-the-Tree posture.

AWARENESS JOURNAL

In "Mapping My Perceptual Conditioning," note what you experienced. Is your social conditioning reflected in the habitual tension in your face? Do you feel more relaxed or freer with a mask on?

Huang motioned for us to spread out. "Now I want you to do the same two-person exercise, this time without the masks. Keep the oil down in that crankcase, keep your faces relaxed. Keep the energy that was flowing out from your face to feed your learned behavior and send it back down to your abdomen."

We paired off with the same partners as before and began to do the exercise. It was incredibly difficult to maintain that connection between my face and abdomen in a continuous way with Keisha right in front of me. I kept wanting to disengage. My face kept wanting to return to its accustomed patterns. I kept wanting to smile approvingly at Keisha.

After I had struggled for a while, the energy seemed to stabilize. I felt a sense of brightness. The world became more dreamlike. My normal manner of experience exploded, and suddenly I found myself swimming in an ocean of sensory stimuli. I found that I had opened myself up to new ways of experiencing my partner. Instead of talking to her face to face, I was engaged in a conversation of body to body, dream to dream. It reminded me my dolphin dreams.

APPLICATION: USE OF THE EYES WITHOUT A MASK

Take the masks off and see if you can maintain a relaxed face while looking into the eyes of your partner. Do this for ten minutes and see what happens.

AWARENESS JOURNAL

In "Mapping My Perceptual Conditioning," note what you realized about yourself while doing the above application.

Chapter 10

THE EYES AND THINKING

After our lunch break, the weather turned sullen, with low clouds that closed off the peaks around us. Octavia, Keisha, Henry, and I went for a walk. We trooped down to the pond to find the surface of the water wind-vexed and choppy. Big drops of rain began to fall, and we trudged back to the meeting hall. It was a good afternoon to be indoors.

Huang drew a pair of eyes on the chalkboard. "The first motion we studied was breathing. The second motion was the actual movement of the body. The third motion is the use of the eyes," he said. "The movement of the eyes reflects learned behavior." Then he pointed to the inside, the outside, and below each eye. "I've drawn this to show you how practically all the meridians of acupuncture meet in the eyes. These meridians move throughout the body and are reflected in our eyes. When we are very young, we are taught to move our eyes in certain repetitive patterns in order to capture the world in the socially agreed-upon way. This is what creates our visual reality or our perceptual conditioning. Our thoughts, our behavior patterns, and our patterns of eye movement are deeply connected. Because we move our eyes in certain patterns, the meridians in our bodies are stimulated in certain repetitive sequences, which in turn affect the entire body. This usually creates an imbalance in our personal feng shui.

"I'm only telling you this to corroborate what you can already feel," he continued, making his eyes bug out so that we all smiled. Huang looked at us and said, chuckling, "I hope you're all smiling from your navels!"

This reminded me to smile from mine.

"I want you to focus on the relationship between the movement of your eyes and your body," Huang continued. "If you can reconnect your eye sense to your navel area, or lower *dan tien*, you can then learn to see with your whole body."

"Is this what its like to have eyes in the back of your head?" Octavia asked in her deadpan monotone that always cracked us up.

Huang laughed along with the rest of us. "This is a very good question as well as a funny one," he said when we had quieted. "Octavia, you're not so far off as you might think. It's like being in a theater with a 360-degree screen. And not just seeing, but hearing, touching, smelling, and tasting. You can expand this kind of superfocused awareness so that it includes your whole world!" Huang gave us a moment to digest this. "That's what we're doing here when we learn to experience the body eye."

I was able to remember, at that point, how my vision had definitely changed when we were doing the exercises with the body eye. My vision had gotten softer, and I had become more relaxed.

Marlene raised her hand. "I don't quite understand the word *outflow*," she said.

Huang turned and smiled. "This idea of inflow and outflow was devised to show a distinction between perceiving as a result of reacting to the outside—our learned behavior—as opposed to perceiving from the inside, which is how we perceive when we're flowing with the Bigger Dream. When I say outflow, I mean your accustomed way of looking at the world, the habitual way you grasp the world with your eyes. When your energy is outflowing through your repetitive patterns, you wear yourself down," Huang went on. "You are putting all of your energy into contacting the world in one limited way, and it's very exhausting. This not only applies to your eye sense, but to all your senses. If you can stop the outflows, you can distance yourself from your learned way of perceiving and begin to see the world as a particle of flow in the midst of the Bigger Dream."

Huang paused for a moment, then began twisting and turning his body in a beautiful motion. His rippling movements reminded me of the flow of wind and water. As I watched, I reflected that what he had just said was very similar to what Esmeralda had been pointing me toward when she explained the true awareness that exists between our daydream and our nightdream.

"What I am talking about is uniting the senses so that, for example, you could hear through your eyes or see through your ears," Huang continued as his movements slowly came to a stop. "A different way of saying this is that there is a point inside, before all the senses become differentiated. From this point you can contact the world directly with your Luminous Essence."

He paused and smiled thoughtfully for a moment, then continued.

"An outflow is reacting to the world in a disconnected, limited way that destroys your unity. When you identify with your sense of unity, you are no longer hooked into the limited action-reaction patterns of learned behavior and the lifestyle and diseases that they engender. Learning to operate from this place of unity and create a feng shui that radiates out from there is what we are after."

He told us to line up, taking a different partner this time, and repeat the same two-person exercise we had done yesterday. This time, in addition to relaxing our faces, we were to attempt to look our partners in the eye, from our abdomens.

"If you let your eyes look back into your lower *dan tien* and keep focusing there, you will get the feeling of being able to see from there," Huang said, as he strolled through the room, checking us. "When you can learn to see from your abdomen, you will begin to directly perceive the world as a particle of flow in the midst of the Bigger Dream."

APPLICATION: RELAXING IN THE MIDST OF CONTACT

Look at another person or yourself in the mirror. Relax your face. Feel that relaxation all the way down to your abdomen. Do you notice how the movements of your mouth are connected to your abdomen in this way? Look at your partner without moving your eyes. Do you notice how, when you think about the world from your perceptually conditioned self-concept, you move your eyes in set patterns? Test it out. If you see the eyes of your partner moving in little patterns, ask what he or she is thinking.

AWARENESS JOURNAL

In "*Embodying My Awareness,*" keep track of how relaxing your face in your everyday life influences how you feel with people and interact with them.

In "*Mapping My Perceptual Conditioning,*" note what relaxing your face in everyday life shows you about yourself. For example, when I look at a wide-eyed baby, I don't feel many expectations coming from the baby, so my face relaxes.

I began moving back and forth with my new partner. This time it was Joseph. I noticed that the expressions I was trying to relax away from were very different than those I had experienced with Keisha, who was, of course, female.

When my face finally did relax, I concentrated on looking at Joseph from my lower abdomen. As I worked with this concept, my vision slowly changed. The world became gelatinous. I could almost see the air as a liquid. I felt like a fish who has just discovered he is swimming in water. I was fascinated. Suddenly I saw the other members of the class as luminous cells of light, moving as patterns of energy.

As I continued practicing with Joseph, I moved in and out of this feeling. It appeared to be connected to how much I could relax all of my senses down into my abdomen. In order to perceive from my abdomen, I had to relax beyond my learned behavior, in this case by keeping my eyes focused inward.

When the exercise was over, Huang told us to take a break. The rain had blown through and I went outside to feel the sun on my face and the breeze against my cheek. It felt great to be outside while I was still moving in and out of the new perception I had discovered. I felt disoriented and didn't want to talk or relate to anyone. I wanted to explore this feeling on my own, so I slipped away from the others and wandered down to a pond. There were some flat dry rocks nearby, warm from the sun. I saw a small black shape moving across one of the rocks. I went over and sat beside it.

It was a stink bug. I had often watched them with fascination when I was a young boy, the way they walked so carefully and slowly, lifting their butts in the air when they were frightened. Something about watching them made me slow down. And right now, as I watched this particular stink bug moving—one step, then another—my mind slowed down until quite distinctly I was listening to him walk. Immediately my rational mind spoke up: *That bug is not making any noise whatsoever. How can you possibly hear it?*

Then it hit me: I was hearing through my eyes.

There was nothing I could compare it to, but somehow I knew what was happening. Although hearing through my eyes was nonsense to my rational mind, here it seemed to be the most natural thing in the world. Was I starting to unite my senses in my abdomen as Huang had suggested?

I looked at my hand and moved a finger. I could hear it move, too. I waggled it back and forth and listened. Then I moved my whole hand and wrist in a circular gesture. I could hear a variety of coordinated sounds. There was a unity to them, somewhat similar to the harmonics of a musical chord. I realized that this type of sensory unity was going on all the time, but that I had been trained to blot it out. With a growing sense of excitement, I now understood what Huang had been talking about when he said hearing with the eyes, and I began to see how the concept of the body eye worked. Not only could I hear with my eyes, I could see with my body!

I looked down at the stink bug and thanked him for bringing me this teaching.

Chapter 11

SOUND

After the break, Huang told us about the fourth motion: sound. This included, he said, the sound that the body makes, both inner and outer. He spoke about how we have isolated our external sound into language and our internal sound into thinking, and that this system creates specific patterns of resonance in the body.

Huang's remarks embellished the meaning of Keisha's term, tactile resonance. I realized that we do communicate with ourselves and with the world at large through resonance patterns.

"In the West," Huang said, "you talk about five senses. In the East, we talk about six senses: the five that you know, plus a sixth sense, thinking. It is very useful to talk about thinking as another sense. It makes it easier not to identify oneself with one's thinking, but to perceive that we are something greater than that. We're not just what we're thinking!" He peered over at me and said with a smile, "Ask Daniel here."

Everybody turned to look at me and laughed. I laughed with them.

"The mistake of confusing the Observer with the thinker is very easy to make," Huang went on. "Normally, you don't have any way to separate yourself from your thinking, so you think of yourself as your thoughts. You learn to identify yourself with words rather than sound. Putting thinking on a level with the other senses allows you to see it as something that you can choose to perceive through or not.

"Let's look at the gestures of thinking," Huang said as he moved his face through a series of pensive expressions. First, he scratched his head, then stroked his chin. Next he scratched the side of his face, then pulled on the lobes of his ears. We all began to laugh as Huang pensively scratched and picked at his nose. When we stopped laughing, he rubbed his eyes and continued.

"We have identified our thinking with who we are. And not only that," he said smiling, "the common belief is that we think from our heads." He began tapping the side of his head. "So we think we *are* our heads." He grabbed both sides of his skull and laughed uproariously. "You see how we can lose energy through thinking," he added, doubling over again in laughter.

I didn't get it—what was so funny? I hoped that one day I would be able to laugh like that with him.

After a moment, Huang began again. "It is important to stop the outflows through thinking as well as through the other senses. Otherwise we lose energy by identifying ourselves with our thinking. Thought runs through the entire body," he continued, "and can be felt as patterns in the connective tissue." He paused for a moment. "We are taught to confine our sound into patterns of thought. These patterns run along lines of connective tissue, throughout the body, forming a web. Our web of thought repetitively uses a limited aspect of our sound. The unused areas become plastered together through disuse. This creates constriction in some areas of our energetic body and gaping holes in others.

"In the same way that our learned respiration creates a wave that keeps us from breathing from our core, the thoughts that are charged by learned behavior keep us from resonating with the greater thought patterns of which we are capable. Thought is concentrated body energy. We need to let our thoughts drop down from the head, then sink through the chest, and settle in the lower *dan tien*." Huang raised his hands to his head, then slowly lowered them to the level of his navel.

He turned to the chalkboard and drew a square block with holes in it that looked like Swiss cheese. We looked at each other with puzzled expressions. "A car engine," Huang said, as if it were obvious.

"Excuse me?" It was Octavia again.

Huang looked at our puzzled expressions and with a smile said, "Ah, Chinese car engine. We'll just let the oil settle down into the crankcase." Amid groans of laughter, he then drew a picture of a torso with a head on top. He darkened the bottom of the torso and drew arrows pointing downward. "Hope you guys get it this time," he muttered. "Let the oil settle down into the crankcase."

He drew another torso with a head, this time with a densely packed dark area in the center of the lower abdomen. "You concentrate that energy in the *dan tien*."

"What do you call the *dan tien* in English?" Keisha asked.

"Gas tank," Joseph quipped.

"There's no word for it in English," Huang answered, "but Joseph's definition isn't bad. The lower *dan tien* is the place in the lower abdomen where we gather energy. It's a place that can be felt, but there's no anatomical corollary." Once again, he rubbed his hand in a circular motion on his lower abdomen. "An easy way to feel it is to swallow and notice where you sense it in the lower abdomen. Another way is to hold your breath until you feel fear rising inside you; then follow the fear down to its source."

APPLICATION: FINDING YOUR DAN TIEN

The *dan tien*, the place where we gather energy, is about four finger widths below the navel, deep inside the pelvic cavity. Huang's suggestions work very well. Hold your breath until you feel uncomfortable. Where does the instinct to draw another breath originate? Now swallow repeatedly until you notice where you feel a sensation in the lower abdomen.

Huang drew a small circle inside the abdominal area and then a thick line that went from the lower abdomen all the way to the top of the head, ending up with a shape that looked something like a thermometer. "When you concentrate energy in this area," he said, pointing to his lower belly, "you can make it flow up through the core of the body."

Huang put down the chalk and looked at us, smiling. "Now let's get back to sound. Words limit our awareness of sound, whether we think them or say them. They usually objectify our perceptions because they are a linguistic structure based on our learned behavior. If we identify too much with words, we lose our sense of flow.

"Language can be useful, allowing us to communicate, but we have

125

to realize what words are. They are vibrational phenomena with a twist. Taken in context, words contain belief structures that go into the far distant past, back to the beginning of time as we know it. Words actually create time." Huang paused to chuckle. "Maybe we'll talk about that someday. But for now, we have to finish talking about the Chinese car engine.

"Our internal chatter restricts us in a great many ways. In fact, the more self-involved we become, the less contact we make with the world at large and the more we are involved in dialogue and projection, both externally and internally. When you see someone extremely involved in their internal chatter, you see a person who is very closed off from the world. They live in a hazy ball of energy, one that doesn't allow much contact. In fact," Huang added, walking over to Joseph and placing a hand on his shoulder, "that's what Joseph was like when I first met him."

Joseph nodded, grinning back at Huang.

"Words and the belief structures that they're attached to impose limitations on our perception, and these limitations color our view of the world," Huang continued. "If we can decharge or break the connection between our old ingrained belief structures and the words we use, we can be in the world of words without limiting our perception. To do this, we need to identify with our sound rather than with our words. But enough of these words for now. Let's take a break and clear the cobwebs out of our heads," Huang said. "Then we'll use the Chinese vacuum cleaner called hard work to get rid of the rest."

I walked outside with Keisha. While we were strolling in the sun, Keisha brought up the idea of how "no thought" could become a way of being in the world. I liked hearing Keisha's observations. I told her how, when Huang was speaking, I had thought about her phrase—tactile resonance—and that I could see how becoming aware of it had to do with being free of my thought processes.

Huang asked us to line up and assume the Horse stance. We moved each of our arms back and forth in front of us in a smooth, undulating, windmill-like fashion. The movement was called Wave Hands Like Clouds. As he walked slowly among us, he said, "Let your thoughts sink down. Let them reside there in your lower abdomen. Collect and unite with the pressure of your Luminous Essence, then let this force spread and fill your whole body. Try to think with your whole body."

As I moved forward and back and from side to side, I kept returning to my habitual patterns of thought. Then I remembered something that Huang had said: "All of the four motions are interconnected. Redirecting any one of them will affect the others."

I found that looking inward helped to dissolve my thoughts, as did creating circulation in my body and opening my joints. Gradually, as the exercise continued, my thoughts spread apart and dissolved. I became the Observer. After I made this important shift, I began to feel bright and full of what I call emotion, as opposed to the emotions: feelings of anger, fear, sadness, or anxiety that I had learned to see through my long years of practice as a healer. These feelings, I had learned, were some of the body's mechanisms for trying to get itself back into a state of well-being.

Being the Observer allowed me to be neutral. I was able to experience in my body that when I allowed my thoughts to go back to their root, I became the Observer. The Observer existed before thought. I then realized that the Observer and Luminous Essence are very connected, if not the same thing.

APPLICATION: FOURTH MOTION—SOUND

Get into the Embracing-the-Tree posture. Notice your thoughts. Do they rise up into your head like noisy sparks? Let them drift down into your abdomen. Feel these sparks as energy and gather the energy in your abdomen; then spread it out through your body as if the energy were warmth radiating from your Center. This may produce a fuzzy, tingly feeling or sensations of warmth throughout your body.

AWARENESS JOURNAL

In "*Embodying My Awareness,*" *describe your physical response to this application.*

"Now," Huang announced, "we will talk about the body that knows. A lot of people spend a lot of time and money trying to remake their bodies into the current fashionable image. But they still retain the same inner ideas and old behavioral patterns. The body that knows is something else altogether. And this body has knowledge and can act more appropriately and quickly in any situation."

Octavia waved her hand. "I'm confused," she said. "I've been living in this body of mine for more than seventy years. It's seen me through some rough experiences, but I've never felt there was more than one of me—although lots of times I wished there had been!"

Huang smiled appreciatively. "I will give you a small demonstration." He pointed to the two biggest and strongest men in our group and told them to attack him at once, using the best techniques they could think of. As the rest of us watched, mesmerized, the two men quickly leapt toward him. But even more quickly they were hurtling away from him, as if they had been shocked by an electric jolt. To my eyes, it looked as if they had literally bounced off Huang.

"That was really relaxing," Huang said, stretching and chuckling as his two attackers dusted themselves off, their faces amused and perplexed.

Nick resumed his place in the group, shaking his head. "I don't get it," he said. "Joseph and I must outweigh you three to one, but you dusted us off like we were mosquitoes. What gives?"

Huang's grin grew to alarming proportions. I thought, not for the first time, that he'd be perfect for toothpaste commercials. Maybe I should advise him to get an agent.

"You don't do this by staying rigid—you have to become soft. When you remain rigid, you limit your options. So, to make any progress you have to explore softness. This does not mean limp, but rather relaxed, resilient. When you are soft and relaxed, you open yourself up to a greater structure and connect to the Bigger Dream. Then you find, in the midst of that softness, a new life and resiliency, and from this Center you create a new idea of your body that includes both your physical and relating bodies. And that is the body that knows. It all starts with exploring softness."

Albert spoke up. "This reminds me of what you said the other day about iron wrapped in silk."

"Good!" he exclaimed. "This is where the concept of iron wrapped in silk originates. The advantage of touching someone softly is that we can penetrate to their deepest intentions. The softness is the silk. The internal circulation that we create within that softness, through relaxation, gives us vertical integrity. That is the iron. The strength and power of iron and the external softness of silk create an intense calmness. This is possible only when the mind is clear. You can't have disturbing emotions and be in this state at the same time."

I thought about how important it is to become emotion rather than emotional.

"What you do is feel the contact, follow it, and trust," Huang continued, walking slowly back and forth.

"Trust what?" Marlene asked.

"Good question, Marlene! Who knows the answer?" He gazed out at us with eager expectation.

I signaled with my hand. "Our Luminous Essence," I said, "at the core of our being."

Huang paused and looked at us, letting the answer sink in. "You permit your assailant to make contact with you," he went on, "but you do not permit yourself to play the role of his own projected shadow."

"But *how* do you do this?" Joseph asked.

"You maintain your integrity and at the same time you maintain contact with them. You stay centered, yet flexible enough that they cannot cast the shadow of their intentions upon you. They cannot make you an object that they can physically project onto."

I looked at the other students in the room, wondering how often I'd made them into objects and what objects they'd made me into.

"Simple, no?" Huang rubbed his hands briskly together and suddenly adopted a traditional heaven-and-earth posture, as if he held a basketball in front of his abdomen.

"There is a way to line up vertically between heaven and earth," he explained, "that allows us to more directly contact our Luminous Essence. On the other hand, the way we have learned to relate to other people around us—what I call horizontal relating—can strip us of that vertical integrity. We want to learn how to relate horizontally while maintaining vertical integrity. If we line ourselves up properly with gravity, then we gather strength from heaven and earth."

I suddenly thought of something that Jake, a chiropractor friend of mine, once told me about the work of a prestigious scientist, Roger Sperry. Sperry's research had shown that, in a well-aligned, healthy body, 30 percent of the motor output of the brain is used to organize the body's relationship to gravity. If the body is not aligned properly, up to 90 percent of the brain's motor output could be used for that function. If we could line up properly between heaven and earth, therefore, we would have a lot more energy for other pursuits. I was beginning to see what Huang was talking about.

Joseph spoke up. "But how do we maintain vertical integrity when we're working closely with others? I know that for me a big problem occurs when I feel like I merge with another person."

"Ah, good question," Huang said. "Remember that what we need to do is to maintain contact with the core of our being and, through that, an identification with the Bigger Dream. When the core of our being is based on the integrity of our Luminous Essence, a structure is then created in the midst of softness."

Joseph nodded.

"On the other hand," said Huang, "when our perceptions are jagged and rigid, we objectify ourselves and think that we have to defend more than is really there. As we become more fluid, the space we have to defend begins to disappear. The area we have to protect becomes smaller and smaller. The less we feel we have to defend, the freer we become.

"What I'm trying to teach you is to move in close without fear. When you first begin to explore being close and a problem arises, you think that you have to be either closed to protect yourself, or open and let the other person do as they will with you. It's either hard or soft, aggressive or passive. If you spend time exploring softness, however, a new kind of integrity develops within you. You will find that you can afford to be soft in your horizontal relations with others because you have developed the strength of your vertical integrity. You need less and less from other people, so you are more yourself around them."

At that moment, I felt very appreciative of all my teachers. Huang was describing what had been slowly gathering momentum within me. More and more, I was able to contact my Center while in close proximity to others. I understood that this new teaching was immense in its ramifications.

Huang extended his arms, palms turned inward, as though he was hugging a big tree, the image of self-containment. "This is what you want," he said, "to feel self-contained and connected to your Luminous Essence in the midst of others. To do this, you first begin to line up with gravity and feel vertically integrated when you are alone. Second, you learn to do this while in the presence of other people, as when we did the forms in class. This reinforces your sense of vertical integrity by bringing it more into a social context. When you can stabilize a way of being in the presence of other people, it is more real to you than if you just do it alone.

"The third step is learning to maintain vertical integrity while face to face with another person. We use the two-person exercises to do this. Although it is challenging, it is still not the same as being out there in daily life, facing the monster of learned behavior toe to toe." Huang stood straight and stretched languorously. "The monster is what we'll deal with tomorrow."

Chapter 12

JAGGED BODIES: THE DAY DREAM

Yesterday, before dismissing us, Huang told us that this morning we would meet as usual in our studio, but that the real work would take place on the streets of the town in the valley. We exchanged puzzled looks, but all Huang would say was "Dress appropriately!"

Now Huang stood before us beaming as though he had some delightful secret to impart. "Today, you are going to do something I think you will find very interesting. You have been somewhat isolated the last few days from the world out there." He gestured toward the window. "Now you are going to go out and take a look at it. I want each of you to walk through town alone. You can use all of the techniques we have practiced and see how they apply to daily life. This will provide a close multisensual look at your perceptual conditioning and enable you to see what shape your personal feng shui is in.

"Unless someone knows what to look for, the people on the street won't guess that you're doing anything different. You will learn to be in the world and not of it, like a duck sitting on water without getting wet. By doing this, you are going to see the reflection of your learned behavior. You will experience how your learned behavior wants to shape you into its way of being. You will sense the jagged shapes of molded, consensualized beings out there trying to shape your behavior. You will learn that your feng shui is formed by a pressure from the outside and a corresponding internal mechanism that you have developed in order to accommodate it. Learned behavior has its uses, but you will experience that it gives you a false sense of security about functioning in the vast world we really live in," he said. "You may feel secure when you're functioning within your learned behavior, but as protection against all the forces in the world, learned behavior is inconsequential. If it's all you've got to protect you and something comes at you from a different mode of perception, you will be squashed like a bug." Huang slapped his hands and rubbed them together with a grin.

"Today, I want you to walk up to people and look them straight in the eye while keeping your eyes focused inside, on your abdomen. Keep your joints loose and keep circulation in your body to bypass your learned breathing wave. This should stop you from talking to yourself. I want you to do this while interacting with both men and women, and if you are lucky enough, a small child. Let's see what happens."

As I walked down the hillside into the wealthy resort town in the valley, I was surprised at the level of apprehension I felt. For the past few days, I'd interacted only with my workshop companions, and I felt strange as I undertook to interact with the people out there. I decided I wouldn't wait until I reached the valley to get started. I practiced walking in a new way, turning my senses inward. I stopped at a little park in order to give myself a chance to integrate all that Huang had taught us. I went over Huang's directions and calmed myself.

It took a while. The feelings that were hardest for me to deal with were the self-consciousness and paranoia I felt about acting differently. They seemed to come and go in waves, but I steadied myself and entered the town.

I walk along the sidewalk of the main street with my eyes on the ground. I find a bench and sit down to watch people. What most astonishes me is the similarity between people; one group evolves into another: babies into young children, children into teenagers, teenagers into young adults.

I see a man scrutinizing me. Instantly I feel a wave of self-consciousness and paranoia. I sense a pressure to stop looking at the world as an Observer and to conform, to be a part of it in the way that I was trained. Part of me longs to settle back into the expected steps of my perceptual conditioning. There is another part that feels suffocated and encumbered by those very emotions.

Now I remember what Huang, Esmeralda, and Eulogio have all taught me about relaxing into the Third Point. When I do this, my sense of self becomes greater than either a positive or a negative reaction toward my learned behavior.

The next thing I notice is a small group of short-haired ladies in their fifties. They are well dressed, seemingly having a good time, laughing, chattering, and looking into shop windows. They are all similar in that they lack fluidity in their bodies. I wonder about the kinds of physical discomforts they must be feeling. I realize that the diseases they are experiencing must be similar, too: breast cancer, osteoporosis, and gynecological problems that result in hysterectomy. I see that the lack of fluidity and the rigid patterns that the body settles into are signals of what surgeries people might have had or the diseases to which they can become susceptible.

I look in another direction. I see the women's husbands, another little group, smug, jingling the change in their pockets, pretending not to watch the young girls go by. Their body motions, too, all seem alike. I realize that a conversation with any one of them would be the same. The subject matter could be different, but there would be similarities about all of them; they'd all talk to me with the same choreography of their bodies. I think about the kinds of diseases and operations they might have had, and know that they too would be similar: high blood pressure, heart disease, prostatitis.

I think about what Huang has taught us about motion. It becomes clear that the kinds of diseases and operations people are likely to have are intimately connected to repetition of motion, lack of spontaneity, and habitual ways of contacting the world.

The idea of calling people's patterns of energy flow their feng shui begins to make sense to me. I start to look at the collective conditioning as a feng shui pattern and at my internal way of relating to it as a corresponding feng shui pattern.

I close my eyes and listen to the sounds around me. I remember Huang saying that, in the Orient, thought is just another one of our senses. A bird sings. During the time it takes me to think "Ah, bird," I blank out the rich auditory texture around me. I realize that I picked only one way of ordering all of the sensual input coming at me. In doing so, I've left out an infinite number of other possibilities of perceiving.

I see that there is a unity and integrity within the cultural matrix that creates "Ah, bird." But this cultural matrix, even in its integrity and unity, limits us from the totality of what we can be. It keeps us from opening ourselves to the full spectrum of sensory input that has the potential to give our bodies elasticity, fluidity, and health. I see that this cultural matrix, or learned behavior, is based on what both Huang and Esmeralda call horizontal relating.

I open my eyes. I look up at the trees and the sky. I make my way through the groups of people, of bodies around me. I still don't feel too safe as an Observer. The idea of interacting with people leaves me a little queasy. I feel exposed to myself, naked, and uncomfortable. I have been walking down streets most every day of my life, and though I sometimes feel uncomfortable, I'm used to knowing what to do. Now something inside me knows that this is going to be different. I can no longer rely on my old way of knowing what to do. I am evolving. My old feng shui pattern will now be revealed. Instead of working through it, I am going to step back and see it.

It helps to remind myself of what Huang told us: People will throw their projections at me and see me as just another person on the street. He also said that people won't know that I am pulling back from collective, agreed-upon behavior patterns, that I am actually stalking myself. Although these thoughts are not very reassuring, they give me the courage to begin.

While people approach me, I notice the difficulty I have in maintaining my focus on what Huang taught us about breathing, use of the eyes, movement, and inner quiet. My old learned ways pull at me like riptides. I squirm. I want to respond in my old ways, and it is very difficult to stay focused. At first I simply can't do it.

Come on, *I chide myself.* Nobody knows or cares about what you're trying to do here. *What do I expect?*

My present experience vaguely reminds me of something I once read about being in two places at the same time. Here I am on the street, looking like a typical Joe, yet I'm really in a different world—concentrating on stalking my learned behavior—from the people around me. Both realities are happening at the same time. My body is their intersection.

Finally I feel strong enough to interact with people the way Huang instructed. I see a man walking toward me. He looks to be in his early thirties. I relax. I allow circulation to build in my body. I relax my face and my joints. I direct my eyes inward as I look him in the eye. He glares back. It is difficult to maintain my posture. As we walk toward one another, it is like paddling a canoe through white water: I am buffeted on all sides. Keeping balance in the midst of it takes everything I have. I feel defenseless; I want to throw up a shield to protect myself; the urge to lower my eyes is nearly irresistible. I feel the projection of his jagged shape trying to mold me into a shape that corresponds to his. I feel a pressure to turn him into an object of anger and violence, an urge to smile or say something. It's hard not to act in the accustomed way and to instead maintain the posture of inner relaxation and circulation.

Then suddenly he is past me. I am centered again. It's incredible! I feel giddy, as though I've just gotten off a particularly hair-raising roller coaster ride. Disneyland, *I think,* doesn't have much to compare with this! *I realize this goes on all the time if only I could tune into it or have the energy and direction to do so.*

I keep walking. I notice a very attractive woman on the other side of the street. I cross the street and follow her unobtrusively. I am able to maintain the internal posture Huang taught us except for intermittent lapses when I become caught up in the sheen of her hair or the round curve of her buttocks.

Suddenly I hear a voice calling from behind me "Julia!" The woman stops, turns, and waves. I am startled but I keep walking. I deliberately make eye contact with her while trying to relax my face and gaze inward. I expect her to glance away, but to my surprise, she smiles at me. The urge to smile back pulls at my face. I want to be cute, attractive. I want her attention! This is a different kind of ride altogether. Although

137

it is not as threatening as the one with the man, it is alluringly more powerful. The waves of energy I have to battle in order to maintain contact with my vertical integrity are more intense.

The urge to look outward and assess what she looks like almost rip my eyes out of their sockets. I nearly panic from the pressure and give into my old ways of being: I want to revert to my old ways. Somehow I continue to maintain my inner focus while looking at her. She briefly raises a hand to her hair and drops her eyes as I pass. When I encounter a rather large older woman, I am surprised to notice that the same things go on inside me. I want to be cute, to be desirable. Most of all, I want her attention.

I noticed that when I pass men and boys of various ages and builds, a similar inner scenario occurs each time. There are differences and peculiarities about the way each person affects me. Some even smile or greet me, but the core of the interaction is always the same: competitiveness, fear, aversion, often flashes of anger and violence, a feeling of being threatened, of having to prove myself.

I pass many more women. Here also, to my great surprise, there seems to be a pattern to my reaction. There is an element of fear involved, but it is based more on attraction than aversion. I fear lack of approval. The impulses that surface have to do with being shy, cute, flashy, or agreeable, the wish to be appreciated and admired. I am surprised that this reaction happens not only with women I'm overtly attracted to, but with women of different ages and shapes. Although there are slight variations in my response, there is a similarity at the core of each interaction. I feel the pressure of wanting to be appreciated and admired.

So this is the living male-female agreement that Esmeralda talked about when we were on the mountain top looking at the people down below!

I try to evaluate which is harder not to react to, men or women. I want to say that it is more difficult to relate to men because of the feelings of having to prove myself against anger, violence, and competitiveness. As I examine my reactions more closely, however, I reaffirm the conclusion I came to earlier: it is much harder to stay in touch with my Luminous Essence with women. Through these observations, I am further able to integrate what Esmeralda told me about how my personal feng shui was related to the male-female agreement within me.

As I muse on these ideas, I see another major opportunity: Poised at a shop window is a woman with her baby in a stroller. I approach the mother and exchange appropriate pleasantries about the child. Then I lean in close to the baby, a beautiful little boy with enormous long-lashed dark eyes and a full head of silky black curls. I feel no pressure from him to be anything; neither do I project anything onto him. I gaze into his eyes and he gazes back, his face relaxed as he drools and bubbles onto his bib.

The baby is unattached to what I am doing. The only challenge to my meditative posture comes from the pressure to make goo-goo faces for the approval of the mother. I feel her mounting tension as I continue to gaze at her child. It is time to go. I compliment the child to put the mother at ease; I say good-bye. As I start away, she scoops the baby up out of the stroller and cuddles him protectively, cooing. She holds up one of his arms and bobs his hand up and down. "Wave bye-bye to the nice man," she says.

My next encounter is with a man wearing cowboy boots, a fringed leather jacket, and a cowboy hat that comes down to the edge of his big sunglasses. His jeans are held up by a belt with a ludicrously big buckle. It spells out the name BUCK. I chuckle as I recall the joke about how, if you live in Texas and someone asks to see your ID, you show him your belt buckle.

I center myself and walk toward Buck in my meditative posture. To my amazement, he smiles at me. I can't see his eyes through the sunglasses, but the smile seems genuine and warm. I smile back. The strange thing is that I expected the usual confrontations with another man, but the interaction was easy and natural. There was nothing pulling on me that I felt inclined to respond to. I was able to be myself.

The longer I work on maintaining my meditative posture, the more relaxed I become. While this increases my confidence in being neu-

tral, I can feel the projections of other people much more powerfully. I am relaxed, full of circulation from the inside. Yet at the same time I'm afraid because my old notions of who I am are crumbling around me.

I walked back up the mountain, exhilarated at the changes I'd gone through. As I entered our meeting hall, I was startled to see Buck in his fringed leather jacket and cowboy hat surrounded by some of my fellow students. He turned. It was Huang! When he saw my facial expression, he began to laugh. I began to laugh, too. He had been in disguise to give us students the opportunity to respond to a "stranger" who was relaxed inside.

After everyone had returned, Huang called us together. At first it was difficult to listen because, although his voice was the same, the outfit didn't match the Huang I knew. "The reason I brought you to a secluded place," he said, "was to stabilize another point, another way to be in the world. I wanted to give you a tactile checklist through which you could reach the Third Point. This enabled you to observe yourselves so that you could experience the motion In-Between, the process of your creation and dissolution, of who you really are.

"When you first went into town, you probably felt empty. It was the feeling of not knowing what you were doing. A similar feeling happens when you learn a new movement in class and have to assume a beginner's mind. However, the learning you did today is on a grander scale. You are learning another way to relate to the world. Of course, at first it will feel uncomfortable. This happens because this new way is bigger than the way that you knew before."

Huang paused for a moment, put his left hand on his hip, shifted his weight to his left leg and, like a cowboy, pulled down the brim of his hat.

Why does he continue this cowboy act? I thought. *He'll use any excuse to ham things up.* I chuckled to myself.

"The learned behavior hits us at a very deep level," Huang continued. "This we were able to experience when we worked with the four motions. However, when you felt me walk by, I wasn't pulling on you with the hooks that you're used to. Your experience with me was probably closer to that which you would experience with a baby. I saw one in a stroller, so I imagine that some of you did interact with it.

"When you stop the outflows and turn your concentration inward, you cancel out learned behavior. The reason that I went to visit you all in town was to show you that it takes two to tango. When you sink back to your Center, quiet your mind, and get close enough to share luminous cells with another person, what you feel is actually their learned behavior hitting you; what you watch is the way that you have been taught to respond—your personal feng shui.

"For example," Huang continued, "let's say that you come up against someone who is in their learned behavior and is trying to activate yours. You check to see if you are beyond your perceptual conditioning by using the techniques of the four motions, as we have done today. In this situation, if you look closely you'll see that it is not you who is the source of the impulses pulling on you to react in a certain way. This helps to clear confusion, because we have been taught to feel that, if we are in an interaction, one half of everything that is going on is ours. It is important to identify where you end and where another person begins. Again, you can use the techniques of the four motions to do this."

Keisha spoke up. "You know, this has always bothered me. I can never tell when I'm with another person whose is what and what is whose." We all laughed.

"And now you know," Huang smiled. "What I have given you is a sensory checklist to determine how much you are involved in a given situation."

"What checklist?" Marlene asked.

"Exactly to the point," Huang said. "I appreciate that you are practical people. Somebody asked me near the beginning of the workshop what are the four motions. And I told you that you'd hear it over and over again. And you have. But one last time we're going to talk about the four motions." His grin ratcheted up a few notches. "By paying attention to your breathing, movement, the way you use your eyes, and the way you talk to yourself, you can at any given moment assess to what extent you are hooked into another person's agenda."

Marlene still looked confused. "I still don't quite get it," she said.

141

"It's simple, especially after you get it," Huang said, smiling. "If you're in the presence of another person and you relax and create circulation on the inside, open your joints, relax your eyes, look inward, and not talk to yourself, then you know that the learned behavior that's going on is not yours. What will happen, however, is that you will be beset by the ways you've been trained to react."

"Okay," Marlene said, "I understand. That makes sense. I like that. But then the question arises: Where do love and affection fit into this?"

Huang looked at her admiringly. "True love and affection *begin* at this point. They radiate outward unimpededly when you act from the Center, from the In-Between. They get very contorted when you act from learned behavior, and that's why sometimes we call the impulse to free ourselves from the tyranny of our learned behavior 'the pressure of affection.'"

"But that's not all," Huang said, going to the chalkboard. He began yet another strange drawing, accompanied by the usual ill-concealed chuckles of his students. He turned to frown at us with an affectation of bewilderment. "What?" he demanded. "You can't recognize a simple chicken?" Huang added a few lines to suggest flapping wings. "A Chinese chicken," he said to our accompanying laughter.

"Now," Huang continued after we had settled down, "when you begin to reclaim energy from your learned behavior, the next stage is to store it, to sit on it, brood on it, like a chicken sitting on her eggs. To do this, you have to relax and be neutral." He drew a few eggs underneath the chicken and we were off again. Huang grinned as he filled the egg ovals in with colored chalk. "Chinese Easter eggs," Huang nodded, satisfied with his effort.

"Eventually, new ways of making contact with the world will arise spontaneously. But, in the meantime, it takes great courage to brood like this chicken," he said, with a grin and a gleam in his eye, "not knowing what's going to pop up next. In this workshop you have been offered the possibility of relating from another position. You began to recognize this other position as a place around which you could create your self-identity. And I am sure you found that you could experience a much bigger sense of self from this central core of your being.

"When you did some of the exercises alone, you began to recognize this new way of seeing yourself. As you did the exercises together in class, you learned to experience relating to another from this new position. You also learned that we can help each other to consolidate a new position from which to operate. It's nice to have help because this is a big undertaking."

Huang paused for a moment, allowing us to absorb his words. "Persistence is the key!" he said emphatically. "Coming to a new idea of the body is a slow, gradual process that meets with great resistance. The consensual reality we live in is very strong. As you have begun to realize through studying the four motions, learned behavior is pounded into us from all sides when we are young and permeates almost to the very core of our being.

"To have even a chance of getting beyond this constant barrage, it is helpful to have other bodies to reinforce another way of being. To put it another way, we need corporeal witnesses to stabilize a new idea of our body."

Huang stopped, took off his cowboy hat, and tossed it on the floor. He wiped his brow with a big red handkerchief and smiled. He pointed his index finger in the air, and said, "One more thing. We are not objects. We are something indefinable. We must change our idea of ourselves as objects and see ourselves purely as flow."

APPLICATION: COMBINING THE FOUR MOTIONS

Remember the applications for the four motions and become aware of the Watcher at the same time. You may need to review them before you try this. Practice each for five minutes.

Now assume the Embracing-the-Tree posture.

◆ Breathing. Create circulation in your whole body. Relax your belly. Notice how this changes the way you breathe.

◆ Opening the joints. Open up the spaces between all the joints in your body.

◆ Use of the eyes. Keep your eyes still. Sense that you have the

143

penetrating eyes of an eagle. Relax your face and feel that relaxation all the way down to your abdomen.

◆ Sound. Gather your thoughts—the noisy sparks of sound. Let them sink down into your abdomen. Feel this energy as warmth or a fuzzy tingle. Spread it throughout your body until it reaches your hands and feet.

Now you are set up to look at your perceptual conditioning or learned behavior. Stay centered by using the tactile applications of the four motions. Practice the four motions while standing for five minutes, or until you can quiet your thinking patterns and bring in the Watcher.

Now practice the four motions while moving your arms like seaweed in water. Continue for five minutes.

Extend the techniques of the four motions to walking naturally around your home. Do this for another five minutes.

Now you're ready.

Walk down the street of your choice and maintain the position of the Watcher, using the techniques of the four motions. As people come toward you, relax your face and look at them directly while maintaining your connection with the Watcher. Observe what happens.

AWARENESS JOURNAL

In "Mapping My Perceptual Conditioning," make notes of what you observed. See if you noticed a difference between what you experienced with men, with women, with a couple, with a baby or child. You will need these later. Do you see the value of using the four motions in quieting your mind in the midst of conditions, and how this can help you in your own self-exploration? Note this in your journal.

PART III

STRATEGY

Chapter 13

HUNTING THE ANIMALS

smeralda sat beside me, humming along with the overture to Rogers' and Hammerstein's *South Pacific* playing from the speakers of her little cream-colored convertible as we wound up a steep road into the mountains. "Some enchaaaanted evening," she suddenly burst into lyrics, and I gave her a quick glance. She had covered her hair with a turquoise scarf. Along with oversize sunglasses, I thought she looked like a sixties film star. I knew her eyes were twinkling behind the dark lenses. "You may meet a straaaaanger . . ." she sang.

"I'll never meet anyone stranger than you," I laughed.

It was a few weeks since Huang's workshop, and I'd taken the weekend off to visit Esmeralda. A lot of what I'd learned from Huang was still sinking in, and I needed to talk it over with her. Now, while I focused on the road, Esmeralda made small talk about books she'd recently read and the state of her garden. I had never realized how much I enjoyed the sound of her voice.

"I'm going to take you up to one of my favorite places," she had announced that morning over tea.

"Where?" I asked.

"It will be a surprise," she winked at me, "but here's a hint: Sometimes it's important to go the top of the mountain to get a bigger picture of where you are going and how you want to get there. An overview can help you orient yourself. With an overview, you can create a strategy." She had tossed me the car keys as we left the house. "I know you like to drive my convertible!" she said. "I know you love it when I give you directions."

Eventually we pulled into a small parking lot. Esmeralda punched a button and the ragtop slid out from a space behind the back seat. As it settled into place, she removed the scarf and loosened her lustrous hair, then smoothed it back neatly from her face and tied it on the nape of her neck with the same scarf. "*Bueno!*" she exclaimed, sweeping off the sunglasses. Gone was the film star; here was Esmeralda once again.

I laughed appreciatively. *Esmeralda the chameleon,* I thought idly, swinging open the car door. From inside the trunk of the convertible we pulled out backpacks and slipped them on. Esmeralda retrieved an immense straw sunhat and nestled it on the top of her head. We started up a steep trail. When we came to a little lookout area, Esmeralda pointed to the town below.

"In that world down there full of rigid bodies talking to rigid bodies, it's easy to lose your sense of direction, especially before you have become accustomed to being fluid." I waited for her to elaborate, but she merely continued to walk.

At the tree line, Esmeralda stopped and pointed with a gesture of her chin off to her left. I saw an eagle circling. We struck out in that direction. In half an hour, we found ourselves at the top of the mountain with a panoramic view on all sides. There was a spot of shade next to a tumbled pile of boulders. Esmeralda dropped her backpack and grinned. "Let's eat!" she said.

From the backpack she pulled a thick red-and-white checked tablecloth. I helped her spread it over the short, coarse grass. Then I sat down and watched as she emptied out the rest of our picnic. There were strips of smoked salmon, pickles, fresh French bread, cheese, potato salad, golden peaches, and a thermos of iced tea, as well as napkins, plates, flatware, and condiments. Once all the food and condiments were spread out, I laughed out loud.

"You're quite a magician at putting these feasts together!" I marveled. "How on earth do you *do* that, anyway?"

"At my age," she rejoined, handing me the thermos, "every woman needs to keep a few secrets."

I poured tea into two cups. "And what that might be?" I asked. "Your age, that is?"

"It's one of the secrets!" she laughed. "But I'll give you a hint."

"Yes?"

"Somewhere between thirty-five and a hundred and sixty-four."

"That really narrows it down," I chuckled. I raised my cup to hers. "To the Bigger Dream!" I toasted.

"To the Bigger Dream!" she echoed, taking a sip. "I love that toast," she added, smiling mischievously. She put down her cup and began heaping potato salad onto a plate. I relished eating with Esmeralda. She knew how to thoroughly enjoy herself. After the long hike, with the view spread below us and the fresh, gentle breeze, the food was incredibly delicious. We ate leisurely, tearing off chunks of bread, talking desultorily, concentrating on the food.

After we had finished, Esmeralda sighed luxuriously, settled back against a boulder, and laced her hands behind her head. "The reason I brought you to the top of this mountain is to give you an overview," she said, "and to help you line up your spirit with the rest of your life. To have a sense of continuity in all your actions, you need a strategy."

"And I suppose you're going to tell me all about it," I grinned, leaning back against another boulder.

Esmeralda waited as I settled down. "In order to give our lives meaning and direction," she continued with a serious expression, "we have to look to our old friend and sacred enemy, Death. It is the fact that we are going to die some day that gives us a sense of time, perspective, and urgency. Death demands that we get into the Center of our feng shui or our Third-Point perspective and stop projecting our false sense of self. Without death, there would be no reason to change at all. It is the knowledge of our approaching death that can motivate us to remove the blinders of conditioned behavior, to move beyond the constricted idea of the body—our learned feng shui, if you will."

Normally, any talk of death stopped me from enjoying my surroundings, since it inevitably produced a tornado of disturbing thoughts. But now, as I looked at the pristine beauty all around me, the idea of death as the definitive force that gives purpose to our lives bolstered my spirit and allowed me to savor the view.

"The realization that death exists has to come from somewhere. When you look at death very closely, you realize that there is something looking at death—the Observer," Esmeralda went on. "This implies that we have a perspective that is greater than death. It is from this perspective that we can create a Center around which to establish a true feng shui."

Esmeralda's statement had a dramatic effect on me. It gave the incredible view before my eyes even more definition and clarity. I told Esmeralda my thoughts, and a big smile crossed her face. We sat for a few moments in silence.

"It is death that requires us to become efficient with our energy," she said at last. "Death demands a strategy, a plan that enables us to see who we are and what we are likely to come up against. The advantage of a strategy is that it provides an effective way of looking at and categorizing the massive inputs coming at us all the time. It also can give us a very practical way of dealing with situations and making choices in everyday life. In fact, it is the major tool for understanding and releasing ourselves from learned behavior.

"You first understand who you are and what you are up against. Then you look very carefully, from an unhurried and calm perspective, at what you have to do, just like Huang's idea of relaxing."

I gazed out, lost in thought, to where the purple hills blended into the horizon. "Go on," I told Esmeralda after some moments had passed.

"The foundation of our strategy is an understanding of the male-female agreement," Esmeralda answered. "In this way we arrange our forces against the tyrannical limitation placed upon us by learned behavior."

"That sounds great," I said skeptically. "But how do we do it?"

"I'm so glad you asked," Esmeralda replied with a smile. She reached into her backpack—which I had thought couldn't possibly hold anything else—and pulled out two small rag dolls, one male and one female. She placed them in front of me. "As I was saying, a very effective way to start the dominoes of our acculturation tumbling is to use the male-female agreement. Practically speaking, this is how we deal with the males in our lives." She reached over and bopped the male doll on the head. "And this is how we deal with the females." She petted the female doll.

Bopping and petting, I thought. *There she goes again.*

"We want to decharge the way we deal with the males and the females," Esmeralda continued. "Then we will begin to accumulate enough energy to explore what's beyond our learned behavior."

Esmeralda looked over at me and added, "You follow so far?"

"Yeah, but I want to hear more."

"And so you shall, *amigo*," she said. "We begin to look inside ourselves and see what's male and what's female—to us. We make lists. We go back to early upbringing and examine our parents: How did they treat each other? How did their parents treat *them*? How did they relate to other males and females and, more specifically, to us?"

"Isn't this how a regular psychologist would approach this?" I asked. "Why don't I just go see one of them?"

"It does sound similar," Esmeralda said, laughing. "But it is different in two big ways. First of all, we are talking about changing our perception of our body, and psychologists rarely deal with the body. Second, we are dealing with how to move beyond our learned behavior once we have gathered back the energy from it. We want to move out into worlds beyond our perceptual conditioning, not just taking the energy released by our realizations and reinvesting it back into our learned behavior."

I took that in, then began thinking about how my own learned behavior had been handed down to me, unconsciously, from generation to generation. Really, there was no one to blame. Since my acculturation had been seemingly innocuous, I hadn't really noticed its damaging effects. Now I could see what I often admired about the overtly damaged people I occasionally saw in my clinic—victims of blatant physical and psychological abuse. At least they were aware of the monster that was sucking their energy. Esmeralda waited, watching me as I thought all this out.

"After we look at how we were related to by our male and female role models, then we look at how we relate to the males and females around us. We begin to see how that connects to the way our parents related to the males and females around them. We don't even have to go searching for the male-female agreement. It's around us all the time. Just stop and take a look."

I recalled, smiling, my experience on the street in the resort town during Huang's workshop. Suddenly, a warning that Esmeralda had once given me about using the male-female agreement popped into my head. "You must continually keep in mind, Daniel, that studying the male-female agreement is not an end in itself; in fact, overstudying it can keep you stuck in it." I reminded her of the warning now.

She nodded, recalling the conversation. "That's right," she agreed. "You have to remember that you are greater than your patterns, remember who you are beyond those patterns, and that the male-female agreement is only a tool for understanding." She peered at me and said laughing, "Once we get a good idea of our psychological landscape, we can begin doing some landscaping."

"And what are my rakes and picks and shovels?" I asked, liking her metaphor.

"Very good. You are getting into the spirit of this. Your main tool is your capacity to look at yourself dispassionately, without judgment." Esmeralda crossed her legs and leaned forward toward me earnestly.

Suddenly, unexpectedly, I was swept with a feeling of deep love for Esmeralda, this funny, wise, simple, beautiful, learned woman who had taken me on at a point in my life when I was not much fun to be with. She had acted at various times as taskmaster, sister, seeress, mother superior, and adversary, and I was just beginning to appreciate how much I owed her. This, I reflected, was a debt that could be paid only indirectly, by healing and loving others. This realization flashed through my head in an instant, and I tucked it away in my heart. Some day I would tell Esmeralda these things, but right now she required my full attention.

"We begin pinpointing," she went on, "who and what situations in our lives have either male or female characteristics. For example, authority figures, directors, situations that directly manipulate our external circumstances, tend to be male. Those issues that have to do with nurturing, comfort, expressing the emotions, tend to be female." She stopped for a moment and smiled at me.

I picked up the female doll and held it closely, like a newborn. Even though I did it playfully, I was struck immediately at the quick shift in my feelings—even the way I positioned the doll in my arms was automatically tender and protective. I related this to Esmeralda.

Esmeralda looked at me and smiled. Then, while holding the female doll in one hand, I picked up the male doll and looked at both of them.

I regarded them as two aspects of my energy.

"When you learn to relax physically," Esmeralda continued, "to be neutral and gather energy in the midst of situations where you're faced with either your male side or your female side, then a major shift in one aspect of your life will impact the others."

"So, Esmeralda," I asked, "is this an example of how we don't have to go around looking for our male-female agreement? It's around us all the time."

"Yes, in a way. We keep creating the same situations over and over again. Thus, a major confrontation with the male side of your learned behavior will create a landslide that clears the weeds and brambles and overgrown shrubs from your internal landscape."

"Okay." I took a deep breath. "Tell me if this is an example of what you mean: I met a woman named Keisha at Huang's workshop. She told me about her father who was an alcoholic and who physically abused her. I can see how this became part of her internal landscape, her learned behavior. In any situation that reminded her of being around her father, she would pull inward and create the same internal wall. She would adopt the same attitude that she had learned as a child and create a pressure to make the current situation repeat her past experience."

I paused for a moment. Esmeralda raised her chin slightly. This was her subtle way of indicating that I should continue.

"Keisha told me how, studying with Huang, she learned to relax physically in the midst of trying conditions. She could then gather energy. After practicing this way of relaxing for several months, she found herself in a bar. There was a large man there who had had a lot to drink and who started to direct his energy toward Keisha. She felt herself begin to tense up. At that point, because of her training with Huang, she remembered to focus on relaxing and maintaining an inward posture of neutrality. When she did that, the energy that she put out changed, and what she then observed was that the drunk no longer had a matching object upon which to direct his energy.

"I think that Keisha had learned to stay neutral in the midst of her learned behavior," I continued. "What she noticed after going through this type of situation a few times was that it no longer happened in the same way. Instead, it was replaced with other ways of relating that she hadn't known before. Is this what you mean, Esmeralda, by changing your internal landscape?"

"Yes," Esmeralda said. "The way she relaxed not only helped her in that situation, but in all other situations of a similar nature. It had a rippling effect throughout her self-concept."

We were quiet for a few moments. Esmeralda stood and stretched. She motioned for me to stand and she picked up the dolls. She put the female doll in my left hand and the male doll in my right.

"Why don't you walk like this for a while?" she suggested.

I felt kind of stupid holding these dolls, but I was starting to get her point, and maybe feeling uncomfortable was a part of that. At the same time that I was feeling uncomfortable, I realized how important physical props sometimes are to make us stop and focus on what's going on inside of us. I was also beginning to realize that feeling stupid could be a doorway into new learning.

The first thing I noticed about carrying the dolls was that I could no longer move in my usual way—my hands were occupied. I began to sense the load of the agreements that I was carrying inside.

Esmeralda noticed my discomfort. "Once you have begun the journey into the Watcher, or Third Point," she said, "studying the male-female agreement will give you a way to measure your progress as you dismantle your learned behavior. Using this technique, you won't get disoriented."

"So is this what's happening to me every time I relax through more of my learned behavior? I'm changing the landscape?"

"Yes, and gathering more energy," she said, chuckling, leading me back toward where we had left our picnic lunch. Once again we sat and admired the view. I felt excited about the possibility of how I could look at my own personal feng shui from the top of my internal mountain.

"Okay, let's continue," Esmeralda said. "First, you have to realize that you are able to see clearly only after you've gone through something. When you look back with the male-female agreement as your lens, then you can see how you're making progress. This imparts strength and confidence, and then when you turn around to face the other direction, it helps you to devise a strategy for the future.

"We'll get back to this in a little bit. But first, I really want you to understand how our learned behavior and its linchpin, the male-female agreement, keep us from experiencing the true affection we have for our world. I want you to know what you're up against. So I'm going to use myself as an example," said Esmeralda.

"In the early days, before I had a strategy, I was very seductive. I would promise my charms," she said, leaning over to flutter her eyelashes dramatically, "my nurturing, my closeness, but not deliver. I did this to get the attention I wanted. Attention is what I was after. But that was a long, long time ago," she said, raising her eyebrows. "I'm sure you can't identify with that at all!" She laughed.

I didn't laugh with her. She was always picking on me for what she called being seductive, or the ways that I used to get the attention I desired by using my learned behavior. It was painful to realize that any time I was attracted to a woman, I couldn't relate in a relaxed way. Something else would take over. *That must be my learned behavior,* I thought, feeling dumbstruck as I looked down at the male and female dolls still clutched in my hands. Then I remembered all the feelings that came up when I was in Huang's class doing the exercise with Keisha where we were up close and personal. What a waste of energy my learned behavior was; how much energy it took to go through all those hoops! And not only once, but over and over.

Then, as if reading my mind, Esmeralda continued. "Fortunately, I learned from someone how to use the strategy of the male-female agreement to gather back some of the energy I was wasting. Then I began to see in others just how seductiveness worked. I don't know if Huang taught you this or not, but when you begin to relax your body energy all the way down into your abdomen, through the sexual centers there, the energy begins to pool and gather and rises up internally into the chest area, and you naturally begin to feel love. What I found out about seductiveness—and I think you will too—is that I was pulling my energy down to those lower areas and promising love, promising closeness, but not giving it. And that in this way I had deprived myself of the love of the world. I had mistaken the energy that I was getting from playing the male-female game of my learned behavior for my true affection for the Bigger Dream, and of it for me."

As Esmeralda paused, I leaned back against a rock. Rubbing back and forth against it, I felt the tenderness with which it caressed me.

"If something happens in the everyday world that causes us pain," Esmeralda went on, "instead of either reacting to it or running from it, we can use our strategy to deal with it. When we have a strategy we can use it to help us trace our learned behavior patterns back through our lives, through the earlier instances that caused us similar pain, back to the original experiences in our very early childhood which set down our patterns of reacting. These are the experiences that limit the flowering of our natural affection."

"So you're saying, Esmeralda, that trying situations can become opportunities."

"Yep," Esmeralda nodded.

I looked up as a huge raven flew by, squawking. "But, you have to remember," I continued, "that studying these male-female agreement patterns is only one wing of the bird. The other is that we are more than these patterns."

"You're getting it now, sonny!" Esmeralda said with a twinkle in her eye. She gathered a handful of small stones from the ground and began balancing them one on top of another. "As you allow yourself to reexperience the pain you went through at a very early age, the limitations of your learned behavior start to fall like dominoes." She poked the bottom stone in the pile and they all fell down. She looked up at me and smiled. I laughed.

"Having a strategy also gives you a way of assessing yourself in an effective way. When you can judge yourself honestly, you create a precise idea of who you are and what you are up against. And another very important thing happens here," she said, looking at me for emphasis. "This produces a sense of clarity in your life, and you begin to merge with the Third Point—the Watcher."

"Are you saying that I haven't been honest with myself and that's why I've been so confused?" I asked.

"Almost," she replied, smiling. "The problem isn't that you haven't been honest with yourself. It's just that you haven't created a stable, neutral vantage point from which to view yourself honestly."

"So what happens when you create a neutral vantage point?"

"Once you establish communication with the Watcher inside, you begin to perceive the world from this point. The true journey is the journey into the eye of the Watcher. As you realize more of who you really are, you then need a way to get that perception out into the world through your physical body and your relating body so that you don't get sick."

I nodded and Esmeralda went on.

"Neutrality becomes your measuring stick. It is neither for nor against your perceptual conditioning. You have to chip away at the delusions about yourself that you have been taught since childhood. It's like hunting."

"Hunting?" I echoed.

"You learn the behavior patterns of your male-female agreement," Esmeralda said with a mischievous smile. "You learn what they eat and when they go down to the water hole to drink, what they do in the twilight hours and in the middle of the night. Then you set traps, and slowly but surely you start to retrieve the energy they have taken from you."

I thought of my discomfort a few minutes before when Esmeralda teased me about my seductiveness. Now, after her explanation, this pattern that I was so ashamed of had become an animal for me to hunt, an object to focus on as part of my strategy.

"Looking at the feeding habits of your learned behavior is at first a terrifying experience. Later it become an endless source of amusement." Esmeralda began to chuckle. "Don't mind me," she said. "I'm just remembering how terrible I used to think those monsters were and how entertaining they are now." She stretched out her legs and leaned back against the rock. "You don't have to look very far for dragons to slay. You are living with them all the time. Your friend Keisha didn't have to go out and set up a special drama to test her neutrality. All she had to do was gather energy and wait. In fact, you can call in the dragons of your learned behavior by becoming relaxed, neutral, and not feeding them." She smiled and growled, animal-like. "Then they will show up, looking for food."

I glanced behind me and laughed uncomfortably.

"So start sharpening your arrows, get ready," Esmeralda said, "get that bow strung." She gestured for me to get up, and we peered down at the distant town. We could see antlike people on the streets below. "You're going to have some hunting to do," Esmeralda said, pointing at the town, "because down below, waiting for you, are the wild animals of your learned behavior."

AWARENESS JOURNAL:
MAPPING YOUR MALE-FEMALE AGREEMENT

You want to see how you work so that you can then use the strategy of the male-female agreement to get a better view of your learned feng shui pattern. To start cataloging your own personal feng shui, make lists in "Mapping My Perceptual Conditioning" as follows:

◆ *Go back and look at the notes you took at the end of Chapter 12 where you combined the four motions. You will now put these feelings in context. On one side of a page write "Male" and on the other side, "Female." Underneath "Male" transfer those experiences from your notes that have to do with men. Then do the same for "Female."*

◆ *For examples of these types of experiences you can refer to Chapter 12. Remember that the male-female agreement is what forms the basis of your learned behavior. Experiences with couples or children are offshoots of this basic pattern. You don't need to list them at this point.*

◆ *Now add to your male and female lists people in your life who have either male or female characteristics. Think of four people—two male and two female—whose characteristics you know well. Under each person's name, jot down a list of things they say often, their body postures, habits, clothes, facial expressions. For instance, under "Mary," you might write: "Swings her hips when she walks, likes short skirts, long polished fingernails, shoulder-length hair, red lipstick, giggles."*

◆ *Now add information to the lists about your early upbringing and relationship to your parents. Describe a time in your childhood when your father seemed most fatherly and a time your mother seemed most motherly. Write a list of the male characteristics that your father showed at that time, and a list of the female characteristics that your mother showed. Note which of these traits you currently identify with.*

When doing these exercises, please don't feel confined by the examples given. Be creative.

APPLICATION: INTEGRATING MALE-FEMALE INFORMATION

Of the traits that you listed in the preceding application, which ones are part of your current personality?

Sit in a comfortable position in a quiet room. Set your lists before you. Start bringing together the separate lists that you made and begin to embellish the deliberate look that you had at yourself while you were walking down the street with the memories of your past.

For instance, as you remember your experience on the street, write four or five expressions that describe the male experience for you. Do the same for the female experience. If you're a man, when relating to other males you may come up with the words such as "competitive, aggressive, fearful." For your female side, the words or expressions might be "wanting to please, being cute, fear of failure." You will have your own.

Your purpose here is to get an overall view and feeling of your learned behavior. It is as if you are on an animal-watching safari. You are observing yourself live, the way you really act in the world, getting a palpable and emotional sense of your perceptual conditioning. You are making the male-female agreement tactile rather than just an abstract concept, documenting the way it is stored in your body. This type of assimilation gives you a bigger view of yourself. You can begin to see how your perceptual conditioning impacts your daily life—when you're alone or with others. You are beginning to put the male-female agreement into a multisensual, living-color context. You are learning to take notes with your body.

Chapter 14

THE PAUSE

The first step of this strategy is to take a pause.

—Esmeralda

U p here on the top of the mountain, I had not only a visual overview, but a feeling of increased awareness and freedom from the
pressures of my life in the world below. "I'd like to pause right
here," I told Esmeralda.

"No, no, no," Esmeralda laughed. "The hunting grounds—" she
pointed to the town below "—are down there."

She must have heard me sigh. "This business of dealing with the
world seems exhausting sometimes, dosen't it?"

I gave a murmur of assent. "Sometimes the task feels overwhelming.
There's so much unlearning to do."

"One step at a time. Take a pause," Esmeralda replied. "It is the first
element in building a successful strategy."

"How so?"

"Because when we take a pause from our normal activity, we stop
the energy drain from our learned behavior. Our energy then can build,
creating a surplus that will seek spontaneous release. This can allow for new
expressions of ourselves that we were unable to access before."

I looked quizzically at Esmeralda. "This makes me think about when
people get sick. They're taking a pause."

Esmeralda waited for me to continue.

"What I see a lot in my practice is that people get so drained by the
clamor of the world or by their habitual patterns that they don't allow themselves space to rest and heal as they go along. Then they end up in my office
with some sort of complaint. It's their bodies saying, 'Hey, pay attention!
You're not taking care of me. Your learned behavior is wearing me down. I'll

make you let me rest!' And illness forces them to take a pause. But they usually don't get the message. They recover and go right back and recreate their world exactly the way it was before. And they get sick again. A more effective way would be to take the energy they build up during the pause and deploy it in a new way . But in order to do that they need a new strategy to live by. And to create a new strategy they have to establish a Center around which to gather energy and make themselves healthy."

"Hey, boy," Esmeralda exulted, "you're getting the hang of this now!"

She got up and began to walk up and down, bristling with energy. "It's important, then, to go back into the world with this pause—let's call it relaxation or neutrality—intact. So the next step is that you learn to maintain this neutrality in the midst of your daily life, which builds even more internal circulation and gives you more perspective. This enables you to observe the wild animals of your learned behavior and to see the patterns they move in while you are among them. They'll keep coming back to eat. You don't have to worry about that."

Esmeralda stopped for a moment to rummage in her bottomless backpack. She withdrew two fat ginger cookies, handed one to me, and took a bite out of the other.

"Don't react—either positively or negatively," she said, munching. "Your only defense is to relax, stay neutral, and learn to operate from this new space. If you can do this, the building energy breaks apart the confining sequence of your learned behavior. Spontaneity begins to leak between the action-reaction patterns, disrupting their continuity and giving you new modes of expression, just like it did for your friend Keisha."

It took a few moments for this to sink in, and Esmeralda watched me intently the whole time, slowly chewing her cookie. I wasn't sure that I had totally grasped it. "So, Esmeralda, what you're saying is that you pull away, create a pause, gather energy, and take this energy back into the world through neutrality. Then you actively learn to relax and stay neutral in the midst of your learned behavior. Is that it?"

"Up to now that's it," Esmeralda replied. "The thing is, once you've taken the pause and are in the midst of it, you can learn to accelerate the process. A proper strategy creates a framework and greatly accelerates the process of growth. By disrupting your patterns, it gives spontaneity a place to come through. It also gives you a place where you can hunt specific patterns," she said, rubbing her hands together, chuckling. "And remember to sharpen those arrows." She ate the last bite of her cookie and licked her fingers. "Take me, for example," she said. "I studied how I behaved around men. I noticed that an important element of my relating to men was—are you ready for this, Daniel?—*giggling!*" Esmeralda lowered her eyes and giggled, putting her hand over her mouth in a perfect mime of a flirtatious young girl.

Of course this made us giggle. The more I tried to picture Esmeralda as a stereotypical giggling girl, the more I laughed. Soon we were howling, riding a rollercoaster of laughter until our stomachs couldn't put up with any more. We collapsed on the ground.

"Do you see what I mean," Esmeralda gasped finally, wiping tears from her cheeks, "by finding the old learned behavior a source of endless amusement?"

I found the thermos and poured out the rest of the iced tea. Esmeralda and I shared the cup. "Go on, I've got to hear this," I urged, trying unsuccessfully to stifle another fit of laughter.

When we were finally able to stop, Esmeralda said, "You see, I would flirt shamelessly, and when these men reacted in an aggressive way, I would start this submissive giggling. So when I decided to disrupt my patterns around men, I stopped giggling. This was my way to start hunting down the whole pattern of how I behaved with them. It was a struggle. But after a while I taught myself to relate to men without giggling."

"Until now," I said, pulling a somber face.

Esmeralda immediately began laughing again. "But seriously," she continued, "what focusing on giggling did was to give me an object of meditation, a reminder to relax even more when I was around men. I became more conscious in my relating. The more consciousness we bring to relationship, the more energy we gather.

"Here you have to be careful because, after a while, your learned behavior will start to incorporate your new pattern. In my case, this *not* giggling became a habit, a feature of my learned behavior. Then it no longer helped me to focus. It had become, simply, part of the way I related to men."

"Okay, so now you have a new habit," I said, smiling.

Esmeralda nodded her head. "You're catching on. I needed something different to keep me aware during these situations. It no longer mattered whether I giggled or not. I had to find something else. So next I used my appearance. The fashion at the time was pancake makeup and lots of eye shadow, eyeliner, mascara, lipstick, blusher—just tons of stuff. Oh, when I think of the *hours* it took to get ready to go out and—and just *buy a damned newspaper!*" Esmeralda threw up her hands, laughing heartily. "Oh, I'm glad not to be so attached anymore!"

I was enjoying this immensely. I'd known little of Esmeralda's young life, and this glimpse of her as a girl added a new dimension to my appreciation of her.

"So you decided to use your appearance," I prompted. "So you're going to tell me you stopped wearing makeup."

Esmeralda nodded vigorously. "I bared my face. The first time I did this, I tell you, Daniel, I felt like I was stepping out onto the street stark naked. In fact, with full makeup and no clothes, I'd have felt *less* naked." She laughed again. "This was a tremendous shock to me, and I used that feeling of nakedness to maintain my awareness until I no longer felt uncomfortable without makeup. Then I could wear it or not wear it, according to my mood or the occasion. If I did, it was because I *enjoyed* it, not because I needed something to hide behind.

"Exactly which actions I chose to focus on were not important in and of themselves. What was important was that they made me more aware and that they were hooked together by a focused strategy for breaking up the male-female agreement. You can get real creative here," she added with a laugh. "What you use is an individual matter. But the specific actions get their charge only because they're part of a greater strategy."

I looked admiringly at Esmeralda for a moment. "Huang is teaching me how to prevent my learned behavior from hooking me when I engage with other people," I said. "I found that not getting hooked takes a lot of energy. My experience was even frightening because of the constant pressure to conform and the magnitude of what was coming at me from the outside.

How do you deal with that?"

Esmeralda smiled, knocked back the last of the iced tea, and made a noise like a horse's lips flapping. We both laughed. "From the inside, it is scary! And that means that you're truly confronting your fears. You have to get used to this place of not knowing who you are in terms of the old coordinates. Since it's an ongoing process, looking at your life in terms of the male-female agreement gives you a sense of where you are and where you're going. It creates a point of focus; it's like a rudder on a sailboat—it keeps you on course in the midst of uncharted waters."

"Uncharted waters! Boy that's where I've been lately," I said. "No rudder—not even a set of oars! And the fog . . . ."

Esmeralda chuckled appreciatively. "The beginning is the hardest time," she continued, "because the state of not knowing is very uncomfortable. The temptation to regress is great. It is especially hard because you have no frame of reference except your relationship to your Luminous Essence deep inside. In order to resist, you have to build confidence and a sense of continuity. This is why a strategy is helpful. If you persevere and tolerate this sense of not knowing, you begin to realize that, when you're in it, you have more energy and feel more complete. There's a feeling of flow. This is what we are looking for."

While we'd been talking, Esmeralda had built up another pile of stones. She was slowly balancing them one on top of the next. She stopped for a moment to find another stone, then went on talking. "Life no longer revolves around either the approval or disapproval of others," she stated. "Instead you learn to dance the mystery of exploring who you are and your relationship to the Bigger Dream."

With a feeling of great clarity, I easily continued to follow everything she was telling me. I told her that. She lifted her hand. "Hold on to that clarity for just another minute. I'm almost done." She placed the new stone carefully on top of the stack. "Bringing you up here to this mountain was part of my strategy in teaching you. I wanted to put you in a receptive mode so that my words could sink in deeply, just like they're doing now." She flashed her mischievous grin. "I never like to work too hard," she said. "I decided to get this mountain to help me rather than trying to communicate these ideas to you in a grocery checkout line."

Esmeralda admired her pile of stones and stretched luxuriously. Then she started putting the remains of our meal into her backpack. We shook out the tablecloth, folded it, gathered the dolls and placed them in my backpack. *"Barriga llena, corazón contento,"* she said. "Full tummy, happy heart." She patted my arm and we started back.

On the way down to the parking lot, Esmeralda entertained me with a series of jokes that she referred to as "jokes not to herself"—stories to tell out loud to another person. These were jokes about what she called the mythic ethnic or professional group that constantly changes personae: Polish, Catholic, Jewish, Mexican, Italian, Black, Wasp, or Protestant; bartenders, doctors and lawyers, and all indigenous tortilla makers the world over.

Eventually we staggered, laughing, into the parking lot. This time, Esmeralda drove. "Let's talk some more about this process of unfolding," she said. I turned slightly toward her to give her my full attention.

"Breaking your learned behavior patterns from the inside, at least at the beginning, is painful. But when you get used to facing this pain, it becomes who you are and you don't think about it anymore. You become very resilient, and what you originally thought of as pain becomes just another opportunity to gather energy. You start to think about the world in terms of energy and maintaining energy, and you start to develop your own ways of moving out of your learned behavior. The pain lives in your belly, born from the male-female agreement. When you build enough pressure to truly experience your pain, you find the exhilaration and joy of being unbound." Esmeralda stopped talking for a moment. I glanced toward the back seat where Esmeralda had sat the male and female dolls, as though they were little passengers.

"We begin to identify ourselves not with our learned behavior," Esmeralda continued, "but with the process of understanding and facing our pain with the strength of our intention. We *become* the process between our natural spontaneity and our learned behavior." Esmeralda glanced over at me with a wink as we continued down the mountain.

APPLICATION: IMPLEMENTING STRATEGY

Pauses in the continuum of your self-concept can occur naturally when you are confronted by separation, shock, illness or death. It's also possible to pull back from life without an outside stimulus. The energy you reap will get you in touch with the Watcher.

This application may seem vague because you will be accessing an aspect of yourself that is not currently a part of your self-concept. Do the best you can with it. Persistence is important.

◆ For thirty minutes a day, take a pause from your normal way of relating. (Remember that the way you perceive is based on the male-female agreement.) Be aware of your living, moving "body notebook."

◆ To give your mind a pause, practice any of the four motions—movement of the eyes, breathing, sound, opening the joints—or any of the practices of earth, air, fire, and water. Notice how, when you do them, you are creating a minipause in your normal perception of the world. This is much like the pause that would be created by the shock of death or separation. Note: If you really are going through one of these shocks right now, try to use this interruption of your normal state of awareness to observe your perceptual conditioning more closely. Often the pain that you feel in these situations is the pain of moving beyond your learned behavior. The saturation of stimuli is more than your self-concept is used to dealing with.

◆ In creating a pause, do you feel yourself gather energy and thus perspective? If you do, note it in your Awareness Journal. You can use this technique to cultivate relaxation and clear perception in the midst of your learned behavior.

◆ Take this pause and your new perspective into your everyday life. The pause helps you to develop a Third Point from which to view your learned behavior. Using the overview of the male-female agreement, study your own action-reaction patterns. Examine your male-female agreement even more specifically, watching for the action-reaction patterns that occur. As an example, recall Keisha's experience with the man in the bar. As a result of taking a pause, Keisha was able to see her pattern with men reflected in that incident.

◆ When you've thought of examples from your own life, you may want to note your particular patterns, both male and female, and write them down in your Awareness Journal under "Mapping My Perceptual Conditioning."

◆ Study your action-reaction patterns until you can see them with some clarity. Then you can choose techniques to disrupt them. For example, Esmeralda first stopped giggling around men, then quit wearing makeup. She disrupted her normal action-reaction pattern, which made her more aware in these situations and, in turn, made more energy available to her.

◆ Note in "Tracking My Awareness" if and how you feel more concentrated, relaxed, or free. Do you feel more spontaneous? Has taking a pause impacted other areas of your life?

Next you will document how going through these experiences impacts other areas of your life. For example, after her episode with the man in the bar, Keisha may have begun to see more spontaneity in her relationship with her male boss, her auto mechanic, a policeman on the street, or even a male bank teller.

AWARENESS JOURNAL

In "Mapping My Perceptual Conditioning," start documenting how, when you changed the pattern in one area of your male-female agreement, it affected the rest of it. Another example: If you change your relationship with a parent, you may notice that it affects how you relate to your spouse.

Begin to see and document how, in the notebook of your living body, working on one area of your male-female agreement affects the rest. The spontaneity in one area will be reflected in others. In your *internal landscape, walls will begin to fall like rows of dominoes.*

Be sure and notice how using a strategy helps you to acquire constancy in your practice and to gain strength, confidence, and perspective. The resulting energy will help you continue your journey without getting lost in your learned behavior.

After you've noticed specific changes in the male-female agreement in your daydream, see if it changes in your nightdream. If so, note it in your journal. The goal is to spend more time in spontaneity and less time in your learned behavior.

PART IV

FENG SHUI FOR THE BODY

Chapter 15

EULOGIO

We are involved in creating a new and more complete idea of our body. Healing is the act of synchronizing our idea of the body—our personal feng shui—with the Bigger Dream.

—Eulogio

After a couple of hours of thrashing around in bed, trying to get comfortable enough to drift off, I gave up. *This is ridiculous,* I told myself. I got up, pulled on my bathrobe, and took some Chinese herbal powders to help me sleep. Then I made myself a cup of tea. I sat now at the kitchen table, blowing on the tea, waiting for it to cool enough so that I could drink it without burning my mouth. I glanced at the wall clock: 2:33 AM. This was the third time in a week that I'd done the Chinese herbs and hot tea ritual in the middle of the night, and I distinctly did not want it to become a habit.

A few months had passed since Huang's workshop, and lately I had begun to experience a strange restlessness. Sometimes I felt frustrated; sometimes I felt sad. And *all* of the time I felt jittery. I had an enormous amount of energy that I simply didn't know what to do with. Esmeralda's wisdom couldn't calm me, and Huang's exercises seemed only to make the situation worse. *I can't go on like this,* I thought wretchedly. *Maybe I need a vacation.*

I got a colleague to cover my practice and headed for Mexico. I lay on the beach to soak up the healing warmth and light of the sun. I walked in the desert to burn off the excess energy, but after a week and a half, nothing had really changed. In fact, I seemed to be feeling worse.

I can't go on like this, I thought wretchedly. *Maybe I need to get back to work.* Even as I packed my bags, though, I suspected that at least part of the problem was that I hadn't fully integrated what Huang had taught me. *So what if I learned what my patterns are from Huang and a way of looking at them from Esmeralda?* I grumbled to myself as I folded clothes into a tote bag and rounded up toiletries from the bathroom. *I still don't have a way to put these teachings into my body and into my life!*

Suddenly I thought of my teacher and mentor, Eulogio. I still had a few days before I had to be back at the clinic, and since I was curious anyway about how what I had learned could relate to healing and the prevention of illness, I decided to stop off on my way to the border and see him.

It was a Friday evening when I drove up to Eulogio's house located in an older part of a town near a river. It was an ancient whitewashed adobe structure with a tile roof, surrounded by flowers and jacaranda trees. Eulogio answered the door himself, looking exactly as he had when we'd last been together: medium height, strong, sinewy build, dark skin, coffee-brown eyes, and black hair, which, I noticed, had begun to show a distinguished touch of silver at his temples. I watched as his handsome face registered first surprise and then amusement. He laughed and threw the door wide.

"Bien venido!" he cried. "Welcome!" First he hugged me, and then, still laughing, stepped back and peered at me critically, head to toe. Eulogio could see things that other people couldn't, and I knew he was assessing the state of my physical, mental, emotional, and spiritual health. "Come in, come in," he said, taking my bags. "I was just thinking about you today, wondering how you were doing." He led me to the same room I had occupied during my last visit. "Have you eaten? Would you like something to drink? What can I get for you?"

I laughed. "To answer your questions in order: no, yes, and a bath towel." It had been a hot, dusty drive, and I longed for a shower and a change of clothes.

Eulogio nodded. "Plenty of clean towels in the bathroom, my friend. While you take a shower, I'll reheat some leftovers and find you something good to drink."

After I cleaned up, I dressed in a clean shirt and pants that Eulogio had laid out on my bed. I went through the house, combing my damp hair with my fingers, to find my friend in the central courtyard, sitting next to a fountain. He waved me over.

"Boy, am I glad to see you," I said as I sat down. Eulogio grinned and handed me a tall frosty glass. I sipped at it gratefully. "Mmmm," I murmured appreciatively. "This is delicious. What's in it?"

"Let's see," Eulgio ruminated. "The usual native shaman's assortment of cicada shells, dried toad skins, earthworms, scorpions—"

"—lizards, centipedes, and bat feces," I chimed in. This was a familiar routine, and it made me laugh every time I heard it.

"So, do you think I could make it as a standup comic?" Eulogio teased.

"Probably," I said, mock-serious. "But don't give up your day job. At least not until you get me straightened out."

"So, tell me, my friend, what's happening to you that has your energy so . . ." Eulogio groped for a word.

"Loco?" I offered.

Eulogio slapped his knee appreciatively. "Sometimes only a Spanish word will do," he chuckled.

"Yeah, my energy feels crazy all right," I confided. I began telling Eulogio what I'd been going through over the last few weeks, mainly that since Huang's workshop, my life had seemed to slowly unravel.

He nodded knowingly, encouraging me to tell him everything. As I listened to myself talking I was relieved to discover that simply describing my predicament out loud seemed to enhance my perspective. It was similar to being with Esmeralda.

"I keep doing Huang's exercises and looking at the world in the way that Esmeralda taught me, yet something is missing. The more energy I gather, the more apprehensive I feel. I worry that something bad is going to happen to me. I'm starting to drop things and lose things. Sometimes I'm downright paranoid, and I want to clamp down, restrict myself. But when I check back over the day-to-day events in my life, the lines that connect me to the world are all intact. I still have my work, I still have a place to live, I still have enough money. I'm not as sensitive to other people's pain as I once was. All of that seems okay. Yet everything is different. The days have gotten so big that every day is like a month. I don't know who I am anymore. I feel like I'm going to burst like an overinflated balloon."

175

Eulogio had a big smile on his face and his eyes were beaming. He reached over and patted me on the shoulder. "You're doing well," he said.

I looked at him, dumbfounded. *Oh, great,* I thought, *another positive thinker; another Esmeralda.* "I'm glad you're enjoying yourself," I said edgily.

"Now, now, my friend, someone has to enjoy your confusion," he said, laughing.

Against my will I started grinning, then chuckling. "Maybe I should start selling tickets," I jibed.

This made Eulogio laugh harder, but in a few moments he continued more seriously. "What makes me laugh, Daniel, is not your pain, but the sense of recognition I experienced when I heard you describing your dilemma. It is an acute crisis that we all have faced," he said, "so you are in excellent company, and it is to be expected. This crisis occurs when we have gathered in enough energy to realize that what our parents taught us is only one way out of millions of ways of being in the world. We find that we can't get angry or sad the way we used to, because anger and sadness are ways of objectifying things and putting the world back in that old order. I think somewhere inside you realize that you can't get angry, frustrated, sad, or morbid the way you used to because your old anger and sadness belong to a way of life you have left behind."

Eulogio's assessment was so right on that I started to laugh, shaking my head.

"You can't even get angry about the fact that you invested your energy into that one way of being for so long," he continued. "You have begun to save energy and are allowing other ways of being to evolve." He looked over and winked at me. "And they haven't evolved enough yet, my friend."

"I guess that's about it," I said.

"Are you going to be around for a while so that you will get a chance to evolve?"

"Is there a fast-forward button?" I said. "I have four or five days. Do you think that will do?"

"Well, we'll make it do. Let's get busy," he said, rising from his chair. "I can teach you some ways to round out your personal feng shui so that the flow of energy that you have accumulated will move through you more smoothly."

Eulogio led me back to my room. "Loosen your clothing and lie down," he instructed, producing a set of acupuncture needles. As I lay on the bed, I felt jagged, hypersensitive. But despite my jumpiness, he quickly and painlessly placed the needles in my arms and legs, chest and abdomen.

Instantly, something surged inside of me, and I changed. I was calm, relaxed, luxuriously tired. I began to dip in and out of a slurpy, deep sleep, the likes of which I hadn't known for weeks. I woke up a bit later, not knowing where I was. There was a languid coolness to the air, and I then dipped in and out of sleep a few more times like a dolphin slipping in and out of the water. The next time I awoke Eulogio was taking the needles out of my body.

"You've been floating in the Bigger Dream and drinking deeply of that spirit," he said. "This type of deep sleep, with the needles in the right places, has allowed you to recontact yourself, to get in touch with a place beyond yourself, In-Between who you perceive yourself to be. From there, you can begin to relate and bring through your being your true feng shui. My being here helps this process because I know what you're going through and what you're looking for. When the needles went in, they opened you to the language with which my body speaks to yours. The needles and my presence helped you to bypass the slow way you normally drift to the core of your being, allowing you to plunge straight down like a stone into a clear pool. That allows you to realign with your proper feng shui. When the ripple happens from the core of your being outward, your feng shui assumes the right shape. I'm telling you this because I know that at this moment you can't remember how you felt an hour ago. Now you have to learn how to get this well-rounded feng shui out into the world."

I murmured agreement and Eulogio motioned for me to stand up. I got up slowly and we walked back to the courtyard and sat by the fountain again. The air felt delicious against my skin.

"In sleep, depending on how deep you go, you allow your world to dissolve as you descend into your core," Eulogio said. "As you return to the waking state, you recreate the world through your perceptual conditioning."

I was still drifting in that luxurious restful state, listening peripherally to everything Eulogio said.

"Your sense of self is involved in the action-reaction patterns," Eulogio continued. "You've been hoodwinked into thinking that in order to be in the world, you have to have all of these emotions and agreements with other people. When you get away from them and sink down into your core, it's scary because you don't know who you are without them. Thus the paranoia."

I told him that Esmeralda had said the same thing, but that knowing hadn't helped me avert the crisis I was in now.

"Knowing something is one thing, incorporating it is another," Eulogio replied. "It's also helpful," he added, "to touch base with people who are used to going through this process."

Eulogio got up and went into the house, and I leaned back in my chair and listened to the fountain. The sound instantly plunged me into the practice of water that Esmeralda had taught me. This perceptual break from my normal mind chatter gave me even more energy. A few moments later, Eulogio returned with two glasses of mineral water and a bowl of stew and some tortillas for me.

As I ate, Eulogio asked me about what I had studied in Huang's workshop. I told him a little bit about Keisha and Huang's explanation of how changing our idea of the body could create a permanent change in us. I described the four motions: breathing, body movement, the use of the eyes, and sound, and how Huang had given us a way to use these four motions out in the world. Eulogio's interest was piqued.

"I'm beginning to get a clearer picture of what's going on with you," he said. "I think you're right. Huang's workshop stirred up some things that you have not integrated yet. But first, let's talk about what you're going through in general terms."

"You're the boss," I said, relieved that Eulogio seemed to know what was going on.

Eulogio smiled. "You still want to be functional in the world. But since you're no longer hooked into functioning in the same way, there are spaces created for spontaneity to come through. This is frightening because you have to build a feeling of confidence that you can deal with the world in the midst of this spontaneity. What you've been doing is clamping down on the spontaneity," he said, "instead of letting yourself flow with it. Your learned behavior has tricked you into believing that it could change. This was just an illusion to keep energy focused on itself." He chuckled. "This created an inner struggle that was very inefficient and allowed your learned behavior to keep attention on itself." He took a sip of water, smiled at me, and continued.

"The process of dissolving and reforming your self-identity is as natural as falling asleep and waking up again. You have to learn to trust it and not become fixated on what is happening around it. Eventually you will come to identify yourself with the Observer inside who is allowing this to happen. This process is revitalizing. It is magical. It has a rhythm of its own."

Eulogio paused for a moment, watching me eat. The stew was delicious, and I mopped the bottom of the bowl clean with the last piece of tortilla and popped it into my mouth.

"It is often our lack of a sense of direction that makes us sick. Have you been looking at your life in terms of the male-female agreement?"

"I thought I had," I said.

"Well, have you been moving the realizations that you've had, the sense of neutrality and gathering energy, back through the tissues of your body as Huang taught you?"

"Well, I don't think Huang really taught me that," I said.

"Then I will," he said, grinning. "Tell me, have you been able to let yourself fall apart?"

"I guess I haven't," I said. "You think that's my problem?"

"Could be part of it, my friend," Eulogio replied. "You have to realize that falling apart or losing your self-identity is the way to gather more energy. It's also the way to feel the rhythm of relaxing and contracting that's going on within you as you gather more energy and let go of your learned behavior. To make it operate efficiently is the next step," Eulogio continued. "If you can help this process work smoothly, you can spend your energy in a myriad of ways of cultivating contact with the world.

"When you reassemble your world, you put back together your idea of the body as well. This is where we begin to move into the area of healing.

One of the things that a healer does is to catalyze this process in others and teach them to allow it to move smoothly in their own lives."

AWARENESS JOURNAL:
TRACKING YOUR ACCUMULATED ENERGY

As you have been accumulating energy, have you noticed that you can't get as angry, frustrated, sad, or morbid as you used to? If so, you may consider that those emotions belong to a way of life you have left behind. Record your observations in "Tracking My Awareness." Keeping an account of the changes you go through and the awareness and energy you acquire will give you direction and confidence.

Chapter 16

THE FENG SHUI OF THE BODY

I woke the next morning looking forward to Huang's exercises. I had been practicing them every day and slowly integrating their principles. They were one of the few activities that lent structure to the new and sometimes frightening spontaneity in my life. Eulogio, who had also studied with Huang as well as Esmeralda, joined me in the courtyard for practice. I was able to pick up subtle but very profound adjustments from Eulogio, with the result that the exercises felt smoother, more natural and real. I was able to learn a lot from the energy emanating from Eulogio.

One movement was called the Bear. Our motions resembled a large bear lumbering along through the forest on its hind legs. As it dragged its feet along the ground, it moved its torso in a twisting fashion. The turning movement evoked the image and power of this animal as well as allowing the body to circulate energy through itself in specific ways that opened up all of the joints.

As Eulogio and I moved side by side, spiraling and turning our bodies together, I realized once again how focusing with a partner creates an incredible amount of mutual concentration. I could feel gravity pulling me downward. It was the embrace of the earth. The more I aligned my body with it and allowed it to pull me down, the more I felt an energy within rising upward and filling me. Those two energies, the downward concentration and the resultant upward surge, created a strong circulation in my body that I was able to move and direct. I saw how the power of gravity—the love of the earth—created the vessel within which I existed.

As Eulogio and I continued the spiraling and turning motions of the Bear, I remembered a patient named Mary. She was recovering from breast cancer. While treating Mary, I had asked about her exercise habits. She told me that she exercised regularly. She ran, walked, lifted weights—

exercise routines typical of our Western idea of the body. What I noticed was that none of those exercises included twisting the torso or extremities. These motions help prevent stagnations such as cancer by increasing the circulation of energy in the torso. "This activates a lot of pumping action in the body and helps it interconnect with itself," I said. I gave Mary a demonstration. I told her that she could accentuate the twisting motion throughout her body while golfing, skiing, playing tennis, swimming, or even fly fishing.

I realized, as Eulogio and I continued our practice, that our movements in day-to-day life reflect our idea of the body and that this has an impact on the body. In Mary's case, there was a definite congestion of energy in her upper torso, and her upper and lower torso were not connecting well. Not only did Mary's exercise regimen not address blockages in the chest and abdomen, it may actually have been exacerbating the condition. The twisting motion that I showed her—and that I hoped she would incorporate into her routine—was a way to connect the upper and lower torso. This would increase energy circulation and help prevent a recurrence of her breast cancer.

Eulogio and I finished our practice and helped ourselves to fresh water. "You look much better this morning," Eulogio said, resting his hand on my shoulder. "When your body gets a taste of well-being, it wants more. Now you have to cultivate and maintain it. You have to become a bloodhound and learn to sniff out well-being."

We strolled over to the chairs near the fountain and sat down. I admired the flowers that I hadn't noticed the night before under the moonlight: big clay pots of red geraniums, their color so brilliant, like neon.

"It's good that you are learning from Huang and Esmeralda," he continued. "Esmeralda has shown you how to connect with the Third Point and how to apply a strategy to your world. Huang has shown you how to observe your perceptual conditioning by centering yourself in your body. Now I'm going to show you how to trace and then fix these patterns through acupuncture and exercise. This is the feng shui of the body."

This aroused my interest. "Do you really know how to trace the patterns of learned behavior and release them?" I asked hopefully.

Eulogio rubbed his hands together as if he were getting ready to do a big job. "Yep, and I guess I'll have to show you," he answered. "But before we do that, we need to have the right perspective. You may not know this, although I'm sure that you've suspected it, that both the science of acupuncture and the science of body mechanics—exercise—are related in that they have to do with the proper realignment of the flow of gravity through the body."

"You've got my attention," I smiled.

"And healing is about dissolving learned behavior into a more fluid way of relating. This is what creates health and provides the proper lens through which to view the health crises of both yourself and your patients. If you don't have the correct lens, even acupuncture won't help," he said.

Eulogio's statement really hit home. I had seen how Western medicine was stuck in the materialistic view of the body. But now I realized that I, too, had often been stuck in my ideas about acupuncture and disease. I told Eulogio this and thanked him. He received my gratitude with the openness of a person who is fully comfortable being himself. He waited a moment in order to digest my admiration.

"As I'm sure Huang and Esmeralda told you, the most important thing is to find a sense of the Third Point or the Watcher inside. From this internal Center, true healing begins. Next, we see how learned behavior works and how it causes disease," he went on. "Then we learn how to relax through a specific behavior, rather than treating it as a so-called Western disease."

I nodded, very interested.

"Another thing," Eulogio continued, "is that we look at a bigger picture of the body in general in order to get a clearer view of how we connect with the world. Remember," he said, "in a real sense the trunk, including the head, is the hub of the physical body. Arms and legs, hands and feet are the way we connect. By having a stronger and more complete flow of energy in our extremities, we can connect more completely with the world. So it is important to stimulate the places where energy is locked in the body and to encourage it to flow back and forth from the trunk to the extremities. When we do this well, we radiate a harmonious feng shui pattern."

Eulogio stood up and began doing the Bear Walk. "Note the importance of the arms, legs, wrists, and ankles. Circulating the energy out to the wrists and ankles is the key." As he sat down, he added, "That's why the so-called source points of acupuncture are around the wrists and ankles.

"Now, let's get more into acupuncture. The charged action-reaction patterns of learned behavior lodge themselves in the body tissues. Through acupuncture, we can release them. The ancients believed that the body is an alchemical treasure trove," Eulogio continued. "They believed that properly aligning the energy currents in the body creates an alchemical transformation that allows us to manifest the urge toward wholeness or enlightenment. It was from these roots that acupuncture evolved."

As Eulogio began walking back and forth, warming to his subject, I felt a thrill of excitement. This was the information I had once hoped would be taught in acupuncture schools. Even in China I had searched without success for someone to teach me the deep philosophy of acupuncture. Now I knew I could get this teaching only from a rare individual such as Eulogio. I was riveted.

"Illness can then be seen as either energy blocks or the body's attempt to become more aligned with its flow," Eulogio went on. "You have to realize that the body has a higher function than work and reproduction, which is all that is important to our learned behavior. We are actually involved in spiritual evolution, and that requires both physical and psychological health."

"You mean," I said, "that we can't hold a meditation posture or work with the flows of energy if we are having a coughing fit or are in the midst of depression."

"Precisely," Eulogio nodded. He pointed out some specific places on his chest and abdomen where memories of learned behavior are stored. Through his explanations, the meanings of acupuncture points around the heart that I had long known—Spirit Seal, Spirit Burial Ground, and Spirit Storehouse—suddenly became clear. He showed me how to access these points by using acupuncture needles to stimulate patterns that would connect them to my extremities, particularly the wrists and ankles.

He said, "For the ancients, healing patients meant driving out the demons that were tormenting them."

"A fitting metaphor for the false perceptions of learned behavior," I said.

"Yes," Eulogio agreed. "The old ways of looking at healing contain seeds of wisdom that are timeless and quite applicable today. Exorcising the demons of false perception and bringing in true perception is really what healing is about. The ancients devised traps by placing needles in the right places on the body, to get energy to flow in new ways and get rid of stuck perceptions. They were very much in tune with how perception and the body are related. Not only did they use acupuncture, they worked with movement as well to repair and evolve the natural feng shui of their bodies."

He stopped, reflected for a moment, then continued.

"Also, right perception is connected to right relating. That is why your work with Esmeralda is so important: right relating is part of getting your life in order so that you can pursue your adventure here in the body." Eulogio sat down again, and for several minutes we sat in companionable silence. I pondered what he had said.

"Eulogio," I began, "all this made me think about the latest theories on balancing the body that I've been using in my practice recently. They're based on the I Ching."

Eulogio's eyebrows went up in an expression of interest. "Oh? Tell me more."

"The area that is actually hurting is seen as a place that doesn't have enough energy. And often the painful place is not even where the acupuncture needle is inserted. Instead, corresponding places on the four limbs are stimulated in order to facilitate energy flow to the site of the pain."

"And because balance is restored, the pain goes away," Eulogio concluded.

"Right. I remember how all this sounded so abstract to me—ho-hum—but when I saw the results, I became a believer. It has given me a much bigger idea of what the body is."

Eulogio nodded.

"For example, I had one patient, Roberta, who had shooting pains on the entire left side of her back. She'd been to many doctors and physical therapists who had tried to treat this area directly. I took a different approach. I calculated that by treating a point on her right forearm her condition would be cured. I inserted a needle into that acupuncture point and, much to her surprise and mine, she immediately felt relief."

"Did that cure her?" Eulogio asked.

"After three more treatments the pain was totally gone." I chuckled. "Sometimes even I can't imagine that sticking a needle in someone is going to have any effect at all. Then, suddenly, they're cured!"

Eulogio smiled. "Yeah, I know. Incredible, isn't it?"

"One of the reasons I enjoy my profession so much," I added, "is that I am continually amazed at the movement of energy in the body and how it works."

"You might not think that changing your idea of the body has any practical effect," Eulogio said, "but you just showed me how it does."

Yeah, he's right, I thought. I could see how, through my work, through the necessity of adapting my perception of the body, and through the results I witnessed in my patients, I had changed my idea of the body without even realizing it.

"I'm glad that you mentioned the I Ching and balance, because they form the central pillar of what I'm about to show you," Eulogio continued. He disappeared momentarily inside the house and returned with a large sketch pad. I watched as he drew the trigrams of the I Ching.

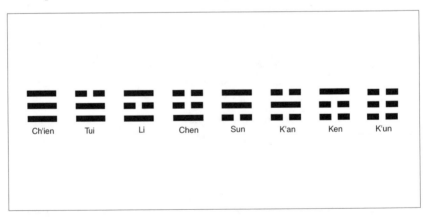

ILLUSTRATION 3: *The ba gua: Trigrams of the I Ching.*

"You probably realize that the trigrams of the I Ching are used in feng shui, too. These trigrams are the *ba gua,* the eight phases. Did you know that the *ba gua* also relate to energy pathways in the body?" I nodded excitedly. I had long suspected these relationships, but I hadn't quite put all of it together yet. I was elated that Eulogio was talking about it.

Eulogio flipped over a page and arranged the *ba gua* in a circular form. "This," he said, tapping the pad with his thick pencil, "is the way the *ba gua* are arranged in feng shui. It's a directional placement representing how our energy radiates into the world."

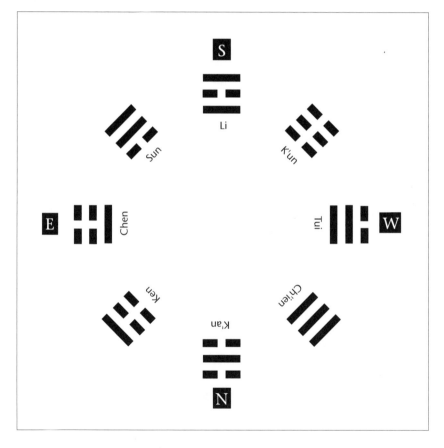

ILLUSTRATION #4: *The ba gua placed in the feng shui pattern.*

"Feng shui means wind and water, or the flow of things," Eulogio continued. "As you probably know, feng shui is also called the art of placement. For example, it is used to determine the placement of a house to capture a balanced flow of energy from the landscape, and the objects inside the house so that the inhabitants prosper. What I'm going to introduce you to is the feng shui of the body," he said smiling, "which is, after all, the house our spirit inhabits. We carry it around with us all the time. If we really want to make deep changes, we have to enhance energy flow through the body."

I was beginning to put together how, through Huang's exercises, Keisha had changed the energy flow in her body, which in turn changed her perception, which in turn changed her life. She wouldn't get the same responses from men as in the past, and she wouldn't be prone to the same diseases. "Wow!" I said. "Do you mean that we can actually change our destiny through acupuncture and body movement?"

Eulogio nodded.

"Then we can use acupuncture and body movement for increased awareness!" I said excitedly.

"Not so fast, Speedy," Eulogio said, smiling as he raised his hand and leaned back against his chair. He ran his hands through his hair and took a deep breath, then began speaking again. "I remember when I was learning this. I wanted to learn it all at once. Fortunately, my teacher wouldn't allow that. Now I can see why." He chuckled again. "For so many reasons, it's of primary importance to first establish an internal Center from which to radiate energy. And I can see right now, " he said, looking at me squarely, "that I'm going to have to explain this to you over and over or you will become very frustrated."

I laughed. "Mind reader!"

"You need to realize that the real house that we live in is our body. So, in general, if we really want to effect a change for the good, we need to change the way we radiate energy.

"Thus, the feng shui of the body," I said.

Eulogio nodded. "Let's start with some basics. The *ba gua* can be used in many ways; for instance, describing how spirit becomes matter. Or, as the Chinese would put it, how the undifferentiated energies of the cosmos manifest as the Ten Thousand Things. Feng shui is the study of how we should align ourselves directionally, how to put ourselves in the right posture so that the undifferentiated can manifest through us properly.

"The *ba gua* are also used medically to describe how incorrect flow manifests as disease or how correct flow manifests as health. To take it one step further, the *ba gua* also relate to the meridians used in acupuncture. Now, as you have learned from Huang, acupuncture is the ultimate science of balancing the energy produced by gravity in the body."

I understood what Eulogio was saying. I remembered how Huang had once told me that acupuncture was a form of specialized body movement.

"The *ba gua* can also describe the basic body movements," Eulogio went on, "and how to get the undifferentiated spirit to flow through the material body. Another use of the *ba gua* is the I Ching—the Book of Changes."

"Right," I said, "the book that's used for oracles or to tell fortunes."

Eulogio's look of incredulity informed me that it was a little bit more complex than that. Once more, I thought, chuckling to myself, I had blundered into the realization that sometimes, if you ask a dumb question or make a dumb statement, you can get a great answer. Your teacher gets so frustrated that he spills the beans.

"The I Ching is a metaphor or an equation that uses the *ba gua* to explain how things manifest. *One* of the ways that it's used is as an oracle," he said pointedly. Then, imitating someone asking a question of the I Ching, Eulogio assumed a deep, serious voice. "What's the next step I should take in my life? Is Daniel ever going to learn how to do things one at a time? Why are my children not like me? What number should I play in the lottery?" He paused for a moment, peered at me, then continued. "When does the bus arrive that carries my *posole?* "

"How many tortillas are there in a short stack?" I was getting into the spirit.

Eulogio intoned somberly, "Why weren't my parents nice to me?"

"The next time I kiss a woman, will she slap me?" Soon we were roaring with laughter.

"So," Eulogio continued after a while, "the I Ching was created thousands of years ago to teach us appropriate action and how to flow in life and which saint to pray to," he concluded, laughing again. "It is about how change happens and how to move with it. You tap into the possibilities generated in a binary system—*yin* or *yang* lines—which, incidentally, is exactly the same system used in computers."

I mulled this over for a moment.

"Using the I Ching," Eulogio continued, "you first fill yourself with the spirit, then ask the spirit to give you the best options. So the first lesson in approaching the oracle is the same as learning to adjust your personal feng shui: learn how to connect with your Center. Only then can you ask the question. When working with the feng shui of the body, you have to first find your Center. Otherwise you only accentuate the patterns created by your perceptual conditioning. Thus the danger." He gave me a moment or two to digest this.

"I'm going to show you an example of how the body, through its movements and alignment with gravity, is constantly radiating an I Ching pattern and how this pattern is related to our feng shui."

Eulogio stood up. "When you throw the I Ching, you are dealing with six lines, two trigrams. An upper trigram," he said, brushing his chest from the diaphragm upward, "and a lower trigram," he added, sweeping his hand across his abdomen. "This is just one example that makes what I'm saying easier to see. When you know how each of these trigrams corresponds to a body movement, you can throw the I Ching with your body. Actually, the body is always creating an I Ching—or radiating a fortune." Suddenly Eulogio laughed as if he had said the funniest thing in the world.

"But how does that work?" I demanded. Naturally I wanted to change my fortune that very minute.

"I'm teasing you," Eulogio laughed. "I'm just showing you this so that you'll know what's waiting for you once you create the proper container. Please keep in mind that all I can explain right now are the main principles. When you visit me again, you will have seen how these principles work in medicine, in your body movements, and in other areas of your life. Ideally you will realize by then that the journey of awareness is what powers the feng shui of the body. Then we can go on."

"But—" I began, still excitedly thinking about the things that I wanted.

I could hear the screech of Eulogio's braking system. "Not so fast, Speedy," he said, putting up his hand like a traffic cop at a busy intersection.

I sighed. "What I hear you saying is that instant enlightenment is not on the spiritual menu today."

Eulogio grinned. "That instant stuff gives you a quick rush but then you're ravenous again an hour later. For sustained nourishment, you need the old-fashioned kind that has to cook slowly, like a good pot of frijoles. Now pay attention because I'm going to show you four ways to move the legs." He demonstrated moving his leg up and down and twisting it in and out in order to extend the hip joints fully. This was followed by four arm movements, all of which corresponded to the eight trigrams of the I Ching and the eight meridian flows in the body. "You want your energy circulating so well that a movement of your arm is felt in your leg." He flicked his right wrist and his left foot sprang outward. Finally he drew the corresponding body postures on the outside of the feng shui diagram.

"And now," Eulogio continued, "you have the task of putting all this together to see how body movement and acupuncture are related."

"Can't you just *tell* me?" I asked.

"No," Eulogio said firmly. "That is not proper cooking."

I threw my hands up in exasperation. "Why does everything have to be done the hard way? I don't get it!"

Eulogio leaned toward me earnestly. "Because that's not proper learning. A teacher does not give you things; he helps you to find them. If you don't work to get learning, that learning becomes trivialized. You'll hear me say it, and it'll go in one ear and out the other because it won't have an internal foundation of hard work and introspection."

I drew a deep breath. I had to accept the importance of learning in the right way. At the same time, I began to glimpse how different body positions or movements could reflect the meridians in acupuncture, the trigrams of the I Ching, and the *ba gua* diagram of feng shui. I could now look forward to going back to my clinic and my life and pondering what he had

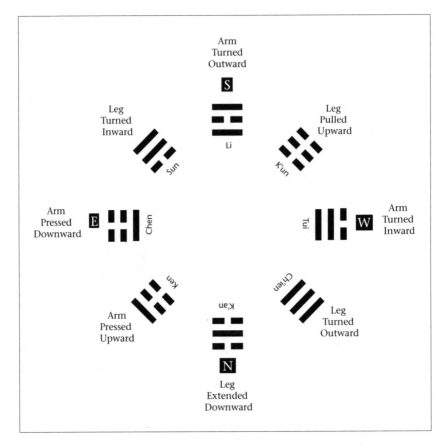

ILLUSTRATION 5: *The feng shui ba gua pattern with corresponding leg and arm movements.*

told me.

Eulogio stretched and looked at me, knowing that he'd gotten his point across..

"The first and most important lesson is how to actively connect with your Center and to mentally and conceptually radiate that into the different aspects of your life. The best way to do that is to practice the Embracing-the-Tree posture that Huang taught you. When you come to see me again, I'll show you the proper movements of the wrists and ankles," he said.

"So this is Feng Shui of the Body 101," I said.

Eulogio nodded. "And I have to tell you one more time," he continued, smiling, "that you must meditate on these principles and feel them in your body. By practicing the Embracing-the-Tree posture, you will begin to get that dynamic moving. This is so important because, if you are not correctly centered, the energy can be misused and get you into even more trouble than you are in already."

I grinned wryly. "That bad, huh?"

"If we apply these trigrams—which relate to a different part of our being—we can understand how, either through acupuncture or body movement, we can change our personal feng shui."

"The way that we flow in the Bigger Dream," I volunteered.

"Yes, my friend. In feng shui, different trigrams relate to different aspects of your life, such as luck or career. The same is true of certain postures and motions." Eulogio went back to his sketch pad and elaborated the previous diagram. "This is what I call the Feng Shui Wheel of Life."

I peered over his shoulder as he continued to sketch.

"For example, you can do a particular exercise every day to bring wealth into your life"— he gave me a sly, sidelong grin—"or to fill your life with admiring women." Eulogio loved to tease me about girlfriends.

"If you do this exercise," he said, quickly showing me a certain movement, "you will bring health and money into your life."

I was startled by what Eulogio was telling me and amazed at how it all fit together. Old Eulogio knew his stuff!

"Or, if you stimulate these meridians enough through acupuncture," he went on, indicating certain points on his body, "you can create the same kind of effect."

I felt my teeth clenching involuntarily. I wanted to change my outer life immediately. Money, girlfriends, health—why was he holding back? Why didn't he just show me everything? "I still don't see why you can't teach this to everyone so that all their problems will be solved," I finally said.

"First of all, they wouldn't do it," he answered. "It's too much work and they wouldn't know what they were doing. Second, it requires the right

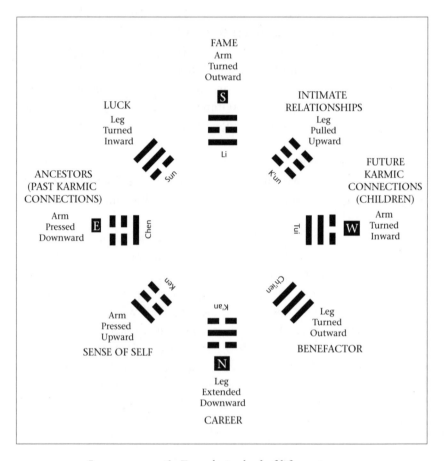

FAME
Arm
Turned
Outward

INTIMATE
RELATIONSHIPS
Leg
Pulled
Upward

LUCK
Leg
Turned
Inward

S

Li

FUTURE
KARMIC
CONNECTIONS
(CHILDREN)

ANCESTORS
(PAST KARMIC
CONNECTIONS)

Sun

K'un

Arm
Pressed
Downward

E

Chen

Tui

W

Arm
Turned
Inward

Ken

Ch'ien

Arm
Pressed
Upward

SENSE OF SELF

K'an

Leg
Turned
Outward

BENEFACTOR

N

Leg
Extended
Downward

CAREER

ILLUSTRATION 6: *Feng shui wheel of life—trigrams,*
body movements and aspects of life.

motivation, or you merely strengthen your learned patterns and accentuate your imbalances. If you focus on certain aspects of your being without a strong Center, you throw off your feng shui even more and affect the people around you in an adverse way."

I smiled, remembering how I had grown close to Joseph at the workshop and what Huang had told us about Joseph and lifting weights. Joseph could get stronger and rise in the beach-boy pecking order, but neither his perception of himself nor the degree to which he could enjoy life would change. In fact, he would become even more entrenched in his learned behavior. Eulogio was telling me the same thing, only in a slightly different way.

"If you don't have a Center and establish a Third Point," Eulogio went on, "you look at the body in terms of your learned feng shui. You overly accentuate a part that doesn't bring balance to your life. The quest for the Center, the journey of awareness, is the reason we're alive."

He asked me to get into the Embracing-the-Tree posture and to connect my body in the way that Huang had taught. "This is the perfect posture through which to establish your Center," he said. "No matter how stubborn you are, Daniel, if you maintain it long enough, gravity will straighten you up, and the thought patterns of your learned behavior won't have a prayer."

"Who, me? Stubborn?" I asked innocently.

Eulogio made an elaborate pretense of looking around the courtyard. "Since you're the only other guy here," he declared, "you can draw your own conclusion." He demonstrated a series that combined all the possible movements of the arms, legs, shoulders, and hips. They reflected the trigrams of the *ba gua* and the flow of energy through the acupuncture meridians.

"I am demonstrating these so that you will realize that what I am telling you is real," he continued. "Moving the energy from your Center out through the feng shui of your body is like throwing a pebble into the middle of a still pool of water. The wave pattern radiates equally throughout the pool. You don't want to accentuate one part of your being over another unless it is absolutely necessary. This is powerful magic and should be treated as such.

"If you do these movements with the wrong intention, you may create a crisis or disease in your life and affect the people around you—and it will double back on you. The only acceptable reason for doing them is to let go of your learned behavior pattern in order to achieve something greater."

Chapter 17

RELAXING INTO CONTACT

*T*he next day for lunch, we walked to a neighborhood *restaurante* that Eulogio insisted served the best enchiladas in all of Mexico.

"Really!" I said, as we ambled down the street. "So do you mean to tell me that you have eaten enchiladas in every *restaurante* in Mexico? That must have been expensive, not to say time consuming." It was my turn to rib Eulogio who, as all his friends were aware, was *un gran exagerado*.

He cast me a dark look. "I didn't have to visit every blasted tortilla place in Mexico," he growled.

"Oh?" I asked innocently. "Then perhaps you read it in guinea pig entrails, like a Peruvian *brujo*?"

"Don't talk like a typical tourist who thinks that every healer who didn't graduate from Harvard Medical School is some kind of sorcerer!"

"And to think I'm your apprentice!" I exclaimed.

"Yep, and soon I'm going to teach you to read coca leaves, the behavior of burrowing insects, the flights of birds, and the faces of people," he said, contorting his face and raising his eyebrows to look like a grotesque monkey. Finally, he twisted his ears for more effect. Nearby, half a dozen little schoolgirls, maybe seven or eight years old, covered their mouths with their hands and shrieked with laughter at his antics. I was laughing too as Eulogio continued with even more outrageous faces, ending with one he called "a chicken's butt."

"Don't worry, Eulogio," I said. "I'll wait until you think I've forgotten all about this." I gave him my wickedest grin.

"I'd think twice about messing with a *brujo*," he said. "That *is* what you called me, no?"

"All right, I apologize," I relented. I winked and grinned at the little girls, sending them into fresh gales of laughter. "You're not a *brujo*. More like a witch doctor—"

"Daniel, you are—what is the English word for *sin vergüenza?*"

"Shameless," I answered. "In fact, that's what my mother always used to say about me."

"Your mother was being charitable!" Eulogio chuckled.

We laughed all the way to the *restaurante,* where we ate what probably *were* the best enchiladas in all of Mexico. With my stomach pleasantly full, I said, "And now I'm ready for that sacred Mexican custom, the *siesta,*" I announced.

"That's the first sensible thing you've said all day," Eulogio chided.

We drowsed for a while, sprawled in hammocks, in the cool shadows of the courtyard. The splash of the fountain lulled me into the twilight of sleep. Just as I was drifting into its music, Eulogio's voice brought me to attention. "Did Huang ever tell you that one way to look at movement is to see that you are moving in a circle based on yourself?"

I roused myself and sat up. I couldn't remember Huang ever saying that, but it did seem to describe his teachings in a nutshell. "No," I said, "but it explains a lot. Tell me more."

"If you look at learned behavior—or your feng shui—as being jagged and angular, thus directional," Eulogio explained, "then when you deal with the world as a circle based on yourself, you can fight this angularity."

I nodded. "So this is also about moving the body from the Third Point, like the radiating ripple caused by the rock tossed into the pool?"

"That's right. If you hold any one idea of the body long enough, it becomes static. But if your idea of the body is fluid, it can adapt to whatever it touches and keep flowing. So we need a group of ideas that interrelate in constant motion."

This reminded me of what Esmeralda had said about using a feature of our learned behavior, such as giggling, as a point of focus: if we practice a new behavior long enough, it becomes incorporated into our habits. Therefore, we need to constantly change our focus—or movement, as Eulogio would say—to stay with the flow of the spirit.

"We need to create a smoothly flowing feng shui," Eulogio said.

"Our lives should move like wind and water." The next thing I knew, Eulogio was breathing softly.

In the early evening before dark, Eulogio and I strolled down to the central plaza and sat on a bench by a fountain. We weren't there long when a man came by, selling balloons. We watched him approach a family and fascinate the children with his wares. Predictably, the children implored their parents to buy one. After seeing this scenario repeated two or three times, Eulogio turned to me.

"Imagine a balloon, not fully inflated, with a structure around it like a shell with holes in it." Eulogio chuckled at the image. "The balloon can't inflate because it is enclosed by this rigid shell," he said, "so it can make contact with the world only where it bulges out through the holes." He laughed again and his eyes sparkled. "It's how a little dog looks when people put those clothes on it, with only its tail, head, and legs sticking out."

"If we start creating circulation from inside our being, we crack the unnatural feng shui structure of our learned behavior. The balloon knows the shape it can grow into, much like our healing body, or the body that knows. If the balloon is inflated properly and consistently, it will neatly shatter the shell, and the balloon can then grow into its wholeness.

"You still have the same places of contact with the world but now you have more. In addition to those places that were exposed to the world before, you have the area that was formerly confined by the shell. The previous areas of contact are not overly stressed because now they are being supported by more areas of contact and the internal integrity of the balloon."

Eulogio glanced at a chubby boy of about four, laughing in delight as the vendor pocketed a few pesos and handed him a brilliant red balloon. The young mother pulled the child close and whispered into his ear. *"Gracias, papá!"* he exclaimed, turning toward his father. The young man nodded and touched his son's face, grinning over the top of the boy's head at his wife.

"There is a natural pressure on the inside of the balloon seeking to make as much contact as it can with the air on the outside, and thus merge with it. Our learned behavior, the structure that limits this contact, causes certain ways of being to bear the total burden of making contact."

Synchronistically, a middle-aged man shuffled by with his hand on his stomach. Eulogio and I watched him pass.

Eulogio continued, "When learned behavior becomes overbearing and doesn't allow enough contact with the Bigger Dream, you get sick. In fact, lack of contact *is* sickness. But contact must come from our true Center so that we're not just accentuating the imbalanced contact that we've been taught. In that sense, sickness can be your ally," he said, his eyes sparkling. "If you listen to sickness carefully, it can teach you how to open up and how to make healthy contact."

"This sounds like what I went though during Huang's workshop when I went into town and interacted with the people on the street."

"What you saw that day was your psycho-emotional reaction to the world—the energetic precursors of physical disease. You need to listen to sickness carefully. If you just patch up the body the way that institutionalized medicine does, then the body continues along the path of learned behavior." He shook his head, a grin on his face. "Your sensitivity decreases and new and more severe illnesses are set into motion."

I remembered, as we walked back to his house, a previous visit with Eulogio when I had gone with him to his clinic. He had explained to me how institutionalized medicine is a coconspirator or a pimp for learned behavior: since medicine is institutionalized it is interested only in maintaining the current learned behavior. This kind of medicine has no center around which to build health.

The result is that it looks at the body as a piece of meat, a functional tool for the perpetuation of learned behavior, and it defines health within this context. It's purpose is to feed the machine, to get people functional again so that they can go back to work.

Eulogio had said that the body has higher functions than merely supporting learned behavior, and that as healers we need to know about the body's potential for higher functioning; that there is an energetic way as well as a spiritual way of looking at medicine and body function that gives our existence much more meaning than the slab-of-meat approach offered by institutionalized medicine. He maintained that both culturally and individually we must evolve and redefine our idea of the body.

APPLICATION: LISTEN TO YOUR BODY

Do you have an ache or a pain somewhere in your body? Listen to what it is trying to tell you. See your body as your teacher. You need to start slowly. For example, ask your body general questions such as: 1) How can I learn to understand the sensations I'm feeling? 2) When this area in my body is painful, what does it mean? 3) How does it relate to my learned behavior or perceptual conditioning? 4) How do my current dreams relate to the pain or joy that I'm experiencing? 5) How does my body feel when I'm lying down as opposed to standing up? Or sitting? 6) When I exercise, at what point does my body feel good and, if I keep exercising, at what point does it feel depleted?

AWARENESS JOURNAL

Take what you have learned and write it up in "Embodying My Awareness." In order to create an ongoing dialogue and a new relationship with your body, do this every time you feel pain. In general, check in with your body every two or three days.

Chapter 18

HEALING SICKNESS

The following day, Eulogio had to see patients at his clinic. We did our exercises as the sun was rising, and I spent the rest of the morning meditating and thinking over what we had talked about on the previous two days. After a late lunch and siesta, Eulogio and I went for a walk along the nearby river. The air was warm and clear. Eventually we found a bench under a huge mango tree and sat in silence, looking out over the water.

Nearby, a magnificent white egret stalked the weeds along the edge of the river. It would stand utterly motionless on its long, delicate legs; then its head would shoot toward the water to claim a small fish, which it swallowed by straightening its neck and throwing its head back. I admired the bird's beauty, patience, and hunting prowess.

"One thing that all illness has in common," Eulogio went on, "is that it represents energy inefficiently trying to express itself. When you trust the wisdom of the body, you learn that illness is the body's attempt at wholeness. Illness makes us dysfunctional in relation to our learned behavior. Illness is often the result of the knowledge of the body trying to break down our learned behavior so that it can make more contact with the world."

"Is that the only reason we get sick" I asked.

"There is another way that illness is created." Eulogio leaned over, raising his index finger. "The way you came to me this time is a good example. It happens when one consciously—but too hastily—seeks to assist the pressure of one's Luminous Essence in uniting with the pressure from the outside, the Bigger Dream. In this case, internal awareness and circulation build up faster than they can find proper expression through the physical and relating bodies. Western medicine can do little to fix this type of illness and the resultant symptomology. The only answer is to find a means of expression for yourself, ideally with the help of someone who has been through it before. Here is where the exercises related to feng shui that I showed you are helpful. It is even very helpful to just get in touch with your Center, realize your intent, and radiate that out toward the different parts of your life while maintaining a vertical integrity." Eulogio leaned back and gave me an odd look. "Have you ever heard of the Humpty-Dumpty theory?"

"What?" I said, definitely thrown off my saddle. "The nursery-rhyme character who looks like an egg?"

"Yeah, that guy," Eulogio said. He stretched out his hands and moved them rhythmically as he repeated the verse. "'Humpty Dumpty sat on a wall./Humpty Dumpty had a great fall./All the king's horses and all the king's men/Couldn't put Humpty together again.'"

"I hope you're not telling me I can't be put together again," I said.

Eulogio laughed. "Illness can be caused when someone, without proper instruction or for some other reason, gathers awareness too rapidly on the inside without a means of expression. This can shatter the outer shell before the learned behavior is integrated into a new way of being. You know, 'Humpty Dumpty sat on a wall/Humpty Dumpty had a great fall.'"

"I'm still having a hard time following you," I told him.

"Okay," he said, looking at me, amused. "Let me put it another way. The undulating energy on the outside wants to merge with the Luminous Essence on the inside. The Luminous Essence on the inside simultaneously wants to merge with the energy on the outside. The learned behavior is what separates them, and our idea of the body is the battleground."

I nodded vigorously. I was beginning to get it. "Pressure from the inside and pressure from the outside," I offered.

"Right. So, if you burst the shell of your learned behavior from the inside, your self-concept has to be put together in a whole new way—the old way isn't going to work anymore. Institutionalized medicine based on learned behavior won't help you. All the king's horses and all the king's men couldn't put Daniel together again!"

"But you could make *huevos rancheros!*" I joked.

Eulogio slapped his leg. "I'll never be able to eat scrambled eggs again without thinking of you!" His laughter was so contagious that I laughed with him.

"All disease is the expression of resistance to this merging happening in the right way," he went on. "So in illness you can either resist merging or use the illness to facilitate it. You have to learn the language of the body. Sickness can move you to a more fluid idea of your body or it can reinforce your rigidity."

I realized that I had seen this happen many times in my clinic. Some people, regardless of their physical condition, gather a great deal of knowledge and transform their lives through the process of being ill. Others use illness only to recharge themselves and create the same problems all over again. "Then disease can be positive, depending on how we deal with it."

"Yes," Eulogio responded. "It's all a matter of focus. If you focus on the disease, you put energy into that which resists growth. If you focus on the opportunity to gain more energy and understanding, then the illness becomes an ally or a set of directives. The art of healing is to understand these directives and assist their implementation."

I was enjoying him so much that I stopped trying to retain what he was saying. I knew that the experience would be stored somewhere in my being. "What about accidents?" I asked. "Are they like a sickness?"

"More Humpty Dumpty again?" he chuckled. "The structure of our learned behavior, one way or another, will start to crack. Illness happens because the body needs more ways to contact the world. Accidents happen for the same reason. People whose personal feng shui is very rigid and does not allow them to merge with the Bigger Dream build up pressure," he continued. "This buildup occurs because the Luminous Essence that wants to freely merge with the Bigger Dream gets bottled up and can't make enough contact to find expression. An accident cracks the pattern and allows a limited amount of contact to take place."

"Yeah," I said, putting my hands behind my head and looking up at the sky, "in an accident, you really make contact."

Eulogio nudged me and pointed. The egret spread its snowy wings and rose silently over the river. The sun had dropped down, and the beautiful white bird glowed golden pink as it skimmed gracefully toward the opposite shore.

"In my own way, I already knew this," I told Eulogio. "A few years ago, a single mother named Lola came to me, all upset over her son. He was always having accidents—falling off his bicycle, getting into scraps with other children, injuring himself at sports. She was afraid for his safety. I told her that perhaps acupuncture could help redirect his energy. In the meantime, I suggested that to discharge the excess energy, she intentionally punch him in the arm—not to injure or frighten him, of course, but just enough to jolt his energy body—every time he left the house. A few days later, Lola reported to me that this had worked remarkably well, and she didn't think she needed to bring him in for a treatment."

"Maybe if someone had made a little crack in Humpty Dumpty, he wouldn't have ended up as *huevos rancheros,*" Eulogio said.

"Let's make sure I've got it," I said. "Sickness is a systemic way of trying to balance the body to create more contact. Accidents are an extreme example of the same process."

Eulogio nodded. "Remember when you were down here last time, we talked about how diseases tend to happen in predictable patterns, making lines up and down the body, relating at the deepest level to the male-female agreement. If you look at people who have been in accidents, you will see that the accidents tend to affect the body along these same lines. And, as you pointed out, certain types of healing can actually circumvent accidents."

"Even a well-intentioned punch in the arm," I added.

"You have to stimulate the energy lines of the body—with either acupuncture or movement—to create a more harmonious feng shui. The pressure can thus be released without violence and the chance of serious injury. Such treatments can also get the body used to energy moving in another way," Eulogio went on. "Then, the whole cycle of building pressure, violently releasing it, and building it up again is redirected. The way of relating with the world also has to change in order to stabilize the new order and not fall back into the old cycle. The actual healing process may even have to repeat a few times. Establishing one way of connecting is not the end of the struggle."

"I know that," I added. "It's like one of those Chinese puzzles. You know, one little carved ivory ball inside of another?"

Eulogio grinned. "One set of action-reaction patterns may have been released, but others are sure to follow, perhaps along those same lines. They are all interconnected. The Watcher from the inside wants total and complete freedom. As healers, we have to streamline this process of release."

"How do we do that?" I asked.

"We have to focus on the process of undoing the patterns and not on the particular pattern we're working on, because one is going to the follow the other. We need to depersonalize them and release our attachment to them. Take, for example, the attachment to being sick. We break down our experience to its essentials and don't waste energy on particulars. In fact, the particulars of the outside world don't make much difference in terms of internal processes. If we look closely at our learned behavior through the male-female agreement, we can see that the pressure it exerts and the way we respond to it are constant. It doesn't matter who you are with. Your male-female agreement is always with you until you relax and move beyond it."

"So not only do I have to deal with one Humpty Dumpty, there's an entire regiment of Humpty Dumpties, one inside the other," I said. "This is getting pretty messy."

Eulogio thought that was the funniest thing in the world. With a mischievous tone in his voice he said, "It will be there even if you are alone. It is the basis of your way of perceiving the world. Looking at particulars is only a distraction." Eulogio started talking very slowly in a very thick Spanish accent. "If your mother isn't around . . . there is your wife . . . or your girlfriend . . . and if they are not around, there is the señorita at the checkout counter."

We both smiled.

"And if none of them is around," Eulogio continued in his normal voice, "the connective tissue in your body still holds the pattern, and you will constantly think about one or the other of them. The important thing is to focus on meeting the world with the awareness of the Watcher."

Eulogio and I sat in silence for a while, gazing reflectively at the river.

He began speaking in a different mood, slowly and softly. "Compassion is the action of love and affection in the world," he said. "Love and affection are constant. Compassion is their tool of expression. But compassion is not always nice."

I was startled. "How so?" I asked.

"To have real love and compassion is to support the true potential or the spirit of what being human is," Eulogio replied. "Consensual reality has constricted the expression of our real love and affection so that we can express it only in limited ways. When you attempt to truly express love and affection, you must go up against the twisted definitions that you have been taught. Watch out: in relating with others, if you don't focus your love and affection in the socially approved way, but instead look at the situation with an overview of real compassion, people will see you as cruel and insensitive. They will do this because you refuse to become a coconspirator in their consensual belief structure. When you feel pressure from others, you may have doubts and think that the concepts that Esmeralda, Huang, and I are teaching you are very cold."

As he spoke, I could remember times when I thought that the result of what they had been teaching me had a very cold undertone. I could remember asking myself, "Where is the warmth in this teaching?"

Eulogio paused for a moment, looking at the river once again. The setting sun had turned it into molten copper. "You have been taught that the only way to express affection is by affirming people in those limited patterns that they have conspired to be a part of," he said. "But," he continued passionately, "when you watch how learned behavior warps people, takes away their spirit, and eventually kills them, it is another matter. It becomes a war. What you learn is that this false sense of niceness and love is very cruel. It is a poison. And you watch people you are very close to, people you really know and care about, get sick and die from it."

We listened to the river and to the breeze that had sprung up. As it murmured in the mango tree, it carried to us the fragrance of jasmine and lemon blossoms.

Eulogio yawned, stretched, and dropped his arms to his lap. He looked me straight in the eye. "Let's make this all simple," he said. "Look at the world in terms of energy. This is a very efficient way to deal with yourself

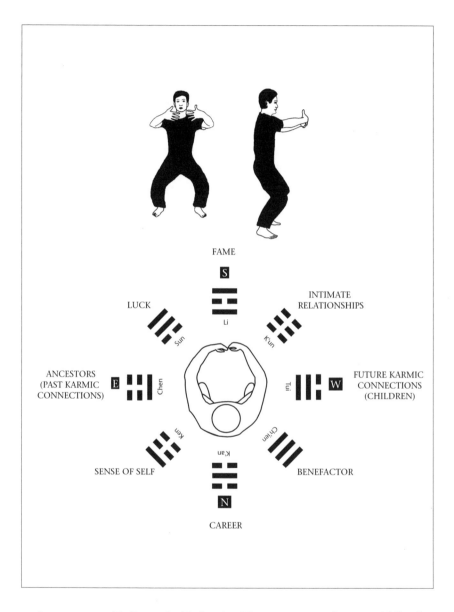

ILLUSTRATION 7: *Person in Embracing Tree posture standing in middle of feng shui ba gua with corresponding aspects of life.*

and to align yourself. Look at what gives you energy and what doesn't, and use what you find to create a strategy. Save your energy and streamline your process. Uncover your true being."

In that moment, through the expression in Eulogio's eyes, I understood all that he was talking about.

We sat as night gathered slowly around us and we absorbed the flow of things—wind and water, the voices of birds, the smells of flowers, the colors of earth and sky. We partook of a meal for the spirit, and when we were full, we got up and walked back to Eulogio's house.

APPLICATION: THE FENG SHUI WHEEL OF LIFE

While facing south, assume the Embracing-the-Tree stance. Relax in this posture for about five minutes, creating a pause in your normal movement patterns and saturating your body with the gravitational pull of the earth.

Are you aware of becoming the Watcher—going beyond your perceptual conditioning? What does it feel like in your body? You may see or feel it as light or warmth or a tingly sensation, or something else altogether.

Imagine the feng shui *ba gua*—the trigrams of the I Ching—arrayed around you as if they are on the rim of a wheel. Begin to see them as the different parts of your life. Imagine that you are the hub of the Feng Shui Wheel of Life. From the center of the *ba gua*—where you're standing—go into each aspect and feel each one. Start at the east, or off to your left. This is where the aspect of your life involving your ancestors resides. Are you aware of how your being is connected to your parents, grandparents, aunts and uncles, etc.—the physical tradition that runs through your body? Come back to your Center briefly, then continue clockwise around the wheel. The next place is the part that has to do with luck. Notice what unexpected and lucky things have happened to you lately. Continue clockwise, looking at each aspect of your life, always coming back to your Center before proceeding to the next.

After you've established a sense or a feeling for these different aspects, go around your wheel of existence again. This time, radiate the feeling of the Watcher or the Third Point—the light or warmth (whatever you felt earlier)—through your body and out to each aspect. To create balance from your Center, direct the feeling of the Watcher through your body into each aspect.

Now combine the two steps. For example, focus on your ancestors in the east and the feelings and visions that come from that spoke of the wheel. Then take the energy from your Center and radiate it to that aspect, filling it with light or warmth. Next, follow the feeling that you've emanated as it comes back down the spoke to your Center, the hub of the wheel. Continue around the wheel.

As a practice, you should do this every day.

AWARENESS JOURNAL

In "Tracking My Awareness," once a week write down any changes that have occurred in the different aspects of your life. These notes should indicate connection and reflection.

Connection: How has your connection with your Center evolved? You may want to write about how the feeling of connection to the Watcher and the Bigger Dream has grown. Have you noticed a change in your connection while you were standing in the Embracing-the-Tree Posture? Any new sensations, feelings, thoughts? Write them down.

Reflection: If you do this once a week, do you begin to see a progression as you unite your life by connecting everything to your Center—the hub of your Feng Shui Wheel of Life? Do you notice a change in how your being is reflected in the eight aspects of your life—the spokes of the wheel? For example, have you noticed more spontaneity, flow, sychnronicity, a sense of wholeness in each aspect of your life? If so, how?

Chapter 19

THE HEALER

*E*ulogio's new housekeeper, Marisol, I learned, took a slapdash approach to most things domestic. Today she had arrived at dawn following a week's visit with an out-of-town brother. I was amazed to find Eulogio rewashing the dishes, remaking the beds, resweeping the floors, and relaundering his shirts, all the while laughing and muttering under his breath in Spanish. Once I caught the word *maldita.*

"I don't get it," I told him finally. "The woman is a complete incompetent. Why don't you find someone else to clean your house?"

"Because," Eulogio explained, as if pointing out the obvious to a slow-witted child, "then Marisol would go away."

I mulled over the possible ramifications of his pronouncement. Since Marisol was old enough to be Eulogio's grandmother, romance couldn't be a factor. "Would that be such a disaster?" I asked.

"Yes," Eulogio said darkly, "it would. Just wait until lunch."

Now, as Eulogio and I lingered over tamales steamed in banana leaves, everything was as clear as a glass of cold water. Marisol may have been a disaster as a housekeeper, but she was an angel in the kitchen. These tamales were filled with a thick, red-brown steaming *mole,* accompanied by divinely seasoned beans and rice so perfect they belonged in a shrine. Dessert was a cold, pitch-black silky compote of some exotic fruit I had never heard of.

"I see what you mean," I sighed.

Eulogio glanced furtively over his shoulder toward the kitchen where Marisol was making an attempt to clean up. I jumped involuntarily as a pot lid crashed to the tile floor. "Her husband died two years ago," Eulogio whispered with a chuckle. Then, in a thick Spanish accent, he added, "Afterward, she had eleven marriage proposals. And some of those men were younger than her sons!"

"Makes sense to me," I agreed, briefly contemplating matrimony myself. "How much do you pay her?"

Eulogio winced. "Too much. She's an extortionist!" He scooped the last of the compote from his bowl and licked the spoon. Then he grinned. "But she's worth every *peso.*"

After such a lunch, we settled gratefully into the hammocks in the courtyard. We drifted in and out of reverie for awhile. When I had regained a semblance of my waking consciousness, a question came to me.

"How does sexuality fit into this?" I asked Eulogio. "When I treat some people, it seems to activate them sexually. They come back and tell me their interest in sex is alive and well since they last saw me. Every man or woman they see looks more appetizing."

"Someone who is feeling a lot of sexual energy is much better off than someone who isn't," Eulogio said, chuckling. "At least they have energy! The reason that they experience it as sexual is because of the male-female agreement. For most of us, our creative energies are very constricted. So if we have more energy, it puts more pressure on this area of constriction—the lower abdomen—and if we don't know what else to do with it, it becomes sexualized."

This was what Huang had said, and I told Eulogio about it.

We rocked in the hammocks a while longer, looking up at the birds, watching the afternoon breeze pass through the tops of the trees. My thoughts wandered, but one thing remained constant: The more I looked up at the trees and felt how they were supporting me in my hammock, the more I loved them. I felt that, in a very real sense, they were the soldiers that held the world together.

The sound of Eulogio's voice brought me out of my reverie. "These hammocks are the perfect place to talk about how gravity affects the body in different postures," he said. "Gravity is what creates our container. It is through gravity that we perceive on this earth. As we hang here in our hammocks, we line up with gravity in a different way than usual. It is much more like being in water. It is very fluid, so our thought patterns flow much more easily."

"I've been noticing that," I agreed.

"In fact, occasionally a friend will come to me, very disturbed, and we will lie in these hammocks, just talking about whatever comes to mind. Eventually his sense of fluidity returns."

"Why do you suppose that is?" I asked.

"Lining up with gravity in a different way breaks apart the usual concrete structures of learned behavior. Actually, sitting is the best posture for concentrating thought. The energy is no longer forced to flow out into your legs by gravity, and not much is pumped into your arms. So movement in the sitting posture is mostly in the trunk of the body.

"In the lying-down posture, gravity pulls on us unimpeded, in a most relaxed fashion. This is where we recede into sleep and make direct contact with the core of our being."

Once again I recalled my chiropractor friend's statement that 30 percent of the motor output of the brain is expended in lining us up correctly with gravity.

"This is why I love these hammocks," Eulogio continued. "It's hard to tell if we are sitting, lying, or moving."

I readjusted my posture, enjoying how fluid my body felt.

"Ah, yes," Eulogio continued. "It is through the moving posture that we most directly contact our relating body. Energy moves to our extremities and back again, from the core of our being out into the world. This is why I showed you the movements for the feng shui of the body. The last posture is standing, the most powerful of all."

"Why is that?" I inquired idly.

"Because in standing, we can move the concentration that we experience while sitting throughout our bodies, from our trunk to the extremities and back. We can focus on the internal motion of gravity. To make real change in our being, we need to alter our perception through all of our postures."

A lightbulb went on in my head. "Wow!" I exclaimed, sitting up. "That's why treating a patient when he or she is lying down doesn't go far enough."

"Precisely," Eulogio agreed. "Go on, Daniel, tell me more."

"They still have to get up and function—deal with the world through all the various postures."

"Very good. So it is important to teach your patients about motion. In fact, I have exercise classes for my patients so that they can learn to bring their new awareness into motion."

My mind raced with the possibilities of incorporating this concept into my own healing practice.

"I also talk to them about their dreams," Eulogio went on, "and ask them to examine their attitude towards the world. Learned behavior has molded our perception throughout all the postures. To heal ourselves we have to move our new awareness back through all of them."

APPLICATION: THE FOUR POSTURES

This application expands on the previous one, The Feng Shui Wheel of Life, about finding our Center or Third Point and radiating it to all parts of ourselves. You did that application from a standing position. Now you'll move your awareness through the other three postures: sitting, moving, and lying down.

While **sitting**, send the awareness of the Watcher out into the different parts of your being as you imagine them on the Feng Shui Wheel of Life. (This is the same procedure as in the last application, except that you are sitting.)

Next, send the awareness of the Watcher out through the spokes of the wheel while **moving** as if you are underwater and your arms are long strands of seaweed. Keep your feet stationary. Radiate from your Center to each aspect of your life, then back again.

Finally, do the same procedure while **lying** on your back. The ideal time is before you go to sleep and when you wake up in the morning.

AWARENESS JOURNAL

After a few days, note under "Tracking My Awareness" if moving your awareness through the different postures has affected the spontaneity of your life.

It was my last evening with Eulogio. Just before dusk, we went again to the plaza. As we ambled around the fountain looking for an empty bench, a little boy suddenly ran into me. "Whoa," I said, grasping his shoulder to prevent him from reeling back. I realized I was in the midst of a group of children at a game of tag. The boy wriggled away and rejoined his playmates.

Eulogio thoughtfully watched the running children. Some of them were clinging to "safe" trees where they were protected, others were running between the trees, shrieking with laughter. "That is what the spirit truly craves," he said. "The freedom and joy of the In-Between."

I always admired how Eulogio let the world come to him and the way he used his observations to amplify the current topic of discussion. As we walked a little farther, a young man approached Eulogio and greeted him.

"I've got my energy back," he told Eulogio excitedly. "I'm my old self again."

Eulogio nodded. "Come see me again! We may not be finished yet."

The man looked puzzled but promised to come to the clinic the following week. As we continued strolling along the path, Eulogio turned to me. "Wanting the energy that you used to have and in the same way is a big trap. It prevents you from going In-Between and exploring new ways of gathering and maintaining energy. It is important to regain energy and then put yourself in the proper posture to continue gaining energy without returning to the old way of expending it. For a real cure, a patient's idea of health and energy has to change. This is the key ingredient to changing the feng shui of the body."

We stopped for a moment and Eulogio continued.

"So many people come to see me wanting their energy the way it used to be. They don't realize that their idea of health and energy—their energy immune system—is based on the action-reaction patterns that made them sick in the first place."

I peered at Eulogio, a bit confused. "Aren't you supposed to make people feel better? Isn't that what a healer does?" I asked.

Eulogio smiled back brightly. The plaza was so full of people there was no place to sit, so we went down to the river and found our bench under

217

the mango tree. After a few moments of contemplation, Eulogio finally answered my question.

"No, a healer is not necessarily supposed to make people feel better," he said, stroking his chin. "A true healer is one who assists the spirit, not one who fortifies a patient's false sense of self." Eulogio paused, gazing out at the river. "In my journey, as I followed the question of what is really a cure," he continued, "I realized that real progress is made from the inside out. From the outside, all you can do is maintenance."

"Like patching an old roof," I said.

"I had to learn to see people in a bigger way than they saw themselves, to teach them a new vocabulary."

"The language of the body," I added.

"You're learning, my friend," Eulogio nodded approvingly. "In illness, the body is trying to fix itself, to line up properly so that Luminous Essence can flow with the Bigger Dream. The healer is there to assist. As the conduit of spirit, the healer acts like a coach. He offers another way of making contact with the world so that the patient can understand his own process. Instead of concentrating on illness, the healer points out that sickness is an opportunity to discover the true self." He gave me a nudge.

"He might even tell jokes and sing to them so that they won't fixate on the idea that they are sick," he said, chuckling.

I laughed, recalling how Eulogio worked with patients at his clinic. He was a veritable jukebox of jokes and zany songs, with numbers just waiting to be punched in response to any story, behavior, or mood that his patients presented. I always enjoyed his performance and how, through it, he was able to change the way his patients thought of themselves, at least during the time they were in his clinic.

"Let's go back to the house," Eulogio suggested suddenly. "There's one more thing I want to show you."

He had me lie down on my bed. Then he lit a candle and pulled a chair up next to me.

"If you are trained properly in the feng shui of the body, you can see the body as patterns of light. Your luminous cell merges with that of the patient, and you are able to perceive where his essence is blocked from expressing itself. This kind of seeing happens through the true understanding of the webs of light that exists between bodies. Then you can correct the patient's movements or place acupuncture needles accordingly." As he spoke, Eulogio placed acupuncture needles on my arms, legs, and the top of my head.

"When you can see and experience the body as a luminous cell," he continued, "and become cognizant of the flow between beings, you are experiencing a new language. By changing your perception, the idea of the body changes from that of a mechanical toy given to us by our learned behavior to a being made of patterns of light. There are rivers of light that connect the cellular integrity of the body. Embryologically, they predate the rest of the body's structure: organs, bones, and so on. These rivers of light interconnect and feed the structures that you normally see."

Eulogio began chanting and the essence of what he was telling me began to flower inside me. Ribbons of light resonated with the sounds of Eulogio's voice. The colors of the light became brighter, more intense, more magical. I was actually seeing sounds, feeling colors, tasting movement, listening to smells. I felt myself dissolving, merging with the Bigger Dream. Sound, movement, energy, light—they all became one, and I simultaneously saw how they all flowed like waves across the womb of creation.

The next morning, Eulogio and I spent some time together going over the correct standing posture and the particular feng shui movements that he had wanted to teach me. As I packed up my things to leave, I felt buoyant and energized with a new sense of direction.

APPLICATION: BECOMING YOUR OWN HEALER

Assume the Embracing-the-Tree posture. Align with gravity and open all your joints.

Align yourself with your true Center—the hub of your Feng Shui Wheel of Life—and notice where you feel it in your body. It may be on top of your head, in the middle of your chest, or in your lower abdomen. For most people, it will be in the heart area.

From that place, create a column of light up and down the middle of the torso from the top of your head to the perineum.

From that column, radiate light out through your extremities: arms, wrists, hands, legs, ankles, and feet. Then send it out through all your perceptual faculties—sight, hearing, smell, taste, touch—to embrace the luminous cell of your perception.

Stretch the membrane of your luminous cell by creating an outward pressure of light as you push energy through your perceptual faculties—your body and your five senses—all you know yourself to be. Feel, merge with, and gather energy from what's on the other side—the Bigger Dream.

Practice this for at least twenty minutes. It is very helpful when you feel either emotionally or physically ill.

PART V

THE PRESSURE OF AFFECTION

Chapter 20

THE PASTA THEORY

I t felt good to be back in Esmeralda's kitchen again, even if I did have to chop onions and garlic. We were making lunch, and my job was a sauce to go over the pasta. As my eyes watered from the onion fumes, I watched Esmeralda filling a pot with water. Today she was dressed in a tiered, full skirt of turquoise cotton and a bright yellow T-shirt. She carried the pot to the stove and flashed a big smile.

"You look like you just came out of a movie with a particularly sad ending," she laughed. "Perhaps the story of Daniel and his girlfriends?" I protested by flicking a tiny chunk of onion her way. I put down my knife and went to the sink. I washed my hands and splashed cool water in my irritated eyes. To my knowledge there is no remedy for onion tears even though everybody professes to have one. As I dried my hands and face with a faded cotton towel, I remembered a question that I wanted to ask.

"Esmeralda," I said, catching her attention, "what do you think change is?"

She raised her eyebrows, waiting for me to elaborate.

"You know—you hear a lot of people talk about changing and growing. And those same people talk about how the world is changing. What do you think about all this?"

"Interesting you should ask," she replied with her cat-cornering-its-prey smile. "Most people who talk about how the world is changing are using this idea to mask feelings of aloneness."

I opened a can of olives and offered it to Esmeralda. She took one and put it in her mouth. "Mmm," she murmured, chewing with delight. "I love these big ripe ones!"

I popped one into my own mouth and held out the can to Esmeralda, who took two this time. "At this rate," I said between olives, "there won't be any left for the sauce."

"Ooooh, give me more," she said happily. "There's another can in the pantry."

I pulled up a stool next to her and we continued working on the can of olives as we talked. "Real change," she said, wagging her index finger, "*real change comes from gathering more energy.*" She disappeared into the pantry briefly and came back with a box of spaghetti. "Have you ever heard of the Pasta Theory?" she asked, looking at me with a twinkle of amusement.

"Unh-uh," I shook my head, munching another olive. Esmeralda reached once more into the can. *First Eulogio and Humpty-Dumpty, I mused, and now Esmeralda and the Pasta Theory.*

"The Pasta Theory states that collective learned behavior—consensual reality—has only so much energy," she said. She opened the box of spaghetti and pulled out a fistful of pasta. "It only seems to change through time. In reality, when it takes on something 'new,' it is only replacing one thing for another and not gaining any energy."

She drew a few strands of pasta out of her hand and placed them on the counter. Then she removed a few new strands from the pasta box and added them to those that remained in her hand.

"This is how the collective learned behavior moves though time, seeming to change because the objects of its obsessions change. But the amount of energy at its disposal remains the same," she continued. Once again she pulled strands of pasta from her hand and placed them on the counter, then replaced them with new strands from the box. "The same thing applies to people who think they are changing," she said.

"What you need to look for, in terms of real change, is whether you have accumulated more energy." She grabbed more and more strands of pasta from the box until her fist was full. "This is more energy," she laughed, shaking the pasta at me. "What is normally perceived as change is merely shifting to a new object of obsession—but with the same amount of energy. The system or person hasn't become more energetic or come closer to expressing more of who they are; they have just changed the way they look at themselves. And because the amount of energy hasn't changed, no genuine change has taken place."

Esmeralda gripped the strands of pasta so that they were condensed into a tight column. She placed the bottom of the column on the counter and relaxed her grip. The pasta splayed out loosely, leaving spaces between the strands. Esmeralda smiled at me.

"When you really do gather more energy, you begin to create more pressure than your learned behavior can handle. Then you enter the In-Between," she said, using her free hand to point to the spaces in between the pasta strands.

"Are you saying then, Esmeralda, that most people don't ever really change, but are only under the illusion of doing so?"

"I think for the most part that's true," she said. "However, everyone at some time or other is given the opportunity for real change. They find themselves in a crisis of some kind where they are forced to open up and be exposed to more energy. It might take the form of a personal encounter with death, disease, or a shock of some type. It might also occur around the separation from or death of a loved one. Everyone has been opened, but few have had the awareness and courage to live in this openness."

Esmeralda lay the pasta down on the counter, then turned and walked towards the cutting board.

"How can we change things on a societal level?" I asked. "What about politics?"

She turned and laughed, and then opened up her hands at waist level, to expose her body.

"The only real politics are the politics that go on between bodies," she said emphatically. "If the way bodies talk to bodies doesn't change, then nothing does."

I opened my mouth to ask another question, but she lifted her hand to wave it off. "Let's get that sauce cooking," she said, "or we'll never eat!"

AWARENESS JOURNAL: GAINING ENERGY

Look at your life energetically. Redefine change as gaining energy. For example, record in "Tracking My Awareness" an instance when you shifted your viewpoint about something. Did it introduce a new spontaneity into your life? Or did it merely reallocate your existing energies? Note and write down a book or a workshop in which the ideas seemed interesting to you. Did the experience give you more energy (allow for new spontaneity in your life)? Or did it keep you at the same energy level but leave you with the illusion that you were changing? Another example might be a change in your political views. Did it give you more energy? What about embracing a new spiritual teaching? Write down your observations.

Lunch had been delicious. I knew that henceforth, I would always think of the sauce I had made as *Pasta a la Esmeralda*. Now Esmeralda and I sat on her patio drinking tea. I gazed up at the beautiful cottonwood trees, golden with autumn's advance. It was then that I noticed a blackened scar on the trunk of one where lightening had struck. It triggered some apprehensive feelings that I'd recently begun to have.

I sat quietly for a moment. "When you open up to more energy to make a better connection with the Bigger Dream," I began tentatively, "and the shields of your learned behavior are shattered, are you then more exposed to negative energy?"

Esmeralda gave me her raised-eyebrow look that meant she needed to hear more.

"The reason I'm asking is because since I've been working with you," I explained slowly, allowing my thoughts to more clearly form, "I've felt something out there that I didn't feel before, and frankly, sometimes it spooks me. It's hard for me to come back into the world the way I used to. Not right now, sitting with you under these trees, but there are times . . . ."

Esmeralda reached over to pat my arm facetiously. "Don't worry, Daniel," she said in a soothing voice. "What you are feeling is merely the acupuncture treatment I gave your voodoo doll." When she saw the look on my face, she threw her head back in a hearty laugh.

I groaned, shaking my head. "Esmeralda, you get me every time! I always think I'll see it coming next time, but I never do." Despite my intention not to, I burst out laughing.

When we had regained our composure, Esmeralda said, "What you are feeling is the opposite of negative energy. You are starting to become yourself. That spooky feeling you describe is about being mesmerized by the objects that your learned behavior has forced you to focus on, the reflections of your own creation. Negative energy is what keeps a person from becoming who they really are. As you gather more energy, you experience the effects of pulling back from your learned behavior, and those effects are more awesome than anything you can imagine. A deep energy is slowing building inside of you, almost imperceptibly. It may feel spooky, but it is not negative. So hang onto your britches, amigo," Esmeralda concluded, smiling, "and get ready for the ride of your life."

I looked admiringly at Esmeralda. She had once again converted my apprehension into something greater. She had my total attention.

"Lend me that pen in your shirt pocket," she said. On her napkin she drew an arrow pointing into an arc. "The arrow is our Luminous Essence in motion, our volition. The arc is that upon which we focus and create," she explained. She made some squiggles on the arc. "These are our creations. You create negative energy when you become attached to results." She pointed to the squiggles. "Whenever we get attached to results, we forget about the impulse inside of us that created them. But this is who we truly are." She tapped the arrow with the pen point. "Since that impulse has no form, it can never be identified with anything. But we can certainly feel it."

I wasn't sure that I totally understood. "Esmeralda," I asked, "are you saying that we are not our creations?"

Esmeralda smiled. "Good question. It's not our creations but our attachment to them that creates a negative drag on our being." She pointed again to the squiggles. "Our attachment to these is like *caca*."

"In other words," I said, "the shit."

She laughed. "Exactly."

Esmeralda sat back and sipped her tea. She gazed up at the leaves for a moment. "You are opening up to being who you really are, which is a process of continual creation," she said. "The mirror of consensual learned behavior that you have been taught to project your results against is beginning to crack. You no longer have your old sense of self to rest in. You are losing your reflection. So what you're feeling—and thinking of as negative energy—is really the insecurity of not seeing your creations mirrored back so that you can attach yourself to them in the same old way. You've begun to pull your energy back." She pointed to the arrow. "You're feeling your Luminous Essence. You're beginning to become aware of your true motive." Esmeralda allowed me a few moments to digest this.

"This is not to say, however," she continued, "that there aren't other things out there in the Bigger Dream, beyond your old shields."

I suddenly felt apprehensive again. "What do you mean, 'other things'?" I asked.

"Other beings have their creations, and they can brush against you," Esmeralda said. "These are real, and they can be very frightening. They can also be dangerous. But after you have begun to heal, to shatter the shields of your learned behavior, you have more energy and a new sense of fullness with which you live your life. You're more whole and you have more energy to deal with these other forces."

"So it doesn't get any easier," I sighed, disappointed.

She laughed, getting up from her chair. "Let's go for a walk." She stacked the cups and saucers and gave them to me to carry to the kitchen while she tidied the table.

As we strolled along the creek, I asked, "So once I start to break up my shields, I'm open to all different kinds of power. How do I navigate?"

"Moving into the layers of the Third Point, the Watcher, will make you constantly redefine your motive. You have desires, you have to make decisions about what to manifest in the world, you have to base your strategy on something." She winked at me as if she were anticipating my next question. "How do you find out what it is and how to use it?"

"Good question," I responded.

"One way is through the examination of your desires," she went on. "What do you want? Examine your reflection." Esmeralda squatted and drew an arc in the sand. "Begin to manifest the objects of your desires." She made squiggles around the arc. "Examine this process of manifestation. Look at it carefully. Then refine and redefine what you want. Use your attachments as your allies. In the same way that the wild animals of your learned behavior will be there waiting, so will be the wild animals of your attachments. If you become aware of an attachment, then work backward from it. Look at what you're attached to, use it as the object of your meditation, refine and redefine your motive.

"As you go through this many times and make it a practice, you will begin to identify more and more with the process that wants to manifest rather than the particulars that are manifested. If you follow your desires down to their root, you will find a force that is continually creating your world."

She drew in the arrow. "It is a deadly mistake to become attached to one's creations: it stops the flow. That is real negative energy! This force wants unimpeded contact with the undulating waves of energy out there, and it does this through the continual process of creation. The closer you unite with this force of creation, the freer you become. It has no shape, is encompassed by no idea, but it has energy and flow."

We had come to a fallen tree and we sat down on it. "When you begin to explore what feels right, you get acquainted with your body of knowledge, or what Eulogio would call your healing body," Esmeralda continued. "You start to see that there's a lot more aliveness available to you. Now, once you have the knowledge that there's more aliveness out there, how do you get your energy back from your creations?" she asked, once again anticipating my question.

"Here is where you use the idea of death," she said, "to get a perspective that is beyond death and learn to operate from there. Death and its handmaidens, suffering and disease, act as your guides, reminding you of what is important and what is not. Eulogio has shown you a lot about that.

"Without the idea of death, all ways of being are equal. We use death to form the basis of our strategy towards life. A strategy is the only thing that can give you a tiller in this endless sea."

Esmeralda found a stick and held it to one side so that, sitting on the log, she looked as though she were piloting a boat. She put her hand to her forehead, as if she were shading her eyes, looking off into the horizon. "Strategy can be seen as motive through the waters of time," she continued, still entertained by her own antics. "We have to examine our motives continually and not get stuck in results; learn to live from right motive, developed from our awareness of our Luminous Essence, instead of learned behavior. We have to make a new life that is fluid, filled with things and relationships that are acts of power. And, of course, enjoy ourselves in the midst of doing it all!

"You begin to navigate between the daydream and the nightdream, gathering energy back, and then deploy it in unimaginable ways. To give this reclaimed energy continuity and direction, you need a purpose beyond the confining world created by learned behavior. Then when you become accustomed to your new direction, you can let go of the tiller." Esmeralda picked up the stick that she'd be holding and threw it away. Then she wiped her hands, smiling.

"Automatic pilot?" I asked.

Esmeralda nodded. "Sort of. Occasionally, you may need to check your bearings or grab onto the tiller when you go through stormy seas. But, with the proper strategy, you will have set a new course in motion," she said, gesturing for me to get up.

We continued walking again. I noticed the stillness in the air and the fallen leaves. I bent over, picked up a leaf that was turning from yellow to brown. "Esmeralda, what happens when we die?"

Esmeralda rolled her eyes toward the top of her head. "Hold on a minute, I'll check with the woman who runs things." With her eyes still directed upward, she spun around once, then stopped to face me. "We're doomed to eat pasta and frijoles forever!" She cackled with delight.

Esmeralda's exuberance was refreshing and contagious. "People die because they no longer have the strength to support their habitual behavior. At first the body gets sick as a way of trying to create new patterns, new ways of contact. When that fails, the physical body collapses, finally allowing that force inside to join with the Bigger Dream."

"Is there no hope?" I asked.

"Death is defined by learned behavior, just as your idea of the body is," Esmeralda said. "From within learned behavior, you cannot conceive of an alternative. But here's a forerunner thought for you," she said, bending over to pick up a cottonwood leaf. "If we can consciously make contact through our body in a total way with that immensity out there, then the body as we know it will disappear."

A shiver shot up and down my spine. Part of me understood what she was saying, but I could not find words for more questions. Instead I asked, "What's a forerunner thought?"

She bent over laughing and then lifted up her finger like Huang. "Good question," she said in a perfect imitation of his voice. She pulled out an imaginary dictionary and pretended to leaf through it. She stopped and put her finger down on the imaginary page. "Oh yes, here it is," she said. "Forerunner thought. The thought that runs out in front."

This time I laughed with her.

AWARENESS JOURNAL: YOUR JOURNEY OF AWARENESS

In "Tracking My Awareness," you can over time record your journey of awareness into the eye of the Watcher, the Third Point, the core of your being—the hub of the Feng Shui Wheel of Life. This writing exercise is designed to make you keenly aware of the twofold process of the journey of awareness. The first part is moving into awareness, focusing on the journey into the hub of the wheel. The second is reflecting that awareness through spokes of the wheel into your life.

This entry in your Awareness Journal focuses on the first part: your journey of awareness into the hub of the Feng Shui Wheel of Life, using your desires as the focus.

◆ *Starting today, once a month sit down and honestly note what's important to you. It could be money, sex, plants, pets, children, career, fame, whatever. Write how you feel about them at the moment. From month to month, notice if the way that you're attached to them has changed. At the same time, jot down what you think are the reasons for your attachments. The reasons may begin to change over time.*

◆ *Does looking at what you're attached to and why you're attached to it refine and redefine your motive and help you gather more energy? Do you notice yourself becoming more focused? For example, let's say you're attached to your career and the attention that come from it. Your focus may change. It could shift from the strokes you get to how it enhances the exploration of your journey of awareness. Therefore, the attention you get is now a pleasant byproduct rather than the main motive.*

Another example might be to ask a question of yourself: Why do I want money? The answer might be travel, to see things. As you become more aware, the answer might become that you want more time for self-exploration on the journey of awareness.

It is important to follow your attachments back to the root of that which creates the reflection that you perceive as yourself. Remember, the things that you want are byproducts of the journey of awareness. You want to change your attachment from things to the journey of awareness—that which begins and ends in this present moment.

Chapter 21

THE GROCERY STORE

Your ego can ingest any realization that you get and make it a part of itself. What you need to do is live in a constant state of realization, which is too much for the ego to handle. This way you can put your learned behavior in its place and let your real self come through.

—Esmeralda

E smeralda and I were on our way to the grocery store. As we drove towards town, I marveled at the beauty around me. I always loved autumn and its mood of melancholy peace. The vibrant fiery colors, the intoxicating smells, and the clarity of the air all reminded me that the end of the year was near.

It seems to me that fall is the time when the veils between the worlds are the most fragile. In my own cosmology, Halloween and All Souls Day mark the end of one year and the beginning of the new one. It's a time of getting everything in order, separating the seeds for spring planting from those to be eaten in winter. It's time to sink into myself and see the obvious, to allow things to settle and sort themselves out, to contemplate what has been accomplished in the previous twelve months and to take aim at the future.

"You know, Daniel," Esmeralda interrupted my reverie, "in many ways, being a teacher is the same as every other position we find ourselves in."

"Oh?"

"A teacher needs a strategy, too," she smiled. "I'm not sure why this is, but in order to claim knowledge as my own, I have to transmit it."

"An interesting dichotomy," I replied. "In order to possess knowledge, you have to give it away."

"It's easy to claim knowledge when you can see it reflected in someone else. As a matter of fact, at this very moment, you are providing me with an excellent opportunity. Thank you."

"And all this time," I joshed, "I thought it was my gorgeous looks and charming personality. Maybe I should bill you at the end of the month."

"Forget it!" she chuckled with a dismissive wave of her hand.

Esmeralda then began to explain the basis of her strategy. "In order to transmit knowledge to you in the best way possible, I have to put you in the right place with the right intention. Then the world provides the appropriate lessons. Setting is very important."

"Like the time you took me to the top of the mountain," I suggested.

"Right. And that's why we're going to the grocery store," she finished enigmatically.

"Excuse me," I said. "I thought it was because you were out of toothpaste and Wheaties."

"Wheaties!" she exclaimed. "I've never eaten Wheaties in my life!"

"That explains a lot," I ribbed. "If you'd eaten Wheaties, you'd probably be a sports star instead of busying yourself giving acupuncture treatments to my voodoo doll."

She pulled a long pin out of her formidable hat and made fake jabs at me, laughing. It was hard to keep driving, avoid her pokes, and stop laughing all at the same time. "Watch out!" I warned. "If you stick that pin in the wrong place, I'll turn into the *brujo* of your dreams!"

The mental picture this evoked made both of us roar with laughter that lasted all the way to the grocery store parking lot. As I unlocked my seat belt, I asked, "What are we really here for?"

Esmeralda swung open her door and climbed out. "This lesson," she said mysteriously, "is about how bodies talk to bodies."

Inside the store, Esmeralda grabbed a shopping cart and began cruising the aisles, carefully examining everything from soft drinks to shaving cream. As we turned down the aisle featuring baby foods, we came upon two men deeply involved in an animated conversation about a local robbery. One of them, a clean-cut blond Anglo in his late twenties or early thirties, was a police officer in uniform. The other man, a handsome Mexican-American of about the same age and dressed neatly in jeans and a sweatshirt, had one hand on the handle of his grocery cart. In the child's seat was a baby about fifteen months old.

Esmeralda made a beeline for the baby. She looked him straight in the eye and started making singsong baby talk, her voice fluctuating up and down. The baby's mouth, plugged with a pacifier, split open in a big grin, revealing two pearly lower teeth, and the pacifier tumbled out. He churned his chubby arms and laughed.

The father's head whipped around as he noticed Esmeralda nose-to-nose with his son. I cringed and tried to blend in with the baby food at my side, thinking, *Does she want to get us arrested?*

"Excuse me!" the man said gruffly.

Esmeralda looked up at him with an innocent smile. "This is your son? He's *so* cute. Tell me, how do you talk to him? Do you say, 'goo, goo, gah, gah' . . . ?"

I watched in fascination as the young father's expression went from authoritative aggressiveness to bewilderment to soft openness. "Uh—well, not exactly," he responded. Then he remembered who he'd been talking to and his face began to stiffen.

Esmeralda looked up at the cop. "Do you have any children, Officer?"

"Er, yeah. Two, actually. But they're not babies anymore."

"How did you talk to them when they were tiny?"

In the battle between maintaining authoritative composure and allowing his softness to surface, the police officer moved closer, shrugged his shoulders, and mumbled something like, "Well . . ."

Esmeralda held her arms out to the baby, and the child, utterly uninhibited, leaned toward her, his own arms wide. She picked him up out of the cart, crooning nonsense words, and handed him over to the officer. "Will you show me?"

The police officer suddenly melted as he looked down at the baby. The father leaned closer, touched his son affectionately, and made coochie-coo noises. He didn't have Esmeralda's touch, but he tried.

Esmeralda waved me over. Sheepishly, I approached.

"This is my friend, Daniel. I think he has a flair for this, too," she said.

I felt really strange doing this in front of other men, and I could understand how they had felt when Esmeralda first spoke to them. The father took the child from the officer's arms and held him out to me. Tentatively I extended my arms and brought the baby to my chest. I did my best to make baby sounds, "Dee, dee, dah, dah . . ." I began experimentally. The baby seemed wholly delighted and rewarded me with a big smile.

The two men relaxed, regarding me with big smiles. I realized suddenly that we were all having fun. After a minute or two, I gave the baby to Esmeralda. She buried her nose in his silky cheek and planted a noisy kiss on it. "Oooh, these baby cheeks are the best! They're so soft, you want to eat them up." She gently lowered the baby into the front part of the shopping cart and turned to the father. "He's a wonderful boy," she said. "I wish you only joy in him." Then she nodded to the policeman and touched his forearm lightly. "Nice to meet you, Officer," she said.

As we turned our cart down the next aisle, the two men and the baby were still grinning after us, their faces glowing. I noticed I had a smile on my face, too, and the products on the shelves seemed to radiate more color.

In the paper-products aisle, we came upon an obstruction. An enormous woman, wearing a white dress printed with faded red roses, was parked in front of us. Her shopping cart, overflowing with food, presented a formidable obstacle. I wasn't sure if she was contemplating the panty hose or the toilet paper, but she was absorbed in something out of this world. She seemed very angry, suffocated, and tired. Her white skin was splotched with red, and her stale body odor and the strong perfume she attempted to mask it with were nearly overpowering.

"Excuse me," Esmeralda said.

The lady didn't seem to hear her. Once again Esmeralda said, "Excuse me." No response.

Esmeralda, with an impish smile on her face, began to squeeze the toilet paper in the woman's shopping cart. Instantly the woman reacted. She took a step towards Esmeralda, towering over her and leaning into her with her protruding belly. "Get your little brown hands off of my toilet paper," she hissed.

People can be very protective about their shopping carts, I thought. *The minute they take a product from the shelves and drop it in the cart, they think it's theirs.*

Esmeralda stood her ground with a charming smile on her face. "But it feels so good! And it's color coordinated. It matches your dress. I like those faded roses. What color is your bathroom? Does it match?"

"Of course it does," the stout woman responded begrudgingly.

"You were so intent on picking out your toilet paper," Esmeralda continued, "that I thought you might be a good person to ask which kind to use. My house guest here just reprimanded me for the roughness of my tissue."

Esmeralda seemed to be enjoying herself immensely. She was playing with this woman the same way she played with me. It was enjoyable to observe her antics, but I was glad that I wasn't the brunt of them this time.

The woman's demeanor began to change. She relaxed. She pulled her belly in by straightening her posture and her face lit up. "Oh, this is my favorite," she said. "It's so soft that you can hardly feel it. It's like sitting on a cloud." She giggled.

"You really know how to pick out toilet paper," Esmeralda chuckled. "I've got to hand it to you." They both enjoyed themselves in another round of laughter. They went on and on, chattering about toilet paper. I felt as though I'd stepped into a television commercial.

After a few minutes Esmeralda introduced me as a famous healer from up north! I joined in the conversation for a bit. The woman and Esmeralda exchanged names and Esmeralda said that she would enjoy seeing Mildred again at the supermarket, for tips. They laughed. Mildred moved her shopping cart and we went on.

Later, as we stood in line at the checkout counter, Esmeralda scanned the tabloids. "This is where you find out about the male-female agreement of the times."

"But people don't really believe that stuff," I said.

Esmeralda rolled her eyes up. "They look at it, read it, and it fascinates them. Or would you rather watch TV?" She handed me the latest *TV Guide.*

As we crossed the parking lot with our groceries, I felt a growing irritation. I stopped, shook my head, chagrined. "Esmeralda, why do you enjoy yourself so much at other people's expense?"

"I don't really enjoy myself at other people's expense," she said, "although I can understand why you might want to see it that way." Esmeralda laughed as she kept walking toward the shade of a nearby cottonwood tree.

I followed her with the grocery cart. Due to a badly worn wheel, it started and stopped and bumped along, increasing my irritation. Finally, I joined her under the tree.

"You empathize with these other people," she said, "because you think I do the same thing to you. And you're right. What you don't see yet is that it's not me who's doing this. It is the spirit shining through me. It is a greater force that finds a way to express itself through me. But I do enjoy observing you and all of your 'specialness,' because it reminds me of when I used to think I was so special.

"You are still relating through the charges given to you by your learned behavior, and I am not. You actually see yourself through the lens of those emotional charges, and I don't. Remember those squiggles back in that drawing?"

I nodded grudgingly.

"Instead of communicating with your whole body," Esmeralda continued, "you become isolated into wanting to communicate in only one way. You're addicted to getting a certain emotional charge off of an object that you create, because it's through these charges that you learned to define yourself. You want to turn me into an object that you can do this to, and the spirit inside me resists," she said, rolling her eyes around and around, smiling. "I flow around it, and you think I'm playing with you. I'm just not falling into your pattern, that's all. I don't want to become just another one of the animals of your learned behavior."

I shook my head, dismayed. "Yeah, Esmeralda, I'm all messed up. How can I get rid of my learned behavior?"

"There's nothing wrong with your learned behavior. It's actually an important way to make contact with the world. What's important is not to get addicted to its emotional charges. You feed off the action-reaction patterns that you've learned and create one crisis after another. Then you believe that these crises define who you are. It is possible to use your learned behavior without being a slave to it."

"What value does my learned behavior really have? What would I be like without it?" I asked.

Esmeralda smiled. "You'd be like that baby we met in the supermarket. You'd need people to take care of you. You wouldn't know the ropes nor the agreed-upon ways that our bodies talk to each other. But you haven't yet realized that going over and over those patterns also impairs your ability to embody a more total way of communicating. It's not the patterns themselves but rather their constant repetition that creates the problem.

"On the other hand," she continued, "if you took away the charge from the action-reaction patterns, you would have the energy to access more of yourself. In other words, instead of being locked in the external perception of your own feng shui, you could be voyaging through the awareness of your perceptual center. I'm talking about changing the perceptual center from which you view yourself and increasing your spontaneity and your ability to flow in the world."

I nodded. "Go on, I'm listening."

"You can use learned behavior to function in the world without limiting yourself to just that way of relating." She pretended to wipe the sweat off her brow, as if talking to me while I was in this mood was a great chore. And it probably was.

"In other words, you can have your tortillas and eat them, too." She chuckled at her own joke and smiled at me.

"How do I discharge my learned behavior?" I asked.

"Throw out those emotional push-pulls based on the male-female agreement. You'll still be able to function through your learned behavior, yet you'll also have the ability to make contact with the world in many other ways. But if you're pimping the perceptual conditioning of your times, the continuum of learned behavior is all that you see."

Pimping! That ruffled my feathers. But just as I was about to say something, the two men we saw in the store walked out with the baby. Esmeralda waved to them and they waved back. I struggled to regain my composure. "Speaking of children," I asked, "how should a parent teach a child to be in the world?"

"It's important to teach children about the learned behavior of their time so they can function, but you also have to remind them that there's more."

"How do you do that?" I asked, pressing my point.

"By embodying it yourself," Esmeralda said simply. "Kids are much smarter than you think. They'll pick up everything you do in a big way." She laughed. "That's another reason why learning the feng shui of the body is so important. Let's put this food in the car and then we'll continue," she said as she started pushing the shopping cart toward the parking lot. I followed her, still a little irritated.

Esmeralda opened the trunk of her car and we put our groceries inside. She told me to take the grocery cart back. The frustration I'd been holding inside flooded out. "Esmeralda, you are one of the most egotistical people I have ever met!" I blurted. "You act like you know everything!"

Esmeralda looked at me, her eyes got huge, and she began to laugh. After her laughter died down, she said, "Being what you call egotistical in a conscious way is actually one of the hardest things to do. You have to put yourself out there beyond learned behavior." She went on to say that there actually comes a point in dealing with our own personal feng shui when, in order to combat the charges of learned behavior, you have to be egotistical.

"The ego can hide behind any bush," she explained, pointing to a small chamisa bush in a nearby planter. "It can even stop you from acting by convincing you that you're being egotistical. It can even hide behind your idea of being humble. Your ego can ingest any realization you receive and make it a part of itself," Esmeralda continued. "You have to live in a constant state of realization and that is too much for the ego to handle. That way you can put your learned behavior in its place and let your real self come through."

I didn't feel angry any longer, but I pretended to be sullen as I wheeled the grocery cart towards the front of the store. As I looked back at Esmeralda, she seemed to be enjoying my antics immensely. When I returned to the car, Esmeralda suggested that we walk down to a grove of cottonwood trees by the river.

We sat under the trees. Esmeralda stretched and began to talk. "It is very important to deal with learned behavior with a minimum expenditure of energy so that you save energy. That will enable you to contact the world in other ways. You need to do things, not for their emotional charge, but because they are there to do.

"When you first begin to decharge yourself from learned behavior, the world seems very empty. And it is, in terms of your learned behavior. However, in terms of your higher purpose, it is just the opening of the door. You learn to fill this void with the journey of awareness into the core of your being. People caught up in their repetitive habits are just missing out. Don't waste time being offended by them. Their habits just aren't important enough, nor are yours."

"Well, that sounds great, Esmeralda. But how do you relate to people then?" I asked, a bit confused.

"You become uninterested in the plight of others in a conventional sense. Instead, you become interested in their struggle to redefine themselves and in your affection for the immensity out there," she said, opening her arms wide. "Also, your struggle to redefine yourself becomes your new way of identifying with others who are struggling to redefine themselves. You begin to see others in terms of the pressure of affection working through them.

"You also need to stop being offended by your own learned behavior," Esmeralda beamed, enjoying herself immensely. "You have to accept yourself, stop fighting with yourself. In this way, you can begin to gather energy."

"Then how am I supposed to think about myself?" I asked.

"The point isn't how you think about yourself," Esmeralda said. "The point is how you make contact with the world. Too often we get stuck on who we are—or aren't. That stops us from making contact with the world.

"When you don't have to go through the idea of yourself and check everything out, you can make more direct contact," she continued. "The thinner the membrane of your self, the more contact you can make. Making contact relieves the pressure created by your Luminous Essence in seeking unimpeded flow with the Bigger Dream. You then begin to ride on the pressure of affection. You want to have many points of pressure, not just the points you've learned to make through your learned behavior. It's the habitual pattern of wanting to keep your sense of self intact that keeps you from maintaining contact with the Bigger Dream all the time," she went on. "By maintaining and trusting the body that knows, you develop another kind of boundary, and this is the boundary that exists through true love and affection."

"What exactly do you mean by a boundary?" I asked.

"It's another level of relating," Esmeralda said, "a natural state of being that's always there. It's who you really are."

"How do you allow that natural being to . . . just be?" I asked, still unclear.

"You go inside and relate from the middle of your being outward, and that starts to be like waves that flow out of you toward the world. And, if you're around another person, deep down they will resonate with that. That's all I'm really doing with you," Esmeralda continued. "Allowing my inner knowingness to contact your inner knowingness, thus giving you the opportunity to relate in a new and expanded way. But sometimes you give me a hard time," she said, chuckling as she lazily rolled her head back and looked up at the sky.

After a minute or so, Esmeralda continued.

"Letting the flow come to life inside of you makes life exciting and spontaneous. You become resilient. The process of falling apart and coming back together becomes almost instantaneous. For example, a while ago you got angry at me, thinking I was egotistical. It's taken you up until now to recharge yourself and to realign with your sense of self. If you do this process faster, you become more resilient. Then you can maintain contact with me, and the world, more continually. When you thought me egotistical, you turned me into an object of your learned behavior. Now, I'm not at all an object in that way. When you got angry, you cut the contact. You threw the word *egotistical* at me to turn me into an object. We're taught to use anger to make the world stop, to freeze things into objects."

Esmeralda stood up and stretched. I did the same. We walked along the river, listening to the sound of the water. We stopped by a pile of leaves.

"I want you to sit here for half an hour," Esmeralda said, "and any time you have a thought about yourself, put a leaf into the water and watch it join the current and float away." Esmeralda walked on down the river.

I sat there, catching my thoughts as they came by, transforming them into leaves, then throwing them into the river. I noticed that the thoughts just passed through. I felt freer and seemed to gain energy. I was able to be with my thoughts from a very deep and relaxing place as I allowed them to flow unimpededly.

Esmeralda's hand on my shoulder brought me back from my state of deep concentration. I got up and we slowly made our way to the supermarket parking lot. When we arrived at the car, Esmeralda gave me the keys and asked me to drive.

AWARENESS JOURNAL:
LOVING THE WORLD AND YOURSELF

In "Tracking My Awareness," once a week make a note about the journey into the core of your being and how it radiates when you are around other people. This is where you really notice how free you are from your learned behavior. For example, if you notice somebody at work beginning to respond differently to you, pay attention and write down the specifics of your interactions with this person. You can notice how well you're reaching out and playing with people and how much you're enjoying yourself with them, as Esmeralda did in the grocery store.

As you gather energy, you become more appealing to others. Your luck may change, or other things may happen. For example, you might notice if any new or interesting situations have occurred with those of the opposite sex. Have new business or career opportunities come your way? Do you have a much fuller experience of relating to specific people around you?

Especially notice how offended you are—or are not—by your own learned behavior. Are you more compassionate and understanding and less judgmental about yourself?

As you gather more energy, spontaneity will leak out through the seams of your learned behavior and give you a fuller life. Streamlining, accepting, and loving our learned behavior is the desired result.

Chapter 22

THE PRESSURE OF AFFECTION

Truth is like water: You can't stop it, you can't possess it. It transforms and changes, flowing everywhere.

—Esmeralda

The half hour at the river had given me a much-needed break from my thoughts. As I drove back from the grocery store, I felt very much at peace. Esmeralda sat next to me quietly, seemingly getting her thoughts in order. When we passed the outskirts of town and got into the flow of driving, she began talking in a very fluid, soft, clear voice.

"Love is a pressure," she said. "It creates more circulation. As we remember more of who we are, we get stronger, and we become full of pressure. As we get stronger in our relating body, we become full of love and compassion. There's an equation between the two.

"When you feel the circulation that Huang talks about as a physical sensation and extend it into the relating body, your habitual learned behavior moves aside and you become a flow of love and compassion. In the same way that Huang would use circulation to become connected with gravity and interact with a person physically without losing his sense of integrity, you can learn to do this same thing with true love and compassion. Huang is able to go down to his real Center and understand the motives of other people. So if you are in touch with the core of your being and relate from there, you can perceive people from the core of their being. This will enable you to understand their pain."

Esmeralda became silent. I looked out the window and enjoyed the big sky, the red rocks, and the golden cottonwood trees. I felt a wave of appreciation for Esmeralda, for all that she had accomplished in her life, and for the opportunity to have spent this time with her.

Soon, Esmeralda began again. "Normally when you interact with people, you feel you either have to react or withdraw because your actions are based on your perceptual conditioning. If you meet someone in terms of awareness, love, and compassion, you can jump to another level of relating. There is a Luminous Essence in us," Esmeralda continued, "a passion for life. It creates the pressure of affection that seeks unceasingly to make contact with the world. This contact is what I call love. Nothing is more devastating than this crushing power of love. Love is the essence. Compassion is its vehicle. There is nothing more devastating to our sense of who we think we are, to our learned behavior, than love and compassion.

"Only by striving for love and perceiving the world through love can you look the contorted beast of learned behavior in eye with compassion. It is your natural being, your seeking to make full contact with the world around you, and your natural expression of love and compassion that allow you to find the Third Point. It is only through love and compassion that you can find freedom and really laugh!" Esmeralda concluded with a grin.

We continued driving in silence. As I looked across the expanse of desert at the vastness of the sky, late afternoon colors began lightly filtering through the clouds. The windows in the car were down and the air passed through. It was cool, crisp, and intoxicating. A few miles from her house, Esmeralda asked me to stop at a lookout point so that we could immerse ourselves in the sunset.

We got out of the car and sat by some rocks on a mesa overlooking the desert. We leaned against the rocks. They were still warm from the sun.

"What I see out there looks like a mirage," Esmeralda said, as if she were reading my thoughts. "It looks like a Hollywood set."

I nodded my head, and she continued. "What's really beyond this illusion is our true love, that for which we have genuine affection. The Bigger Dream is a soft, smooth, womblike texture full of sublime affection. In its vastness, it includes being human, yet it is far beyond that. It's much more rarefied than we can experience through our human interactions." Esmeralda paused for a moment." Once you have tasted your connection with the Bigger Dream, it has a lure that is beyond anything you can conceive of."

"How," I asked, "do we relax in this warm affection and still be in the world of constant clamor and glaring brightness? How can we blend this ultimate knowledge, this sublime sense of affection, with the dichotomy of being in the human form?" I looked at Esmeralda, wondering.

"When we are in the womb, we are surrounded by warm affection. When we come out, we look for this feeling again. To reunite with it, we have to disentangle ourselves from the false sense of affection that we have learned, acknowledge the pathways of affection that are given to us. We have to accept our learned behavior. But we need to take away its limited focus and expand beyond our idea of humanness, expand beyond anything we know of, to merge with our true love, the Bigger Dream."

Esmeralda's words washed over me. We were quiet for a while, and then Esmeralda continued softly. "What drives our search for bliss is our affection for the waves of existence that undulate out there. This is the pressure of affection."

We watched, at ease with one another, as the sun dropped below the horizon. The clouds flared red, orange, magenta, purple, and violet, and overhead the first stars began to glow. Time flowed without end behind us and ahead of us. The only time that mattered, though, was the present moment.

Rain was unusual in the fall, but on this particular evening, a few weeks after I had visited with Esmeralda, a slow downpour fell. I had hiked far into the mountains and located a small cave where I had been camping for several days. I had wanted to be alone, to probe the Center of my own feng shui pattern. I wanted to go the top of my inner mountain to get an overview.

I sat now in silence inside the cave, a blanket over my shoulders, before the fire. As the storm rumbled beyond the mouth of the cave, the fire settled, scattering sparks. Although I was very much alone, I was much less lonely than I used to be. I had learned a lot from Esmeralda, Huang, and Eulogio. As I dropped more and more of my perceptual conditioning and radiated energy outward from my Center, I was more comfortable with myself. As I moved away from the idea of my body that was given to me by my learned behavior, I was able to gather more energy and live in a bigger world.

After gathering more energy, I learned to radiate it out through my body into the way that I relate to the world.

I had learned that the journey of awareness has two basic parts. One is to continually explore and redefine our Center of awareness; the other is to radiate our Luminous Essence outward correctly through the feng shui patterns in our bodies.

I recalled a conversation I had with Esmeralda just before I left her house.

"What is it that you and Huang and Eulogio are trying to teach me?" I had asked. "You talk about gravity, you talk about pressure, you talk about sickness, disease, compassion, and affection. How does it all fit together?"

Esmeralda had smiled at me. "Huang, Eulogio, and I provide you with three ways that you can move In-Between. We are trying to remind you of who you are. Gravity, health, affection, love—these are just different words for the same thing. They are all about flow.

"It's really quite natural. When you take away the veneer of who you think you are and begin to flow In-Between, you allow gravity to pull you down to earth. This is being humble; this is true humility, and it creates an outward pressure. Through it, you begin to appreciate the wonder and magic of this very moment."

Drifting out of the memory, I felt the warmth of the fire on my face. I slowly shifted the blanket, picked up a stick, and rearranged the fire. I looked affectionately at the flames, watching their lights and shadows caress the contours of the cave around me. A bolt of lightning branched through the sky and lit the cave. Crashing waves of thunder rolled.

Esmeralda's words had catalyzed a movement in me that allowed me to sink below my aloneness, below my idea of death, to just sit and feel the earth beneath me. *Humility is just being here*, I thought, *just being who you really are. It's so simple.*

I opened to the Bigger Dream and it filled me.

Acknowledgments

I would like in particular to thank Andrew Elliott for his help in rewriting this book and for his constant support in bringing this project to completion. Thanks are also due to Rhoshel Lenroot who helped me put this material down originally, to Joseph Durepos my literary agent for his counsel, to Brenda Rosen who first took a chance on me, to Quest Books for their support of my work, and especially to Jane Lawrence for her editing skills.

QUEST BOOKS
are published by
The Theosophical Society in America
Wheaton, Illinois 60189-0270
a branch of a world organization
dedicated to the promotion of the unity of
humanity and the encouragement of the study of
religion, philosophy, and science, to the end that
we may better understand ourselves and our place in
the universe. The Society stands for complete
freedom of individual search and belief.
For further information about its activities,
write or call 1800-669-1571, or consult its Web page:
http://www.theosophical.org.

The Theosophical Publishing House
is aided by the generous support of
THE KERN FOUNDATION,
a trust established by Herbert A. Kern
and dedicated to Theosophical education.